What experts say about this book!

While there are many SAT resources in the market, very few organize their content so that students can work specifically on the areas that correspond to the cross-test score areas in which they are struggling. *SAT Math Practice Questions* offers an organized set of practice questions so that students can develop their skills in the specific areas in which they are weak. The questions are very close to the actual SAT questions, both in scope and difficulty. I look forward to using the book with my students who are seeking high SAT math scores.

– Keith Wilkerson, Lead Teacher & Founder,
CollegeThoughts

This book has a ton of ranked-difficulty questions that will hone any student's skill in math for the SAT. Dividing the problems into their respective test-given categories helps the student choose which areas to focus on for the maximum point values.

– Bob De Dea, Owner,
Good iDeDea

Vibrant's SAT test prep series can help the student view the test from a different lens and accelerate their learning process. The book does a good job by describing what concepts and ideas are tested in each SAT section, and provides useful guidance around strategies you can employ to improve your chances of answering the questions correctly. You'll be reminded how silly errors can lead to incorrect answers and how to avoid them (i.e. focus specifically on what the question is asking and make sure you complete final steps such as converting from inches to feet, etc.). We recommend considering this book as part of your SAT prep process.

– Mark Skoskiewicz, Founder,
MyGuru SAT Tutoring

There is so much that I like about this math resource for the SAT. First, it's divided in the same way that the College Board has chosen to set the division of categories (Heart of Algebra, Passport to Advanced Math, etc.) and within each category, every angle is fully explored so that there will be few if any surprises when taking the exam. The questions are neither too simple nor too difficult so that they provide a realistic gage as to how you'll perform when you take the test. Overall, I'd recommend this resource for students to add to the resources they are using when preparing for the math section of the SAT!

– Sean Silverman, Tutor,
Silverman Test Prep

What experts say about this book!

My initial reaction to this book is, I love it! It is very smart the way you have the book formatted. I can break down the test into different sections with varying skill levels as well. Brilliant! That makes the test prep easier for both teachers and students, and as a prep coordinator, I can give students different levels even in the same lesson. I like the way you have structured the problems to look like the test and included opportunities for students to practice their bubbles and grid in questions on the same page. Students definitely need help there!

– Zachary Baca,
Arvada High School

The *SAT Math Practice Questions* book is a fantastic resource for students and tutors alike. The layout of the book, divided by the subscores of the PSAT and SAT, works well to allow students to analyze their scores and then concentrate on the skills where they need most practice. The list of topics in the answers is also helpful for tutors who appreciate focused practice, as it gives a quick resource for precision in lesson planning. I very much enjoyed the book, and I think it's a great resource to have.

– Dr. Laura Jarvis-Seibert, Manager and Academic Tutor,
The Fluency Factory

Loved the very useful and concise information in Chapter 1, SAT Overview; it will definitely add to a higher score if the student follows this advice. The Calculator/ No calculator icon at the top of the page is also useful. Dividing the questions into 3 categories of difficulty - easy, medium, and hard, is brilliant! This makes studying much more effective for the student.

– Judith Sargent, Branch Manager,
Las Vegas-Clark County Library District

SAT®

MATH PRACTICE QUESTIONS

2023

350 SAT Math
Practice Questions

1 full-length timed
Math test

Elaborate Solutions and
Answer Explanations

Extensive Range of
Questions

SAT® Math Practice Questions

Paperback ISBN-10: 1-63651-094-9
Paperback ISBN-13: 978-1-63651-094-1

Library of Congress Control Number: 2022933143

This publication is designed to provide accurate and authoritative information in regard to the subject matter covered. The Author has made every effort in the preparation of this book to ensure the accuracy of the information. However, information in this book is sold without warranty either expressed or implied. The Author or the Publisher will not be liable for any damages caused or alleged to be caused either directly or indirectly by this book.

Vibrant Publishers books are available at special quantity discount for sales promotions, or for use in corporate training programs. For more information please write to **bulkorders@vibrantpublishers.com**

Please email feedback / corrections (technical, grammatical or spelling) to **spellerrors@vibrantpublishers.com**

For general inquires please write to **reachus@vibrantpublishers.com**

To access the complete catalogue of Vibrant Publishers, visit **www.vibrantpublishers.com**

Table of Contents

This page is intentionally left blank

Dear Student,

Thank you for purchasing **SAT Math Practice Questions** We are committed to publishing books that are content-rich, concise and approachable enabling more students to read and make the fullest use of them. We hope this book provides the most enriching learning experience as you prepare for your **SAT** exam. Should you have any questions or suggestions, feel free to email us at **reachus@vibrantpublishers.com** Thanks again for your purchase. Good luck for your SAT! - Vibrant Publishers Team

ACT/SAT Books in Test Prep Series

Math Practice Tests For The ACT

ISBN: 978-1-63651-085-9

Winning Strategies For ACT Essay Writing:
With 15 Sample Prompts.

ISBN: 978-1-63651-049-1

Practice Tests For The SAT

ISBN: 978-1-63651-087-3

For the most updated list of books visit

www.vibrantpublishers.com

This page is intentionally left blank

How To Use This Book

SAT Math Practice Questions is divided into four chapters focusing on specific areas of math questions that appear in the SAT: problem-solving and data analysis, heart of algebra, passport to advanced math, and additional topics in math. These four chapters contain practice questions that you need to keep solving and revising until you get it perfect. Chapter 6 contains a Math Practice test that you can solve once you've gone through the questions in the book and feel thoroughly prepared to take a practice test.

Heart of Algebra: In Chapter 2, you will be practicing linear equations and solving functions. You'll also be solving and interpreting systems of linear inequalities in 1 and 2 variables.

Passport to Advanced Math: Chapter 3 will expose you to more complex math, like quadratic and exponential functions. The focus here is on solving quadratic equations with rational coefficients, as well as the addition, subtraction, and multiplication of polynomial expressions. You will also practice sketching graphs by using your knowledge of the zeros and factors of polynomials.

Problem-solving and Data Analysis: In Chapter 4, you'll find questions on ratios and percentages, word problems, and questions that need to be solved by analyzing relationships in graphical and statistical data. You will use scatterplot, linear, quadratic, or exponential models to describe the relationship between variables.

Additional Topics in Math: There are six additional math questions in the SAT test, three in the calculator section and three in the non-calculator section. Here, you will be solving questions on geometry, trigonometry, and complex numbers. You will be practicing questions on volumes, congruence, similarity, and radian measures.

In each chapter, you will be solving two broad types of questions: multiple-choice questions that require you to choose one answer, and grid-in questions that need to be marked in a grid.

All questions are divided into two parts: questions that require a calculator (Calculator questions) and questions that need to be solved without a calculator (No-Calculator questions). For detailed instructions on the type of questions, please refer to Chapter 1.

Difficulty level of the questions

Within each chapter, the questions have been divided into MCQ questions and Grid-in questions with three levels of difficulty- **easy, medium,** and **hard**- to help you practice effectively. Remember that each question has equal weightage when it comes to marks- it's only the level of difficulty and the time spent on each question that differ.

The amount of time spent on each question is subjective, but try to follow the average time limits set out below so that you have sufficient time for each question on the test.

Easy: These questions are fairly basic and can be answered quickly if you have a strong grasp of the fundamental math concepts. These are straightforward questions that don't require much calculation or brainstorming. These types of questions will take 40-30 seconds to complete, on an average.

Medium: These questions are at an intermediate level of difficulty and require you to think carefully before answering. They are slightly more complex than the questions in the easy section and involve a series of steps in the process of finding the final answer. On an average, these types of questions will take a minute or a minute and a half to complete.

Hard: These questions require careful attention and may take up a significant portion of your time. They require a clear understanding of the exact answers required, so it is best to approach them with an analytical frame of mind. Read between the lines as you investigate the details and the exact requirements set out in the question. These questions generally take 3-2 minutes to complete.

Chapter 1
SAT Overview

So, you've decided to take the SAT. At this point in your life you probably have a lot of important decisions looming in front of you. What college would I like to attend? What do I need to get in? What classes should I be taking? What's a good GPA? Of course, you are also wondering about the SAT. This chapter provides an overview of the SAT as one of the data points considered for college entrance standards. It also provides the outline of the test, grading overview and some helpful hints to get you started. The most important first step is to know what to expect, so you can make the best-informed choices as you look forward to your exciting future. Congratulations on taking that first step.

What is the SAT

The SAT (Standardized Aptitude Test) is one of the two primary tests which colleges use to gauge whether or not you might be ready for college. It is a test that reflects the things you should have learned in high school and relies on strategic questioning to actively represent those skills and knowledge that are essential as you enter the world of college. But what is it really? The SAT is a measure of how well you can take what you learned and apply it to a timed testing environment. It shows how well you take tests and how well you do in a stressful situation. It does not however, measure your intelligence. In fact, once you learn the tips and tricks of the test, one might argue it measures your testing ability more than what you know.

If that's what it is, why do colleges use it for a standard for admission? Colleges use this as a *predictive analytic tool* to try to figure out if you have the basic abilities required of a college freshman. They want to make sure you can comprehend reading at a level that is expected in your classes. Same with math: do you have a basic understanding of mathematical concepts so you can succeed not just in math class but in other required classes such as economics? Many colleges also want to see if you can write in a way that is conducive to the college classroom. Again, they are not testing whether or not you CAN write but whether or not you can follow instructions and apply what you read to create an essay that would be appropriate for the college classroom. Finally, they are assessing your ability to take lengthy, timed tests. This testing situation mirrors what you might encounter in your college classes. They want to make sure, when they check that box for YES, they will be admitting someone with the tools to succeed. Colleges and universities must report their success rates with students and if all their students drop out, because they are not prepared to succeed, then the college itself cannot succeed. That is one reason why the admission process is so rigorous.

Preparing for the SAT

Knowing all that, it is essential to understand the tips and tricks of this assessment. The SAT is a great vehicle to show what you know. It has recently been realigned with the current high school college readiness curriculum, so it does reflect what you have seen in your classroom. But like any other test, it requires preparation and planning to do your best. It is important to note that you can take the test more than once. It won't count against you to try again, and in the end, you can choose the test you would like to send to your chosen school. Some schools *superscore,* which means you can combine the best sections into one final score. (You can read more about that in the "Words to Know" section). All these options are handy, especially if test taking isn't one of your strengths, but the real goal should be to go into your first testing situation with a plan to succeed.

SAT Math Practice Questions

Here are some tips to prepare for that first testing day:

- Learn strategies, tips and tools
- Practice, practice, practice. The more questions you see; the better you will do
- Learn math and reading formulas
- Create a study group and learn from your friends

You also need to:

- Understand the purpose of the test
- Outline the standards and requirements of each section
- Learn strategies and practices that will help you do your best on the test
- And above all, know what to expect and develop a plan to succeed

On the day of the test here are some things to remember:

- Get a good night's sleep and relax. Remember it is not the end of the world if you don't have your best testing day. You can always take the test again.
- Gather your testing supplies. Take several sharpened number 2 pencils and your calculator (make sure it follows the guidelines set forth by the College Board).
- It is always smart to take a snack with you for your breaks. This will help energize you and keep you going.
- Don't forget your picture ID and your testing ticket. Make sure to double check all the requirements on the College Board site. They will give you a detailed account of all the documents you need to bring.

Words to Know

College Board: The College Board is the manager of the SAT. This organization provides great resources to better understand the application process, the meaning of your score, and the components of the test.

Standardized: Standardized means the same for all. Everyone taking the SAT will be tested on standardized material. There is no truth in the old myth that a red cover is a harder version, or if you take the test in June, it's easier than if you take it in January. Whenever you take it, regardless of the color of your test, the content is the same.

ACT: This is a test similar to the SAT. When the SAT was redesigned, it became more aligned with the content of the ACT. Now the two tests are pretty similar. Both tests are equally important, and you should consult your colleges of choice to see which they prefer.

Data Point: You might hear the SAT mentioned as a data point. This means it is just one measure, one point of data that is used to predict whether or not you will be a good fit for the college or university. Remember, they are using a predictive analysis formula to find the best fit for their programs and campus mission.

You'll notice that every institution rates data points differently so that those skills they value most will be the biggest data points to consider.

Old SAT vs. New SAT: In 2016, the SAT made some major changes to its format, grading formula and essay. For the first year that these changes were in place, students could choose which format they would like to take. However, now there is just one SAT. When you sit for the exam, you can be assured that everyone else sitting for the exam that day is receiving a similar version of the test.

Superscore: A Superscore is when after taking the SAT multiple times, you combine the best scores for each section to create the Superscore that you send to your school. For example, if you rocked the first math test but just bombed the reading, if you chose to take it again, and did great on the reading, your score could be composed of the math from the first test and the reading from the second. This sounds great, right? However, this is not a College Board thing. This is a school-to-school decision. You need to check with the schools you intend to apply to and see if they Superscore. If they do not, then you will use the total scores from each individual test. This is an important distinction.

Who takes the SAT

The typical test taker is a student planning to enter an undergraduate program in the United States or Canada. The SAT may be a requirement for admission, but it is important to check with your colleges of choice to see if they prefer the SAT or ACT. It is also essential to see if they require the essay. Typically, this test is taken in the 11th and 12th grade.

Who gives the SAT

On the day of the test, your exam will be administered by trained proctors. They are employees of the College Board and they specialize in test security. They are not able to answer questions about the test but can answer your logistical questions such as where to take a break and when the test starts. They read their instructions from a script so the College Board can ensure that every test taker is receiving the same information. They are also responsible for watching for testing anomalies or misadministration issues.

The SAT is administered by the College Board. The College Board is an organization which writes, evaluates and manages the registration for the exam. They are your one stop shop for anything you need to know about actually taking the test. You can register through their site as well as receive your final score. Once you register and choose your schools, the College Board will also send your scores directly to your schools of choice. They also provide a thorough explanation of your scores, so you can see your highs and lows and make plans for improvements, if you are considering retaking the test.

Remember, even though you may take the test at your high school, it is not your school that is responsible for the test. The College Board creates, grades and secures all tests, so they can ensure test security. In other words, they can guarantee that you took the correct test with the correct results.

What is tested?

The SAT is divided into three sections:
- Reading
- Writing and language
- Math

Reading

The Reading test consists of 52 multiple choice questions and you have 65 minutes to complete it. You'll encounter passages or pairs of passages that are taken from the fields of literature, historical documents, social sciences and natural sciences. The biggest advantage you have in this test is to choose the order you attack the passages. The best strategy is to practice. Your strategy will improve as you begin to understand your strengths and opportunities. That understanding comes with practice. For example, if you are good at historical documents, you might want to do that passage first and get it out of the way, so you can focus on the natural science passage that you know is a passage that will require more of your time.

You can also learn about question types and develop strategies for each one. The question types you will see include;
- Main idea/big picture questions
- Detail questions
- Inference questions
- Author's purpose and technique questions
- Vocabulary questions
- Analogy questions
- Data reasoning
- Use of evidence support

Each question type carries with it its own strategies and tips. The first step is to be able to decide which question type you are encountering. After you know what type of the question it is, you can decide first what kind of answer you are looking for and next how to use the passage to find the answer. However, as you are deciding these strategies, the clock is ticking, which is why practicing is essential.

Here are some quick tips to get you started:

- Know what to expect: format, time, expectations.
- Choose the order of passages.
- Read the passages in a way that makes sense to answer the questions. You don't have to necessarily read every word to answer these questions.
- Remember this is a passage-based assessment. They are not looking for what you think or what you know. Focus on what the passage says. That's all that matters.
- Save main idea questions for the last. By that time, you will have lived with the passage long enough to get the gist of what it is saying.

Writing and Language

You will have 35 minutes for the 44 multiple choice questions in this section. Questions cover grammar, vocabulary and editing. You will start with four passages and work through the questions in context. What this means is that every question offers you a chance to practice real skills such as editing, choosing the best word and reordering sentences. You will be also asked several reading comprehension questions mostly relating to topic sentences and details. Don't get too caught up in reading the passages but make sure as you are working through the questions, you have a general idea of what is going on in the passage. That makes it much easier to answer those tricky reading comprehension questions. You also may need to interpret graphics, so make sure you understand their role in the overall passage.

Math

The math section is divided into two parts with a total of 58 questions. Note that in the first section, you cannot use your calculator for the 20 questions. This section takes 25 minutes. The second section has 38 questions and lasts for 55 minutes. In this part, you can use your calculator.

The math section covers four main topics.

- Heart of Algebra
- Problem Solving and Data Analysis
- Passport to Advanced Math
- Additional Topics in Math

The most important thing in this section is to know what the question is asking. Make sure you have worked through all the steps to reach the answer the test really wants. Sometimes, not completing that last step or not converting inches to feet or pounds to ounces is the difference between a correct and incorrect answer. Also read the word problems carefully. Use your reading strategies to find keywords and again, make sure you understand what type of answer is required. Finally make sure you are able to use and apply the basic math formulas required for this test. The College Board website provides a comprehensive list of those formulas. Knowing what formula goes with what problem is a big first step towards math success.

Scoring

The SAT has two main scores: Reading and Writing, and Math.

For each section you can score between 200 and 800 points. A perfect final score is 1600.

Here are some terms to better understand your score:

Your **total score** is the sum of the Reading and Writing and Math sections. This can range between 400 and 1600. A **section score** is the score you receive on each of the separate sections: Reading and Writing and Math. Remember Reading and Writing are scored as one section. This can be helpful to students who have strengths in one of the sections but struggle in the other. They will eventually balance each other.

A **percentile** is the comparison between you and the rest of the students who took the SAT in the year of your test. This is a test that 11th and 12th graders can take, so you will be compared with all students, not just those students in your grade.

A **cross-test score** shows how you performed on select questions that represent knowledge in science and history. Finally, a **subscore** is reported as a number from 1 to 15 and it shows how you perform on basic knowledge questions that specifically relate to what you learned in high school. Topics include: a) Command of Evidence, b) Words in Context, c) Expression of Ideas and d) Standard English Conventions for Reading and Writing and Language tests and a) Heart of Algebra, b) Problem Solving and Data Analysis and c) Passport to Advanced Math for Math test.

The calculation of your overall score is a bit tricky. First there is a raw score. A raw score is found through how many questions you got right. You are not penalized for skipping or guessing questions, but you should always attack each question with your best strategies. Then your score is "equated." What this means is basically your score is curved. The way the curve is determined is far more complicated than you need to understand to figure out your score, but here is the gist. The College Board takes all the tests and determines a high and low scoring range. Based on those highs and lows they set their scale. This scale tries to smooth out all the different testing situations, so everyone's curve is pretty much the same. The bottom line is that the curve never really makes that much difference in your final score. If you have a high raw score, you will have a high SAT score. So, the best strategy is to get as many right answers as you can.

Now that you know the basics you are ready to get started. The key is to practice and know what to expect. Good luck and get practicing.

Directions for Questions

Following are some general instructions for solving the questions.

1. The use of a calculator **is not permitted** for **no-calculator questions.**

2. The use of a calculator **is permitted** for **calculator questions.**

3. All variables and expressions used represent real numbers.

4. Figures provided in this test are drawn to scale unless otherwise indicated.

5. All figures lie in a plane unless otherwise indicated.

6. Unless otherwise indicated, the domain of a given function f is the set of all real numbers x for which f(x) is a real number.

Reference

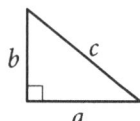 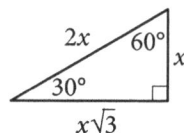 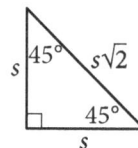

$A = \pi r^2$ $A = \ell w$ $A = \frac{1}{2}bh$ $c^2 = a^2 + b^2$ Special Right Triangles

$C = 2\pi r$

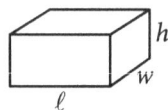 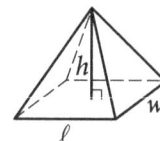

$V = \ell wh$ $V = \pi r^2 h$ $V = \frac{4}{3}\pi r^3$ $V = \frac{1}{3}\pi r^2 h$ $V = \frac{1}{3}\ell wh$

For Multiple-choice questions

Solve each problem, choose the best answer from the choices provided, and fill in the corresponding circle on your answer sheet.

Answer: A   A ●   B ○   C ○   D ○   Answer: B   A ○   B ●   C ○   D ○

Answer: C   A ○   B ○   C ●   D ○   Answer: D   A ○   B ○   C ○   D ●

For student-produced response questions, solve the problem and enter your answer in the grid, as described

below, on the answer sheet.

1. Although not required, it is suggested that you write your answer in the boxes at the top of the columns to help you fill in the circles accurately. You will receive credit only if the circles are filled in correctly.

2. Mark no more than one circle in any column.

3. No question has a negative answer.

4. Some problems may have more than one correct answer. In such cases, grid only one answer.

5. **Mixed numbers** such as 3½ must be gridded as 3.5 or 7/2. (If 3½ is entered into the grid, it will be interpreted as 31/2 instead of 3½.)

6. **Decimal answers:** If you obtain a decimal answer with more digits than the grid can accommodate, it may be either rounded or truncated, but it must fill the entire grid.

Answer: $\frac{7}{12}$ Answer: 2.5

Write answer in boxes.   ← Fraction line   Grid in result.   ← Decimal point

Acceptable ways to grid $\frac{2}{3}$ are:

Answer: 201 – either position is correct

NOTE: You may start your answers in any column, space permitting. Columns you don't need to use should be left blank.

This page is intentionally left blank

Chapter 2
Heart of Algebra

MULTIPLE CHOICE QUESTIONS

1

What is the slope of the line perpendicular to the one shown below?

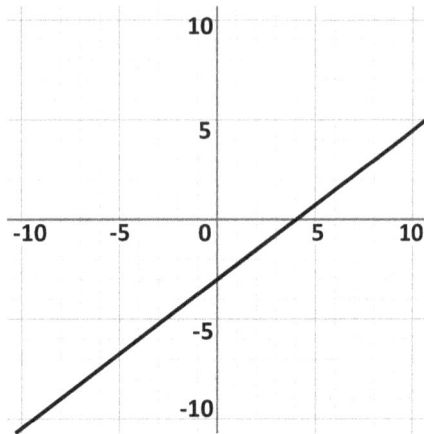

A) $\dfrac{3}{4}$

B) $\dfrac{4}{3}$

C) $\dfrac{-4}{3}$

D) $\dfrac{-3}{4}$

A B C D
○ ○ ○ ○

2

Mark runs a tutoring service where he charges $7 for each new client and $20 per hour. His new client gets 4 hours of tutoring and pays Mark $100. Which of the following statements is correct?

A) Mark was overpaid

B) Mark was underpaid

C) You cannot determine if he was overpaid or underpaid based on the information given.

D) Mark was paid the correct amount for his services.

A B C D
○ ○ ○ ○

3

Which of the following lines has an undefined slope?

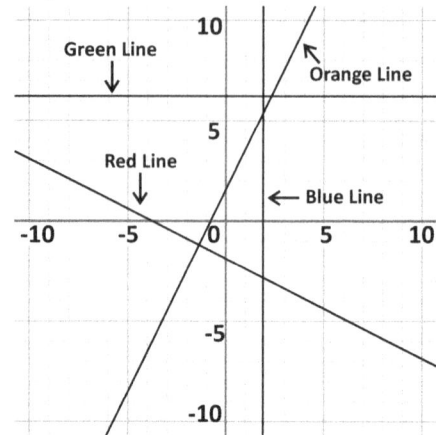

A) Red line

B) Green line

C) Blue line

D) Orange line

A B C D
○ ○ ○ ○

4

Megan and her friends all go to buy candy at the store. Mark pays $15 for 3 chocolate bars, Megan pays $20 for 4 chocolate bars, and Cindy pays $100 for 20 chocolate bars. Which equation below represents the price per chocolate bar related to the total price of each order? Please note that y represents total price and x represents number of chocolate bars.

A) $5y = x$

B) $y = 5x$

C) $y = x + 5$

D) $15y = 3x$

A B C D
○ ○ ○ ○

5

Samantha bought M&Ms from the store. She is told that the amount of sweet M&Ms and the amount of bitter M&Ms is represented by the following system of inequalities, where s is the number of sweet M&Ms and b is the number of bitter M&Ms:

$$s + b \geq 25$$

$$5s - 10b < 2$$

Which of the following solutions, in the format (s, b) could be a possible solution for the number of M&Ms in Samantha's bag?

A) (6, 10)

B) (2, 30)

C) (1, 1)

D) (50, 10)

A B C D
○ ○ ○ ○

6

What is the solution to the system of linear equations demonstrated in the graph?

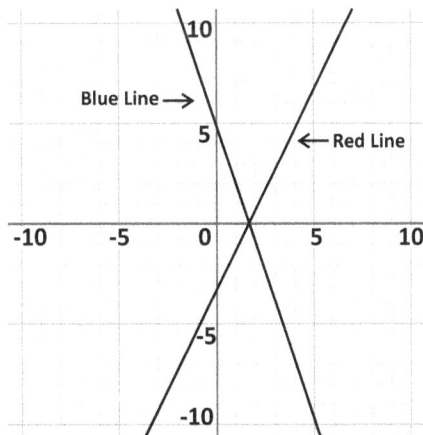

A) (0, 2)

B) (0, 0)

C) (2, 0)

D) (2, 2)

A B C D
○ ○ ○ ○

7

The following graphs represent a system of linear equations. The lines shown are parallel. How many solutions will this system of equations have?

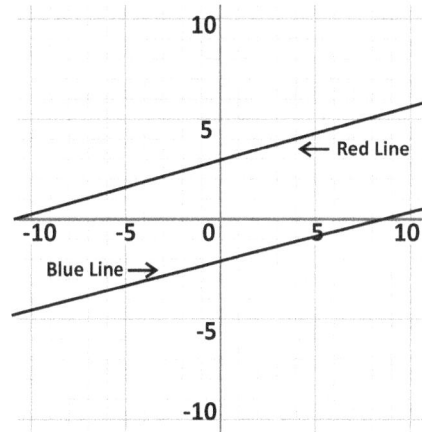

A) No solution

B) One solution

C) Infinite solutions

D) Because we are not given the equations of the lines, it is impossible to know.

A B C D
○ ○ ○ ○

8

Which of the following graphs demonstrates a system of linear equations with no solution?

i.

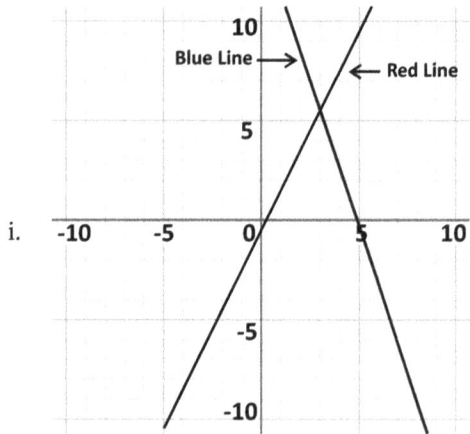

ii.

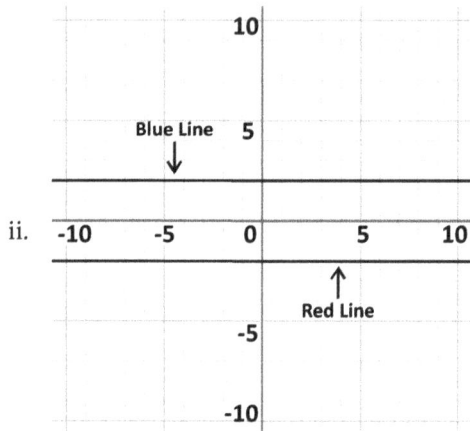

iii.

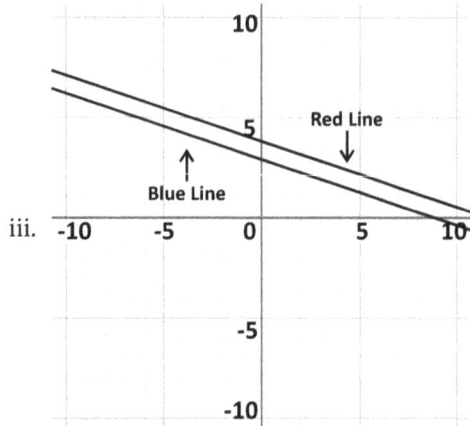

iv.

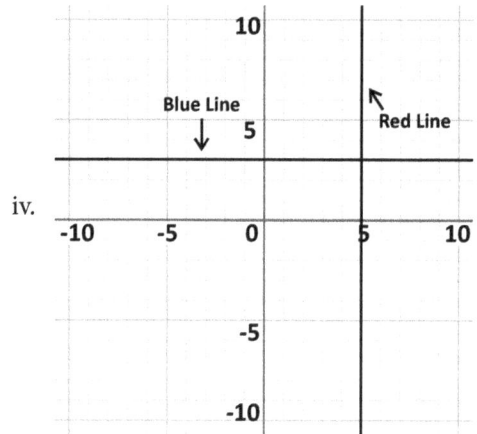

A) i & ii

B) ii & iv

C) iii & iv

D) ii & iii

A B C D
○ ○ ○ ○

9

If $a + 2b + 3c = 24$ and $3a + 2b + c = 36$, what is the value of $(a + b + c)$?

A) 8

B) 12

C) 15

D) 60

A B C D
○ ○ ○ ○

10

In a factory, the number of units manufactured in a month follows the linear function $N = 231D$, where N is the number of units produced in the month and D is the number of days elapsed in the month. Which of the following represents 231 in the above equation?

A) The number of units manufactured only in the first day

B) The number of workers working in the factory

C) The number of units manufactured each day of the month

D) The increase in the number of workers in the factory per day

A B C D
○ ○ ○ ○

11

A man buys a apples and g oranges, each costing 80 cents and 60 cents respectively. If the man buys less than 18 fruits and spends less than \$12, which of the following is the correct inequality representing the above information?

A) $a + g = 18$
   $4a + 3g = 60$

B) $a + g < 18$
   $4a + 3g < 60$

C) $a + g \leq 18$
   $4a + 3g \leq 60$

D) $a + g \leq 18$
   $4a + 3g = 60$

A B C D
○ ○ ○ ○

12

If $5a - 7 = 2a - 22$, what is the value of $a + 2$?

A) 4

B) −3

C) 0

D) 2

A B C D
○ ○ ○ ○

13

$$P = 89 + 12t$$

The number of vehicles in public transportation in City X between 2005 and 2014 is modeled by the equation above. In the equation, P is the number of vehicles and t is the year (assuming 2005 is $t=0$). What does the 12 mean in the equation?

A) The number of vehicles in public transportation was 12 in 2005.

B) The number of vehicles in public transportation increased by 12 vehicles each year between 2005 and 2014.

C) The number of vehicles in public transportation increased in total by 12 between 2005 and 2014.

D) The number of vehicles in public transportation was 12 in 2014.

A B C D
○ ○ ○ ○

GRID-IN

14

$$f(x) = x^2 + px + q$$

If $p = 2q$ and the function has a value of 16 at $x = 3$, what is the value of p?

15

In the TAS aptitude test, three marks are awarded for a correct response and one mark is deducted for an incorrect response. John took the test and secured 76 marks. If there are 40 questions in the test and John attempted all questions, how many of his responses were incorrect?

1. **Topic:** Misc

   The correct answer is C

   The slope of the perpendicular line is the opposite reciprocal of the slope of the line shown above. The slope of the line above is $\frac{3}{4}$. This is determined by looking at one point and finding the rise/run.

   For instance, if you take the point $(0, -3)$, the rise is 3 and the run is 4 to get to the point $(4, 0)$. Therefore, the opposite reciprocal is $\frac{-4}{3}$, which is answer choice C.

2. **Topic:** Misc

   The correct answer is A

   Mark was overpaid. Mark should have been paid $\$20 \times 4 = \$80$ for his hourly rate, and then $\$7$ more for the new client fee. Therefore, he should have been paid $\$87$. Because he was paid $\$100$, he was overpaid.

3. **Topic:** Graphing Linear Equations

   The correct answer is C

   The blue line is a vertical line. A vertical line has an undefined slope because the change in x is zero. The formula for slope is *"The change in y divided by the change in x"*. Because the change in x is zero, the denominator of the slope is 0. In mathematics, you cannot divide by 0 and the result is an undefined slope.

4. **Topic:** Linear Function Word Problems

   The correct answer is B

   $y = 5x$ because the cost per chocolate bar is $\$5$, as seen by $\$15/3 = \$5$, $\$20/4 = \$5$, and $\$100/20 = \$5$. The cost per chocolate bar needs to be multiplied by the number of bars purchased to get the total price of the order. Therefore, the equation is $y = 5x$.

5. **Topic:** Systems of Linear Inequalities Word Problem

   The correct answer is B $(2, 30)$

   In order for an answer to be a possible solution, it must make both equations in the system of inequalities true. For the first equation, plugging in the values makes it $2 + 30 \geq 25$, and simplified it turns into $32 \geq 25$, which is true. For the second inequality, it becomes $5(2) - 10(30) < 2$, which simplified is $-290 < 2$. This is also true. Therefore, this is a possible solution.

6. **Topic:** Solving Systems of Linear Equations

   The correct answer is C

   The solution of the system of linear equations is the intersection. On the graph you can see the intersection at $(2, 0)$. Therefore the correct answer is C $(2, 0)$.

7. **Topic:** Linear Equations and Inequalities

   The correct answer is A

   No solution. Parallel lines will never intersect, so a system of linear equations that contains two parallel lines will have no solution.

8. **Topic:** Linear Equations and Inequalities

   The correct answer is D

   A system of linear equations has no solution when the lines are parallel. Here, the lines are parallel in iii and ii. Therefore, these are the two systems with no solution. The answer is therefore D.

9. **Topic:** Solving linear equations and inequalities

   The correct answer is C

   $a + 2b + 3c = 24$ ...(i)

   $3a + 2b + c = 36$ ...(ii)

   Adding: $4(a + b + c) = 60$

   $a + b + c = 15$

   The correct answer is option C.

10. **Topic:** Interpreting linear Functions

    The correct answer is C

    As 'N' represents the number of units produced in the month and 'D' represents the number of days elapsed in the month, the 231 getting multiplied to the number of days implies:

    $N = 231$, for $D = 1$

    $N = 462$, for $D = 2$

    And so on...

    This means that the number of units manufactured each day of the month is 231

    Hence option C.

11. **Topic:** Systems of linear inequalities (word problems)

    The correct answer is B

    Since total number of fruits is less than 15, we have: $a + g < 18$

    Since total amount spent is less than $12, we have: $80a + 60g < 1200 => 4a + 3g < 60$.

12. **Topic:** Solving linear equations and inequalities

    The correct answer is B

    $$5a - 7 = 2a - 22 => 3a = -15 =>$$

    $$a = -5 => a + 2 = -3.$$

    Hence, the correct answer is B.

13. **Topic:** Interpreting linear functions

    The correct answer is B

    In the given formula t is multiplied by 12, then it follows that each year the number of vehicles P increases by 12 for given years.

    Hence, the correct answer is B.

14. **Topic:** Functions

    The correct answer is 2

    Since $p = 2q$, we have: $f(x) = x^2 + 2qx + q$.

    Again, the function takes a value of 16 at $x=3$, we have:

    $$16 = 3^2 + 2q \times 3 + q => 16 = 9 + 7q => q = 1.$$

    Thus, $p = 2q = 2$.

    Hence, the answer is 2.

15. **Topic:** Linear inequality and equation (word problems)

    The correct answer is 11

    Let the number of responses that John got correct be c and the responses that he got incorrect be i.

    Thus: $c + i = 40$ ... (i)

    Also, since he secured 76 marks, we have: $3c - i = 76$ ... (ii)

    Adding (i) and (ii): $4c = 116 => c = 29$.

    Thus, $i = 40 - c = 40 - 29 = 11$.

    Hence, 11 of John's responses were incorrect.

    Hence, the answer is 11.

MULTIPLE CHOICE QUESTIONS

16

Using the following equation, what value of "A" makes the following system of equations have $(-4/7, -1/7)$ as a solution?

$$Ax + 5y = -3$$
$$-8x + Ay = 4$$

A) 3

B) 5

C) 4

D) –4

A B C D
○ ○ ○ ○

17

Choose the answer choice that best graphically displays the following equations:

$$y < 2x + 4$$
$$y \geq \frac{-1}{3}x - 2$$

A)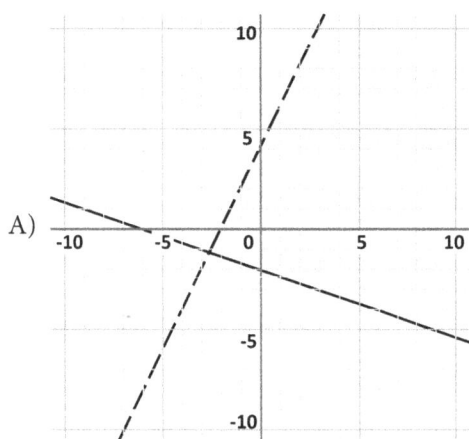

B)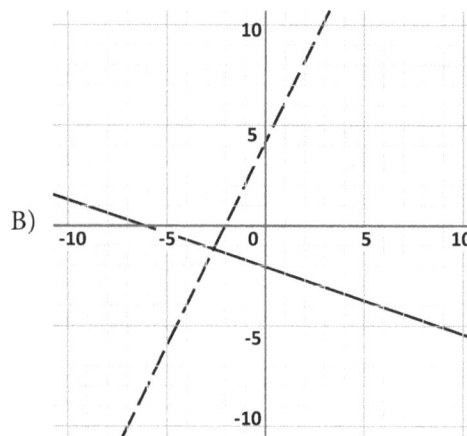

C)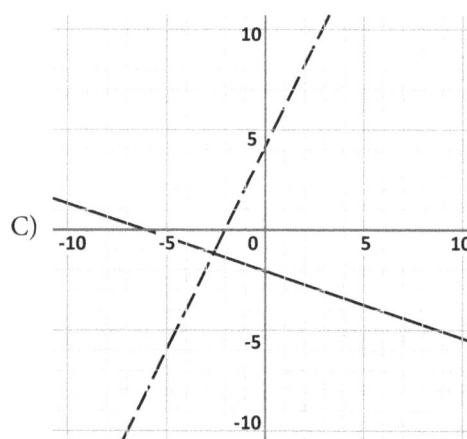

D)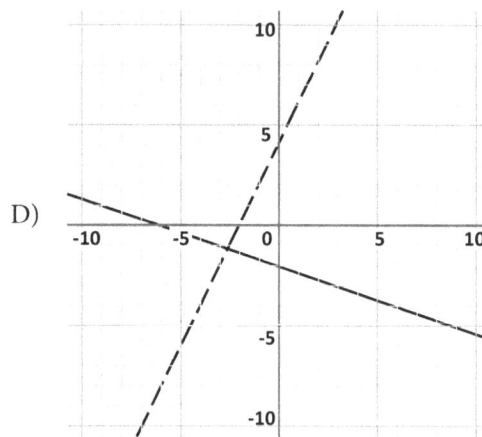

A B C D
○ ○ ○ ○

18

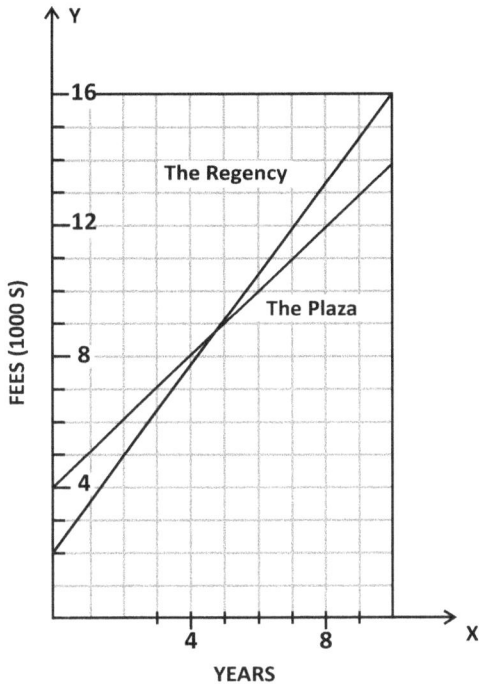

The membership plans of two health clubs, The Plaza and The Regency for ten years are shown in the graph above (membership fees are in thousand dollars). For the initial registration, each club requires an upfront payment of registration fees and every year thereafter one needs to pay a fixed annual membership fee. What is the difference between the annual charges of the two clubs (in dollars)?

A) $0

B) $200

C) $400

D) $1400

A B C D
○ ○ ○ ○

19

Adam bought 23 pencils, 15 erasers and 20 sharpeners from a stationery shop and spent a total of $111. Bob bought 12 erasers, 4 pencils and 7 sharpeners from the same stationery shop and spent $51. What is the price of 1 pencil, 1 eraser and 1 sharpener, respectively?

A) $4, $2, $1

B) $5, $1, $2

C) $2, $5, $2

D) $2, $3, $1

A B C D
○ ○ ○ ○

20

What is the sum of all the possible values of x if $|x-1|+|x-7|=10$?

A) 0

B) 3

C) 6

D) 8

A B C D
○ ○ ○ ○

21

The IKEA Store made a special promotion where the price of a set of 7 chairs and 13 tables would cost $1060, while the price of 13 chairs and 7 tables would be $940. If all chairs and tables are identical, what is the combined cost of two chairs and one table?

A) $40

B) $60

C) $100

D) $140

A B C D
○ ○ ○ ○

22

Fred visits a car showroom. Being concerned about safety, he wanted cars with automatic braking system (ABS) or adaptive cruise control (ACC). Among the cars he checked, six did not have ABS and seven did not have ACC. Also, nine cars had one of the safety features and none had both features built–in. How many cars did Fred check?

A) 5

B) 10

C) 11

D) 13

A B C D
○ ○ ○ ○

23

The cost, in dollars, of producing tires by a manufacturing firm is determined by the following equation: $C = 120 + 90 \times W + 78 \times N,$ where 'C' represents the cost incurred, 'W' represents the number of workers, 'N' represents the number of units produced. If 10 units have to be produced, what is the maximum number of workers that can be employed so that the total cost doesn't exceed $2700?

A) 18

B) 19

C) 20

D) 21

A B C D
○ ○ ○ ○

24

Joseph, the primary school teacher of Illinois Public School, distributed some sweets among the students of his class on his birthday. After distributing three sweets to every student, he found some sweets were still left over with him. He doubled the number of sweets with each student and found that he still had M sweets left over. However, instead of doubling, had he given only one sweet extra to every student, he would have been left with N sweets $(N>M)$. How many students (S) are there in his class?

A) $6S + M$

B) $4S + N$

C) $N - M$

D) $\dfrac{N - M}{2}$

A B C D
○ ○ ○ ○

25

For how many positive integer values of n will $(n^2 + 5n + 12)$ be divisible by $(n + 5)$?

A) 1

B) 2

C) 3

D) 5

A B C D
○ ○ ○ ○

26

Joe distributed some pens among the other students of his class. The number of pens that each student got was 3 less than the number of students who got pens. If the total number of pens distributed is less than 21, which of the following is the correct inequality for the total number of students, s, in the class?

A) $s^2 - 5s - 16 < 0$

B) $s^2 + s - 23 < 0$

C) $s^2 - 5s - 17 < 0$

D) $s^2 - 3s - 21 < 0$

A B C D
○ ○ ○ ○

27

If $x^2 - 4x - 32 > 0$ and $|x - 2| < 7$, how many integer solutions of x exist?

A) 0

B) 3

C) 9

D) 2

A B C D
○ ○ ○ ○

GRID-IN

28

The value of x is related to y through the following equation:

$$2y = x$$

What is the value of B in the following equation if $y = 5$?

$$3x + 10y = 2B + 2$$

29

What is the slope of the line perpendicular to the line depicted below?

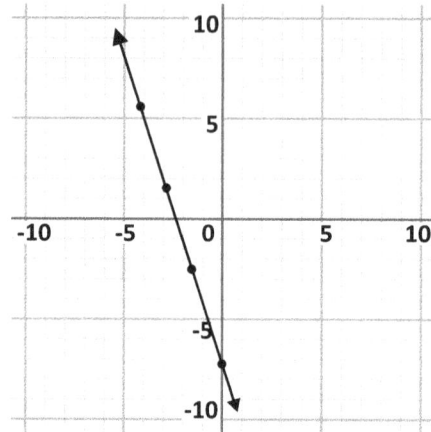

| *SAT Math Practice Questions*

30

A man earns $40 per hour as a consultant. Additionally, he also earns $6 per hour as a content writer. He is only allowed to work 15 hours per week, but wants to make $450 per week. If n represents the integer number of hours he works as a consultant, what is the least integer value of *n*?

31

The average of thrice the cube of a number and twice the square of the same number equals eight times the same number. Given that the number is a positive integer, what is the number?

32

What is the minimum value of the expression $|x+3|+|x-1|$?

33

abcd is a four–digit number such that *a+b+c=d* and *a+c=5b*. What is the value of *a+b+c+d*?

34

Given that the system of equations $3x+ky=1$ and $6x+3y=2$. For what value of k does this system have infinite solutions?

16. Topic: Solving Systems of Linear Equations

The correct answer is C

Add the two equations together and then substitute the (x, y) point given into the resulting equation. When you add the two equations together, you get $Ax - 8x + 5y + Ay = 1$.

Plugging in $x = \dfrac{-4}{7}$ and $y = \dfrac{-1}{7}$ gets you

$\dfrac{-4}{7}A + \dfrac{32}{7} - \dfrac{5}{7} - \dfrac{1}{7}A = 1$. Solving for A

and combining terms: $-5A = -20$, $A = 4$.

So, Choice C is correct.

17. Topic: Graphing linear equations

The correct answer is A

The dotted line represents $y < 2x + 4$. The line needs to be dotted because it is less than, not less than or equal to. The shading needs to be downward because it is less than. The line corresponds to $y \geq \dfrac{-1}{3}x - 2$. The line is solid because it is greater than or equal to. The shading is above the line because it is greater than. The intersection, represented by the shading, represents all of the values that are in the solution of the system of linear inequalities

18. Topic: Graphing linear equations

The correct answer is C

We can see that the registration fees of The Regency and The Plaza are $2000 and $4000 respectively.

At the end of 5 years, the total amount spent for membership of either club is equal to $9000.

Thus, the annual charge for The Regency =

$$\frac{\$(9000 - 2000)}{5} = \$1400.$$

The annual charge for The Plaza =

$$\frac{\$(9000 - 4000)}{5} = \$1000.$$

Hence, the difference between the annual charges of the two clubs =

$$\$1400 - \$1000 = \$400.$$

Hence, the correct answer is C

19. Topic: Linear function (word problems)

The correct answer is D

Let the cost of a pencil be a, the cost an eraser be b, the cost of a sharpener be c, then Adam should have spent $23a + 15b + 20c$, which must be equal to *$111*

$23a + 15b + 20c = 111 \ldots(\text{i})$

Also, Bob must have spent $12b + 4a + 7c$ and as he spent $51, we have:

$4a + 12b + 7c = 51 \ldots(\text{ii})$

Adding, we have:
$27a + 27b + 27c = 162 => a + b + c = 6 \ldots(\text{iii})$

Only option D satisfies (iii).

The correct answer is option D.

20. **Topic:** Solving linear equations and inequalities

    The correct answer is D

    We know that $|x-a|$ refers to the distance of the point x from the point a on the number line.

    Based on the above expression, we can divide the number line in three regions as shown below:

    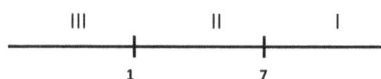

    Region I:

    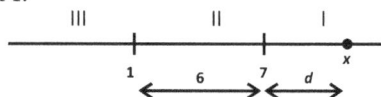

    $|x - 1|$ and $|x - 7|$ refer to the distances of the points 1 and 7 from x respectively. The distances between any two consecutive points have been marked (*in bold*) in the diagram.

    Thus,

    $|x - 1| + |x - 7| = 10 =>$

    $(d + 6) + d = 10 =>$

    $2d + 6 = 10 =>$

    $d = 2.$

    Hence, the value of $x = 7 + 2 = 9.$

    Region II:

    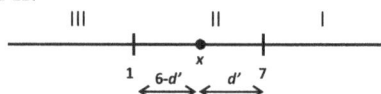

    Here,

    $|x - 1| + |x - 7| = (6 - d') + d' = 6 \neq 10.$

    Thus, no value of x is possible in this region.

    Region III:

    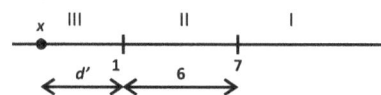

    Here,

    $|x - 1| + |x - 7| = 10 =>$

    $(d') + (6 + d') = 10 =>$

    $6 + 2d' = 10 => d' = 2.$

    Hence, the value of $x = 1 - 2 = -1$ (we subtract since x is to the left of 1).

    Thus, there are two possible values of x, namely $x = 9$ or $x = -1$.

    Thus, the sum of all the possible values of

    $x = 9 + (-1) = 8.$

    Hence, the correct answer is D.

21. **Topic:** Linear inequality and equation (word problems)

    The correct answer is D

    Let the price of a chair be $\$c$ and that of a table be $\$t$.

    Thus, we have:

    $$7c + 13t = 1060 \,...(i)$$

    $$13c + 7t = 940 \,...(ii)$$

    Since we see that in the equations, the coefficients have reversed positions, we would make two new equations by adding and subtracting the given equations.

    Thus, by adding (i) and (ii), we have:

    $$20c + 20t = 2000 => c + t = 100 \,...(iii)$$

    By subtracting (ii) from (i), we have:

    $$-6c + 6t = 120 => -c + t = 20 \,...(iv)$$

    Adding (iii) and (iv):

    $$2t = 120 => t = \$60.$$

    Substituting the value of t in (iii):

    $$c = 100 - t = 100 - 60 = \$40.$$

    Thus, the price of two chairs and one table =

    $$2c + t = \$(2 \times 40 + 60) = \$140.$$

    Hence, the answer is D.

22. **Topic:** Linear inequality and equation (word problems)

    The correct answer is C

    Let the number of cars that Fred checked be x.

    Number of cars that did not have $ABS = 6$.

    Thus, the number of cars that had $ABS = x - 6$.

    Again, the number of cars that did not have

    $$ACC = 7.$$

    Thus, the number of cars that had

    $$ACC = x - 7.$$

    Since no car had both features, we can say that the cars having ABS and the cars having ACC are all different cars.

    Thus, total number of cars having a safety feature

    $$= (x - 6) + (x - 7) = 2x - 13.$$

    According to the problem, we have:

    $$2x - 13 = 9 \Rightarrow 2x = 22 \Rightarrow x = 11.$$

    Therefore, Fred had checked 11 cars.

    Hence, the correct answer is C.

23. **Topic:** Interpreting linear functions

    The correct answer is C

    $$C = 120 + 90 \times W + 78 \times N$$

    For 10 units, total cost

    $$= 120 + 90W + 780 = 900 + 90W$$

    Thus: $900 + 90W \leq 2700$

    $W \leq 20$

    The correct answer is option C.

24. **Topic:** Linear inequality and equation (word problems)

    The correct answer is D

    Let the number of students in the class be S.

    After doubling the number of sweets with each student, each student receives 6 sweets (*initially they had 3 sweets each, which when doubled would imply 6 sweets for each student*).

    Thus, total sweets given away by Joseph = $6S$.

    Since there were M sweets left, total number of sweets with Joseph = $6S+M$.

    Had Joseph given one extra sweet to each student, he would have given 4 sweets to each student.

    Thus, total sweets given away by Joseph = $4S$.

    Since there were N sweets left, total number of sweets with Joseph = $4S+N$.

    Thus, we have:

    $$6S + M = 4S + N \Rightarrow 2S = N - M \Rightarrow S = \frac{(N - M)}{2}$$

    Thus, the number of students in the class =

    $$\frac{(N - M)}{2}$$

    Hence, the correct answer is D

25. Topic: Quadratic and exponential (word problems)

The correct answer is B

Rewrite the given expression

$$n^2 + 5n + 12 = n(n+5) + 12$$

Thus, we see that the first term i.e. $n(n+5)$ is divisible by $(n+5)$.

In order that the entire expression i.e. $n(n+5) + 12$ has to be divisible by $n+5$, we must ensure that 12 is also divisible by $n+5$.

Thus, $n+5$ must be the factors of 12. The factors of 12 are 1,2,3,4,6, and 12.

Since n is a positive integer, $n+5$ can either be 6 or 12.

Thus, $n = 6 - 5 = 1$ *or* $n = 12 - 5 = 7$.

We conclude, there are two values of n which satisfy the condition given.

Hence, the answer is B.

26. Topic: Systems of linear inequalities (word problems)

The correct answer is C

Total students in the class = s

Thus, number of students other than Joe = $(s - 1)$

Thus, number of pens each student got = $(s - 1 - 3) = (s - 4)$

Thus, total number of pens =

$$(s - 1)(s - 4)$$

$$(s - 1)(s - 4) < 21$$

$$s^2 - 5s - 17 < 0$$

The correct answer is option C.

27. Topic: Solving linear equations and inequalities

The correct answer is A

$$x^2 - 4x - 32 > 0 =>$$

$$(x - 8)(x + 4) > 0 =>$$

$$x > 8 \text{ or } x < -4 \dots \text{(i)}$$

(Note: if the above had been an equation, the roots would have been 8 or – 4. Since the inequality is of '*more than*' type, the solution can be remembered easily as: "*greater than the greatest or less than the least*". Here, the bigger root is 8, hence $x>8$ while the smaller root is – 4, hence we have: $x<-4$).

$$| x - 2 | < 7 =>$$

$$-7 < x - 2 < 7 =>$$

$$-5 < x < 9 \dots \text{(ii)}$$

(Note: if the above had been an equation, the roots would have been 9 or – 5. Since the inequality is of '*less than*' type, the solution can be remembered easily as: "*in between the greatest and the least*". Here, the bigger root is 9 while the smaller root is – 5, hence we have: – $5<x<9$).

Now, we need to combine the solutions from (i) and (ii) and find the common region (intersection) as shown in the number line below:

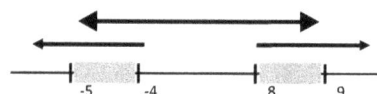

Hence, we see that the common regions are:
$$8 < x < 9 \text{ or } +5 < x < -4.$$

However, in the above regions, there is no integer value present.

Thus, there are no integer solutions for x.

Hence, the answer is A.

28. **Topic:** Solving Systems of Linear Equations

    The correct answer is 39

    Substitute $2y$ in for $3(2y) + 10y = 2B + 2$.
    Then substitute in 5 for y. $30 + 50 = 2B + 2$.
    Combine constants and get $78 = 2B$. Divide by
    2 and get 39. Solution is 39.

29. **Topic:** Graphing linear equations

    The correct answer is $\dfrac{1}{3}$

    The slope of the line depicted is –3. You can
    find this by taking the x and y difference of two
    points. One option is to use (0, –5) and
    (–1, –2). The change in y is $-2 - (-5) = 3$

    and the change in x is $-1 - 0 = -1$. The slope is

    therefore $\dfrac{3}{-1} = -3$. The slope of a perpendicular

    line is the opposite reciprocal, which is $\dfrac{1}{3}$.

    Therefore, the answer is $\dfrac{1}{3}$.

30. **Topic:** Systems of linear inequalities (word
    problems)

    The correct answer is 11

    The man works n hours as a consultant. Let he
    work x hours as a content writer.

    Thus: $n + x \leq 15$ ...(i)

    Also: $40n + 6x = 450$ ...(ii)

    Multiplying (i) with 6 and subtracting (ii):

    $$-34n \leq -360$$

    $$n \geq \frac{360}{34}$$

    $$n \geq 10.59$$

    Since n is an integer, we have: $n \geq 11$

    The correct answer is '11'.

31. **Topic:** Quadratic and exponential (word
    problems)

    The correct answer is 2

    Let the number be x.

    Thus, we have:

    $$\frac{3x^3 + 2x^2}{2} = 8x =>$$

    $$3x^3 + 2x^2 - 16x = 0 =>$$

    $$x(3x^2 + 2x - 16) = 0$$

    $$x(3x^2 + 8x - 6x - 16) = 0 =>$$

    $$x\{x(3x + 8) - 2(3x + 8)\} = 0$$

    $$x(x - 2)(3x + 8) = 0 => x = 0, 2, -\frac{8}{3}.$$

    Since x is non–zero and an integer, we have $x=2$.

    Hence, the correct answer is 2.

32. **Topic:** Solving linear equations and
    inequalities

    The correct answer is 4

    We know that $|x–a|$ refers to the distance of the
    point x from the point a on the number line.

    Based on the above expression, we can divide the
    number line in four regions as shown below:

    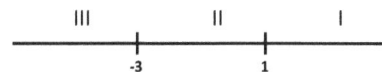

    Region I:

    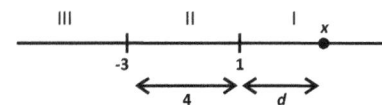

    $|x+3|$ and $|x–1|$ refer to the distances of the
    points –3 and 1 from x respectively. The
    distances between any two consecutive points
    have been marked (*in bold*) in the diagram.

    Thus,

    $$|x + 3| + |x - 1| = (d + 4) + d = 2d + 4 \geq 4$$
    (since d≥0).

Region II:

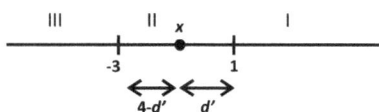

Here,

$$|x+3|+|x-1| = (4-d') = d' = 4.$$

Region III:

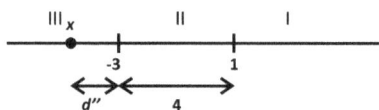

Here,

$$|x+3|+|x-1| = (d'')+(4+d'') = 4+2d'' \geq 4.$$

Thus, from the above, we can conclude that the minimum value of the expression is 4 (which occurs at any value of x from -3 to 1).

Hence, the correct answer is 4.

33. **Topic:** Solving linear equations and inequalities

The correct answer is 12.

We have:
$a+b+c = d$ ...(i)

$a+c = 5b$ ...(ii)

From (i) and (ii): $b+5b = d => 6b = d$ ...(iii)

Since b and d are single digits, the only possible solution is $b=1$ and $d=6$ (if $b=2$ or higher, then $d=12$ or higher, which is not a single digit).

Thus, we have:

$$a+b+c+d = (a+b+c)+d = d+d = 6+6 = 12.$$
Hence, the answer is 12.

34. **Topic:** Solving systems of linear equations

The correct answer is 1.5

$$Ax + By = C$$

$$Px + Qy = R$$

For infinite solutions: $\dfrac{A}{P} = \dfrac{B}{Q} = \dfrac{C}{R}$

$$\frac{3}{6} = \frac{k}{3} = \frac{1}{2} => k = \frac{3}{2} = 1.5$$

The correct answer is 1.5

MULTIPLE CHOICE QUESTIONS

35

Use the following system of equations for this problem.

$$2x + 3y = 10$$
$$10x - Ay = B$$

What is the value $A - B$ that would make this equation have infinite solutions?

A) −15

B) 15

C) 13

D) −65

A B C D
○ ○ ○ ○

36

How many of the following cannot be a solution to the system of linear inequalities if A is a positive constant?

$$Ax - 2y < 10$$
$$-4x - Ay < 20$$

A) $(1, 5)$

B) $(-10, 2)$

C) $(4, -3)$

D) $(9, 8)$

A B C D
○ ○ ○ ○

37

N is a two-digit number having sum of digits as S and product of digits as P.

How many such two-digit numbers exist such that

$$2N = 2S + 3P$$

A) 0

B) 1

C) 9

D) 12

A B C D
○ ○ ○ ○

38

Four friends, Ann, Bob, Charlie and David together have $200. The amount with Charlie is twice of that with Bob. The amount with Ann and Bob together is $40 less than the amount with David. Charlie has $30 less than what David has. What is the amount with Ann?

A) $20

B) $30

C) $40

D) $60

A B C D
○ ○ ○ ○

39

On his birthday, Joseph bought some lozenges to distribute among his N friends. He tried giving x lozenges to each friend but had 7 lozenges left over. Had he tried giving one more lozenge to each friend, three of his friends would have been left without any lozenges; however, no lozenges would be left over. Which of the following is the correct relation between N and x?

A) $N = 3x + 10$

B) $N = 3x + 7$

C) $N = x + 10$

D) $N = x + 7$

A B C D
○ ○ ○ ○

40

With $30 in his pocket, Ron wanted to buy some chocolates priced at $3 per piece and some pencils priced at $4 per piece. How many different ways can he purchase the items if he must buy at least one chocolate and one pencil and he must spend the entire amount he has?

A) 1

B) 2

C) 3

D) 4

A B C D
○ ○ ○ ○

41

In five years, Alfred would be 20 years more than twice his son's age. Ten years back, Alfred was 30 years more than thrice his son's age. After how many years would Alfred be exactly twice as old as his son?

A) 5

B) 10

C) 15

D) 25

A B C D
○ ○ ○ ○

42

A part of the graph shown beside has been shaded. The lines which form the boundary are the two axes and two lines (the integer coordinates through which the lines pass are shown by dots). Which of the following options correctly depicts the shaded region?

A) $2x - 5 \le y \le 2x + 3, x \ge 0$

B) $2x - 5 \le y \le 2x + 5, x \ge 0, y \ge 0$

C) $2x - 3 \le y \le 2x + 5, y \ge 0$

D) $2x - 3 \le y \le 2x + 3, x \ge 0, y \ge 0$

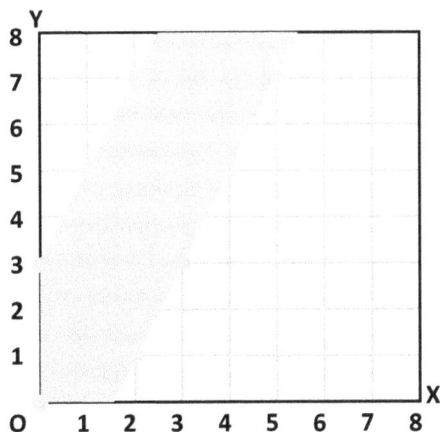

A B C D
○ ○ ○ ○

43

If $6a + 5(b - a) = 24$ and $5(a + b) - 2b = 10$, what is the value of $(a + b)$?

A) 3

B) 4

C) 5

D) 6

A B C D
○ ○ ○ ○

GRID-IN

44

In Year 10, there were 50 miles of road paved in Long Beach. In Year 40, there were 110 miles of road paved in Long Beach. In Year 0, which represents the first year that the town was established, how many miles of road were paved

35. Topic: Solving Systems of Linear Equations

The correct answer is D

To have infinite solutions, the x and y coefficients need to be the same (*or multiples of each other*), and the constant also needs to be the same. This represents a common y intercept and the same slope, which would create the same line. In this situation, you would multiply the first equation by 5 to get the second one. The first equation would then by $10x + 15y = 50$. To equate the two equations, the $10x$ as the first term for both would match. The second term would equation $15y = -Ay$.

So, $A = -15$.

The third part is the constant, where $50 = B$.

So, $A - B = -15 - 50 = -65$.

This is Choice D.

36. Topic: Solving Linear Equations and Inequalities

There are a few methods to solving this. One way is to solve for A and then combine the restrictions on A. For the first equation, if you solve it for A you get $A < \dfrac{(10 + 2y)}{x}$ and if you solve the second equation for A you get

$$A > \dfrac{(-20 - 4x)}{y}$$

Combining these, you get

$$\dfrac{(-20 - 4x)}{y} < A < \dfrac{(10 + 2y)}{x}$$

You can then try each solution to see which ones satisfy the equations. For (1, 5), you can plug in to get

$$\dfrac{-24}{5} < A < 20.$$

This is therefore a possible solution, because A can both be less than 20 and greater than $\dfrac{-24}{5}$

For the next possible solution, you plug in $(-10, 2)$ to obtain $10 < A < \dfrac{-7}{5}$,

which is impossible. Therefore, $(-10, 2)$ is not a solution. Next, plug in $(4, -3)$ and obtain $12 < A < 1$, which is impossible, so $(4, -3)$ is not a solution.

Lastly, plug in (9, 8) and obtain

$$-7 < A < \dfrac{7}{3},$$

which is a possible solution. Therefore, there are 2 listed possible solutions that cannot be solutions to our system of linear inequalities.

37. Topic: Linear inequality and equation (word problems)

The correct answer is C

Let the two–digit number be $N=10x+y$ where x and y are the digits.

We know that $1 \le x \le 9$ and $0 \le y \le 9$.

The sum of the digits of the number =
$$S = x + y.$$

The product of the digits =
$$P = xy.$$

Thus, we have:
$$2(10x + y) = 2(x + y) + 3xy =>$$
$$20x + 2y = 2x + 2y + 3xy$$
$$18x = 3xy => y = 6.$$

Since we cannot determine the value of x, it implies that x can take any value from 1 to 9.

Thus, the possible numbers are 16, 26, 36, 46, 56, 66, 76, 86, and 96.

Thus, there are 9 such numbers.

Hence, the correct answer is C.

38. Topic: Linear inequality and equation (word problems)

The correct answer is A

Let the amounts with Ann, Bob, Charlie and David be a, b, c and d respectively.

Thus, we have:
$$a + b + c + d = 200 \,...(i)$$
$$c = 2b \,...(ii)$$
$$a + b = d - 40 \,...(iii)$$
$$c = d - 30 \,...(iv)$$
Substituting (iii) and (iv) in (i):
$$(d - 40) + (d - 30) + d = 200 =>$$
$$3d = 270 => d = 90 \,...(v)$$
From (iv): $c = d - 30 = 90 - 30 = 60$.

From (ii): $2b = c = 60 => b = 30$.

From (iii):
$$a + b = d - 40 => a + 30 = 90 - 40 => a = 20.$$
Hence, the answer is A.

39. Topic: Linear inequality and equation (word problems)

The correct answer is A

We know that Joseph has N friends. Also, each friend receives x lozenges initially.

There are 7 lozenges are left over.

Thus, the number of lozenges = $Nx + 7 \,...(i)$

Had he tried giving one more lozenge to each friend, i.e. each friend received $(x+1)$ lozenges; and he could have perfectly distributed them among $(N–3)$ friends.

Thus, the number of lozenges =
$$(N - 3)(x + 1) = Nx - 3x + N - 3 \,...(ii)$$
Hence, from (i) and (ii) we have:
$$Nx - 3x + N - 3 = Nx + 7 =>$$
$$N - 3x = 10 => N = 3x + 10.$$
Hence, the answer is A.

40. **Topic:** Linear inequality and equation (word problems)

    The correct answer is B

    Let Ron buy c chocolates and p pencils.

    Thus: $3c + 4p = 30$ ...(i)

    The number of chocolates and pens must be positive integers. To find the integer solutions to the above equation, we need to find any one solution (*by trial and error*) and use that to find the other solutions.

    The first solution is easily obtainable: $c = 10, p = 0$ (*it does not matter that p is not a positive integer*).

    It is clear that we need to increase p and as a result, the value of c would decrease. Thus, to get the other solutions, we increase p by the coefficient of c, i.e. 3 and decrease c by the coefficient of p, i.e. 4.

    The other solutions of the above equation are shown below:

c	p
10	0
6	3
2	6

    Beyond this, the value of c would become negative and hence inadmissible.

    Thus, there are only two ways in which Ron can spend the amount to buy chocolates and pencils (*the first solution in the table above is inadmissible since the number of pencils is zero while the problem states that he needs to buy at least one of each*).

    Hence, the answer is B.

41. **Topic:** Linear inequality and equation (word problems)

    The correct answer is D

    Let the age of Alfred's son ten years back be x years.

    Hence, Alfred's age at that time was $3x+30$ years.

    Thus, the present age of Alfred =

    $3x + 30 + 10 = (3x + 40)$ years.

    Also, the present age of Alfred's son = $(x+10)$ years.

    Now, in five years, Alfred would be $(3x + 40 + 5) = (3x + 45)$ years old.

    Also, in five years, Alfred's son would be $(x + 10 + 5) = (x + 15)$ years old.

    Thus, $3x + 45 = 20 + 2(x + 12) = x = 5$.

    Thus, the present age of Alfred = $3x + 40 = 55$ years and the present age of Alfred's son = $x + 10 = 15$ years.

    Let in y years, Alfred would become exactly twice as old as his son.

    Thus, we have: $55 + y = 2(15 + y) => y = 25$.

    Thus, Alfred would become twice as old as his son in 25 years (*the ages of Alfred and his son would be 80 and 40 respectively*).

    Hence, the answer is D.

42. **Topic:** Graphing linear equations

    The correct answer is D

    We see that point $(2, 1)$ belongs to the right line, hence $y \leq 2x + 3$.

    Also, point $(3, 0)$ belongs to the left line, hence $2x - 3 \leq y$.

    We also see from the graph that x and y are positive.

    Hence, the correct answer is D.

43. Topic: Solving systems of linear equations

The correct answer is B

$$6a + 5(b - a) = 24$$

$$a + 5b = 24 \ldots(i)$$

$$5(a + b) - 2b = 10$$

$$5a + 3b = 10 \ldots(ii)$$

From $(ii) \times 2 + (i)$:

$$11a + 11b = 44$$

$$a + b = 4$$

The correct answer is option B.

44. Topic: Linear Function (word problems)

The correct answer is 30

The slope of the equation is

$$\frac{(110 - 50)}{(40 - 10)} = \frac{60}{30} = 2.$$

So far, the equation is $y = 2x + b$, where b is the y intercept. Plug in a point to find the y intercept. For instance use $(10, 50)$. Now the equation is $50 = 2 \times 10 + b$.

Now, solve for b, which is 30. Therefore, the y intercept is 30. Therefore, at Year 0, the amount of road paved is 30 miles

MULTIPLE CHOICE QUESTIONS

45

The dog park charges $10 for a membership and $3 per hour for your dog to run around in their park. Mindy brings her dog to the park and spends less than $40. Which of the following inequalities represents Mindy's situation, where h is the number of hours at the park and C is the total amount Mindy paid?

A) $3h + 10 < 40$

B) $3C - 10 < 40$

C) $3h + 10C = 40$

D) $3h + 10 > 40$

A B C D
○ ○ ○ ○

46

In Los Angeles, Mario is a delivery driver. He makes $5 per delivery and has to pay $20 for gas each week. If Mario does 20 deliveries in one week, how much does he make, in dollars, when accounting for the deliveries and the gas?

A) $100

B) $25

C) $200

D) $80

A B C D
○ ○ ○ ○

47

Mike owns a bike shop and has at least 15 total bikes. He has green bikes and blue bikes. Each green bike can be rented for $3 per hour and each blue bike can be rented for $5 an hour. If Mike makes no more than $80 an hour in total from renting his bikes, which system of inequalities represents his situation? Please note that b represents the number of blue bikes and g represents the number of green bikes.

A) $b + g \geq 15$ and $b + g < 80$

B) $b + g \geq 15$ and $3g + 5b \leq 80$

C) $b + g \geq 80$ and $3g + 5b \leq 15$

D) $b + g \leq 80$ and $3b + 5g \leq 15$

A B C D
○ ○ ○ ○

48

Is the solution (25, 11) the solution to the following system of equations?

$$y + x = 36$$

$$2y + 8x = 140$$

A) Yes, (25, 11) is the solution because it satisfies both equations.

B) No (25, 11) is not the solution because it does not satisfy the first equation.

C) No, (25, 11) is not the solution because it does not satisfy the second equation.

D) More information is needed in order to answer the question.

A B C D
○ ○ ○ ○

49

What are the coordinates of the solution to the following system of linear equations?

$2y = 7.8x$ and $2x + 3y = 10$

A) (2.85, 3)

B) (0.73, 2.85)

C) (2.73, 0.85)

D) (7.8, 2.85)

A B C D
○ ○ ○ ○

50

On Tuesday, a winter storm passed through Blizzardville. Snowfall in Blizzardville can be represented by the equation $S = 2.7H + 8.8$, where H is the number of hours since Midnight, and S is the total amount of snow, in inches, on the ground in Blizzardville. What is the best interpretation of the value of S at $H=2$?

A) At 2:00AM, there are 8.8 inches of snow on the ground in Blizzardville.

B) At 2:00AM, there are 5.4 inches of snow on the ground in Blizzardville.

C) At 2:00AM, there are 14.2 inches of snow on the ground in Blizzardville.

D) 2 inches of snow have fallen since Midnight in Blizzardville.

A B C D
○ ○ ○ ○

51

The profit of a company is determined by the following equation: $P = 50.2 \times N - 236.8$, where '$P$' represents the profit of the company and 'N' represents number of units manufactured by the company. What is the minimum number of units produced so as to have no loss incurred?

A) Minimum number of units manufactured is 3

B) Minimum number of units manufactured is 4

C) Minimum number of units manufactured is 5

D) Minimum number of units manufactured is 6

A B C D
○ ○ ○ ○

52

The waiting time, t, in minutes, for the nth person in a queue, is given by the relation: $t = 12.5n - 15$. If each person takes 10 minutes to be serviced, what is the time gap, in minutes, between when the service for a person is completed and the service for the next person begins?

A) 1.5

B) 2.5

C) 3

D) 4

A B C D
○ ○ ○ ○

53

If $-5m + 9 = 7m - 15$, what is the greatest possible value of $3m + 2$?

A) 2

B) 6

C) 8

D) 3

A B C D
○ ○ ○ ○

54

The road company uses the function $g(x) = 400x + 600$ to estimate the cost $g(x)$, in dollars, to modify x linear feet of roads. The company plans to spend $121,000 for road modification, how many linear feet of roads will be improved?

A) 301

B) 408

C) 250

D) 323

A B C D
○ ○ ○ ○

55

What is the slope of the red line?

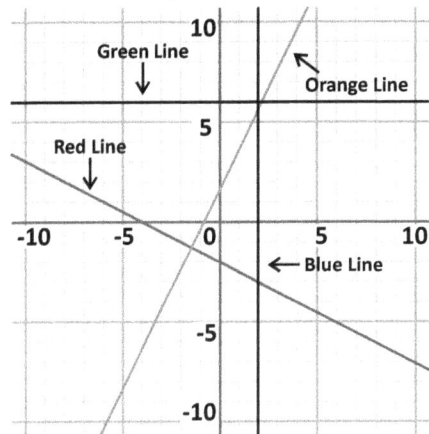

A) 2

B) -2

C) 1/2

D) -1/2

A B C D
○ ○ ○ ○

GRID-IN

56

What is the y value of the solution to the following system of linear equations?

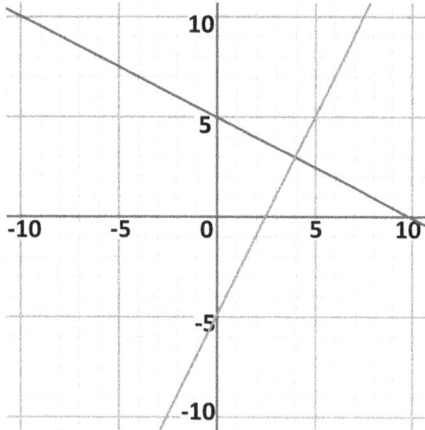

57

What is the y value of the y intercept of the equation $y - 2 = 10(x + 5)$?

58

The population of Whoville increases yearly according to the following equation: $y = 250x + 450,$ where x represents years since 2000 and y represents total people in the town. What is the population of Whoville in 2050, which is 50 years since 2000?

59

Georgia makes $6 an hour babysitting and $10 an hour editing essays. She works less than 30 hours a week and makes more than $180 a week. If she works 25 hours babysitting, how many whole hours could she have edited essays this week?

60

The reduction in speed, r, in miles per hour, of an engine having n bogies attached to it is given as: $r = 4\sqrt{n}$. The final speed, s, in miles per hour, at which the engine can pull the n bogies attached is given as: $s = 40 - r$. What is the speed of the train, to the nearest tenths, in miles per hour, when there are 15 bogies attached?

61

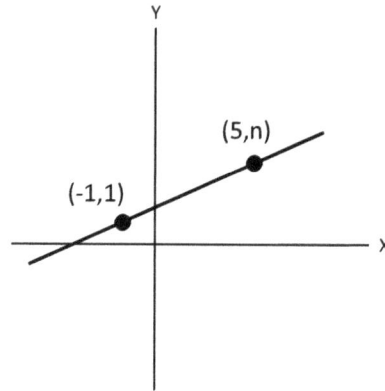

The graph above depicts a straight line passing through *(–1, 1)* and *(5, n)*. What is the least integer value of n if the slope is greater than $\dfrac{2}{3}$?

62

If $x - (3 + 2x) = 7 - 3x$, what is the value of x?

63

Alice is selling homemade cupcakes for $2.30 each. The materials to bake one dozen (12) cupcakes cost $4.20.

How much is Alice's net profit if she will sell 3 dozen cupcakes?

64

The point (M,19) is a solution to the following system of equations.

$$2x + 1 = y$$
$$y - x = 10$$

What is the value of M?

45. **Topic:** Misc

    The correct answer is A

    The solution is *A* because this represents the total hours Mindy spent at the park with her dog multiplied by the cost per hour, to give you the total she paid for the hours at the park. Then, the $10 membership fee is added to this to give you the total cost paid to the dog park. We are told that she spends less than 40, so the expression of $3h + 10$ needs to be less than 40.

46. **Topic:** Linear Function Word Problems

    The correct answer is D

    $80 because the situation is dictated by the equation $y = 5x - 20$, where x represents number of deliveries and y represents the total Mario made. By plugging 20 into the equation, you get $5(20) - 20 = 80$, which is answer choice D.

47. **Topic:** Systems of Linear Inequalities

    The correct answer is B

    The first inequality represents the total number of bikes being greater than or equal to 15. The second equation represents the total cost Mike makes per hour, with the total cost of the blue bikes being rented for $5 per hour times the number of blue bikes added to the total cost of the green bikes being rented for $3 per hour times the number of green bikes. In the problem statement it mentions that the total Mike makes per hour is less than $80, so the sum of the blue bike income and green bike income should be less than $80.

48. **Topic:** Solving Systems of Linear Equations

    The correct answer is C

    (25, 11) is not the solution because it does not satisfy the second equation. When you plug (25, 11) into the first equation, you get 11+25=36, which simplifies to 36=36, which is

true. For the second equation, you plug in to get 2(11)+8(25)=140.

When you simplify the left side you get 222=140, which is not true and therefore incorrect.

49. **Topic:** Solving Systems of Linear Equations

    The correct answer is B

    First, divide the first equation by 2 to get $y=3.9x$. Then use the substitution method to plug $3.9x$ in for y in the second equation. The second equation then becomes $2x+3(3.9x)=10$. Distribute the 3 and then combine like terms to get $2x+11.7x=10$, which becomes $13.7x=10$. Solve for x by dividing by 13.7 to get $0.7299...$, which rounds to 0.73.

    Then plug in the x value into $y=3.9x$ to get $y=3.9(0.73)$, which rounds to 2.85.

    Therefore, the solution is B, (0.73, 2.85).

50. **Topic:** Linear Inequality and Equation Word Problems

    The correct solution is C

    By plugging $H=2$ into the equation given to represent snowfall, we get $S=2.7(2)+8.8$, so $S=14.2$. S was defined as the amount of snow that has fallen since midnight, so this means 14.2 inches have fallen 2 hours after midnight, which is 2:00AM. Therefore, C is correct.

51. **Topic:** Interpreting linear functions

    The correct answer is C

    Since there is no loss, we have:

    $$P > 0$$
    $$50.2 \times N - 236.8 > 0$$
    $$N > 4.72$$

    Minimum integer value of N should be 5

    The correct answer is option C.

52. Topic: Interpreting linear functions

The correct answer is B

For the nth person, there are $(n-1)$ persons ahead of him.

So, time for servicing $= 10(n-1)$

For those $(n-1)$ persons, there would be $(n-2)$ gaps

If each gap is of k minutes, we have:
$$10(n-1) + k(n-2) = 12.5n - 15$$
$$k(n-2) = 2.5n - 5 = 2.5(n-2)$$
$$k = 2.5$$

The correct answer is option B.

53. Topic: Solving linear equations and inequalities

The correct answer is C

First, let us solve the equation
$$-5m + 9 = 7m - 15$$
$$-12m = -24$$
$$m = 2.$$

The greatest possible value that satisfies the given inequality is 2. Therefore, the greatest possible value of $3m + 2$ is $3(2) + 2 = 8$.

The correct answer is option C.

54. Topic: Linear inequalities and equations (word problems)

The correct answer is A

Since the total cost is $g(x) = 121,000$, we have
$$400x + 600 = 121,000 =>$$
$$400x = 120,400 =>$$
$$x = 301$$
Hence, 301 linear feet of roads will be modified.

The correct answer is option A.

55. Topic: Graphing Linear Equations

The correct answer is D $\dfrac{-1}{2}$

In order to find the slope, you need to take the change in y and divide it by the change in x. Using the points $(-4, 0)$ and $(0, -2)$ on the red line, you can find the slope. The change in y is $-2-0=-2$. The change in x is $0-(-4)=4$. So, the slope is $\dfrac{-2}{4}$, which reduces to $\dfrac{-1}{2}$. This is answer choice D.

56. Topic: Misc

The correct answer is 3

The solution to the system of linear equations is the intersection of the two lines. The intersection is at $(4, 3)$ by inspection. Therefore, the y value of the solution is 3.

57. Topic: Graphing Linear Equations

The correct answer is 52

The y intercept is found when the x value is 0 in the graph. Plugging in $x=0$ leads to the following equation: $y - 2 = 10(0 + 5)$, which simplifies to $y - 2 = 10(5)$. Multiplying 10×5 and adding 2 to the right side gives you a y value of 52. Therefore, the answer is 52.

58. Topic: Linear Function Word Problems

The correct answer is 12,950

In order to solve this, you must plug in 50 for x and obtain the equation $y = 250 \times 50 + 450$. Do the multiplication first and then the addition to get 12,950. So the population in 2050 in Whoville is 12,950 people.

59. Topic: Systems of Linear Inequalities

The correct answer is 4

If b represents hours babysitting and e represents hours editing, the system of linear inequalities that represents this situation is as follows:

$$6b + 10e > 180$$

$$b + e < 30$$

The question states that she works 25 hours babysitting, so this can be plugged in for b. The system of linear inequalities now becomes the following:

$$6(25) + 10e > 180$$

$$25 + e < 30$$

These linear systems now simplify to $e>3$ and $e<5$. Because the question asks for the whole number of hours she worked, e must be 4. Therefore, the answer is 4.

60. Topic: Interpreting linear functions

The correct answer is 24.5.

$$r = 4\sqrt{n}$$

Also: $s = 40 - r = 40 - 4\sqrt{n}$

For $n = 15$: $s = 40 - 4\sqrt{15} = 24.508 \approx 24.5$

The correct answer is 24.5

61. Topic: Graphing linear equations

The correct answer is 6

Slope of the line = $\dfrac{(n-1)}{(5+1)} = \dfrac{n-1}{6}$

$$\dfrac{n-1}{6} > \dfrac{2}{3}$$

$$n-1 > 4$$

$$n > 5$$

Thus, the least integer value of n is 6.

The correct answer is '6'.

62. Topic: Solving linear equations and inequalities

The correct answer is 5

$$x - (3 + 2x) = 7 - 3x =>$$

$$x - 3 - 2x = 7 - 3x =>$$

$$x - 2x + 3x = 7 + 3 =>$$

$$2x = 10 => x = 5.$$

The correct answer is $x=5$.

63. Topic: Linear inequalities and equations (word problems)

The correct answer is 70.20

Alice gets $(12(2.30) - 4.20)$ dollars profit per dozen of sold cupcakes. Hence, for n dozens of sold cupcakes she will get $n(12(2.30) - 4.20)$ dollars profit.

If Alice sells 3 dozens cupcakes, her net profit is

$$3(12(2.30) - 4.20) = 70.20 \text{ dollars.}$$

64. Topic: Solving Systems of Linear Equations

The correct answer is 9

You can do this problem two ways. Both are outlined below.

In Method 1, solve the system of linear equations. Do this by solving for y in the second equation to obtain $y = 10 + x$. Plug the expression $10 + x$ in for y in the first equation to get $2x + 1 = 10 + x$. Move the x over to the left side and the 1 over to the right side to get $x=9$. Therefore, the x value of our solution is 9. $M=9$.

In Method 2, plug 19 into either equation, because it is the solution to the entire system. Plugging 19 for y into the first equation becomes $2x + 1 = 19$.
Subtract 1 and divide by 2 to get $x=9$. Therefore $M=9$. You can also plug into 19 for y the second equation to get $19-x=10$. Add x to the right side and subtract 10 to the left side to obtain $x=9$. Therefore, $M=9$.

MULTIPLE CHOICE QUESTIONS

65

Gerald and Lee know that they have the same amount of blue and red marbles in their collections. Gerald knows that the weight of his marbles is less than 48 ounces. He also knows that his blue marbles are 3 ounces, and his red marbles are 2 ounces. Lee knows that his marbles weigh over 60 ounces, but he added extra weight to his marbles, so his blue marbles weigh 8 ounces, and his red marbles weigh 4 ounces. Which the following answer choice(s) demonstrate possible combinations of red and blue marbles each boy could have?

i) 8 red marbles, 8 blue marbles

ii) 30 red marbles, 16 blue marbles

iii) 2 red marbles, 14 blue marbles

iv) 18 red marbles, 10 blue marbles

A) iii and ii

B) i and iii

C) ii and iii

D) i and iv

A B C D
○ ○ ○ ○

66

Rachel and Mike are performing a science experiment using ice. Mike starts with 3 pounds of ice and leaves it out in the science classroom. The ice melts at a rate of 0.53 pounds per hour. Rachel puts 30 pounds of water in the freezer, and it turns to ice at a rate of 0.27 pounds per hour. If the experiment started at 12:00, at what time will each student have an equal amount of ice?

A) 12:05

B) 9:45

C) 2:30

D) 3:45

A B C D
○ ○ ○ ○

67

The average of the temperatures recorded by the National Climatic Centre in New York in a particular week for Monday, Tuesday, Wednesday and Thursday was 60°F. The average for Tuesday, Wednesday, Thursday and Friday in the same week was 55°F. If the ratio of the temperatures for Monday and Friday was 13 : 9, what was the temperature on Monday?

A) 45 °F

B) 55 °F

C) 60 °F

D) 65 °F

A B C D
○ ○ ○ ○

68

The demand of a particular product decreases as the price goes up. A company researched that when the product price is $45, the demand for the product is 1000. For every $5 increase in the price of the product, the demand falls by 15. What will be the demand for the product when the price is set at $80?

A) 890

B) 895

C) 985

D) 995

A B C D
○ ○ ○ ○

69

The entry fee of an amusement park is $10. Each ride in the park costs $2.50. If Chad has $25 with him, what is the maximum number of rides he can get on?

A) 6

B) 8

C) 9

D) 10

A B C D
○ ○ ○ ○

70

The relation between the temperature readings of the Celsius (C) and Fahrenheit (F) scales is given by: $F = 9/5\ C + 32$. If the temperature in Fahrenheit increases by 36 degrees, what is the corresponding increase in the Celsius scale?

A) 12°

B) 20°

C) 32°

D) 52°

A B C D
○ ○ ○ ○

71

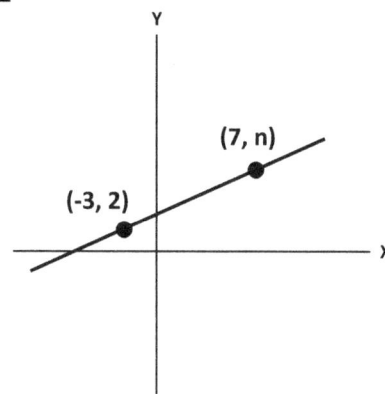

The graph above depicts a straight line passing through (–3, 2) and (7, n). If the Y–intercept of the line is given by k, which of the following is the correct expression of k in terms of n?

A) $k = 2$

B) $k = 0.3n - 0.6$

C) $k = 0.3n + 1.4$

D) $k = 0.1n + 1.8$

A B C D
○ ○ ○ ○

72

Harry got $350 as his salary. He puts $M in his savings account, and then spends the rest of the money on buying presents for his family members. If Harry has 8 family members and he spends $A amount on each member, which of the following equations represents the amount Harry spends on each member?

A) $(45–M)

B) $(350–0.125M)

C) $(43.75–M)

D) $(43.75–0.125M)

A B C D
○ ○ ○ ○

73

A class of 50 students belonging to the Kindergarten is divided in two sections A and B, having students in the ratio 2 : 3 respectively. The average weight of the students of the entire class is 40 lbs. The average weight of the students of section A is 2 lbs. less than that of the students of section B. What is the average weight of the students of section B?

A) 32.6 lbs.

B) 36.4 lbs.

C) 38.8 lbs.

D) 40.8 lbs.

A B C D
○ ○ ○ ○

74

To complete a particular task Dave charged $50 for the first 3 hours and thereafter $10 per hour. If '$A$' represents the amount that Dave receives after working for 'H' hours, which of the following expresses the amount he earns after working for 'H' hours, where $H>3$?

A) $A = 10H$

B) $A = 10H + 10$

C) $A = 10H + 20$

D) $A = 10H + 50$

A B C D
○ ○ ○ ○

75

In an exam, 3.5 points are awarded for every correct answer and 0.45 points are deducted for every wrong answer. If out of N questions, a boy answers at least 4 questions wrong and at most 8 questions wrong, which of the following correctly gives the correct range of scores, S, he can get in the exam?

A) $3.5N - 31.6 \le S \le 3.5N - 15.8$

B) $3.5N - 31.6 \le S \le 3.5N$

C) $15.8 \le S \le 3.5N - 31.6$

D) $3.5N \le S \le 31.6$

A B C D
○ ○ ○ ○

76

The demand of a particular product decreases as a linear function as the price goes up. A company researched that when the product price is $45, the demand for the product is 1000. For every $5 increase in the price of the product, the demand falls by 5. Which of the following correctly represents the demand, D, for the product as a function of the product price, p?

A) $D(p) = 1000 - \left(\dfrac{-4}{5}\right)p$

B) $D(p) = 1000 - (p + 45)$

C) $D(p) = \dfrac{1000}{45} - \dfrac{5}{4}p$

D) $D(p) = 1000 - \dfrac{5}{4}\left(\dfrac{4p}{5} - 36\right)$

A B C D
○ ○ ○ ○

77

A grid is made up of 13 rows of squares, each having 14 identical squares. Bob comes and wants to draw some more squares to the grid. So, he draws 3 additional rows and adds 'n' additional squares in each row, including the ones he added himself. Which of the following expression correctly represents the increase in the total number of squares in the grid?

A) $11 + 5n$

B) $42 + 16n$

C) $60 + 12n$

D) $224 + 16n$

A B C D
○ ○ ○ ○

78

A man travels by bus to work. For each trip, the man pays $x. He has an option of purchasing a monthly pass for $P which would reduce the fare for each trip by $r. If n be the number of trips he must make per month so that purchasing the pass is a profitable to him, which of the following is the correct inequality satisfying the above information?

A) $n < \dfrac{P}{r}$

B) $n > \dfrac{P}{r}$

C) $n < \dfrac{P}{x - r}$

D) $n > \dfrac{P}{x - r}$

A B C D
○ ○ ○ ○

79

If $2a - 3b = a + 2b,$ then what is the ratio of $a : b$?

A) $4 : 1$

B) $5 : 1$

C) $4 : 3$

D) $8 : 3$

A B C D
○ ○ ○ ○

80

A local contractor installs windows and doors. He charges $230 per window for installation and $340 per door for installation, plus a fee of $180 for the project. He got the second project from John and decides to give him a 12% discount as a returning customer. Which of the following expressions represents John's total bill, in dollars, for buying w windows and d doors?

A) $0.88(230w+340d)+180$

B) $1.12(180+230w+340d)$

C) $0.88(230w+340d+180)$

D) $(180+230w+340d)-0.12(230w+340d)$

A B C D
○ ○ ○ ○

GRID-IN

81

A system of inequalities describing Emily's exercise habits is described below. In the equations, h represents the number of hours hiking and b represents the number of hours playing basketball.

$$2h + b < 10$$

$$200h + Ab > 1000$$

What value of A creates no solution to this system of inequalities?

82

What is the y intercept of the following linear equation?

$$(y - 3.5) = -2.4(x - 2.8)$$

83

Abe reads a book every day, some pages in the morning and some in the evening. He reads 23 pages every morning and 31 pages every evening. The number of pages, N, completed by Abe after some number of days can be written as a function of the number of mornings, M, and the number evenings, E. How many number of pages will be read by Abe just after 11 mornings have passed?

65. Topic: Linear Inequality and Equation (word problems)

The correct answer is B

The equations that represent this situation are $3x + 2y < 48$ and $8x + 4y > 60$, where y is the number of red marbles in each collection, and x is the number of blue marbles in each collection. You can either plot each equation in a graphing calculator and look at the overlap, as shown below, or plug in each answer choice to see if it makes each equation valid. Answer Choice B is correct.

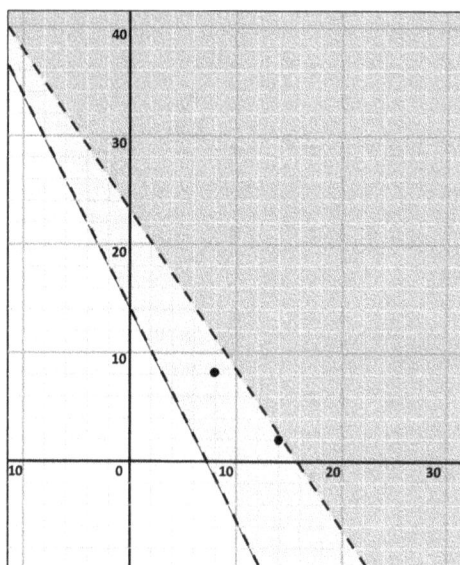

66. Topic: Linear Inequality and Equation (word problems)

The correct answer is D

The equations that dictate this experiment are $y = 3 - 0.53x$ and $y = 0.27x$, where y is the amount of ice in pounds and x is the number of hours that have gone by since 12:00. Setting them equal to find when Mike and Rachel have equal amounts of ice gives us the following equation: $3 - 0.53x = 0.27x$.

Move the $0.53x$ over to get $3 = 0.80x$.

To isolate x, divide by 0.80 on both sides. Thus, $x = 3.75$. This means 3.75 hours have passed in order to get the same amount of ice. Convert 3.75 hours to hours and minutes, to get 3 hours, 45 minutes. Add this to 12:00 to get 3:45. Therefore, the answer is Choice D, 3:45.

67. Topic: Linear inequality and equation (word problems)

The correct answer is D

Let the temperatures on Monday, Tuesday, Wednesday, Thursday, and Friday be denoted by M, T, W, H, and F respectively.

Since the average of M, T, W and H is 60, we have: $M + T + W + H = 60 \times 4 = 240$ ...(i)

Again, since the average of T, W, H and F is 55, we have: $T + W + H + F = 55 \times 4 = 220$ ...(ii)

Subtracting: (i) – (ii):

$$M - F = 20 =>$$

$$M = F + 20 ...(iii)$$

We know that

$$M : F = 13 : 9 =>$$

$$(F + 20) : F = 13 : 9 =>$$

$$\frac{F + 20}{F} = \frac{13}{9} => 9F + 180 = 13F$$

$F = 45$.

Thus, $M = F + 20 = 45 + 20 = 65$.

Thus, the temperature on Monday was 65°F.

Hence, the answer is D.

68. Topic: Linear function (word problems)

The correct answer is B

We know that, when the price is $45, the demand is 1000 units.

For every $5 increase in price, the demand falls by 15 units.

Thus, when the price is $80, the price has gone up by $(80 – 45)=$35

Thus, the demand falls by $\frac{35}{5} \times 15 = 105$ units

Thus, the demand = 1000 – 105 = 895

The correct answer is Option B.

69. **Topic:** Linear function (word problems)

The correct answer is A

If Chad takes 'R' rides in the park and spends 'A' amount on it, then $A=10+2.5\times R$

Here, $A = 25 => R = \dfrac{25-10}{2.5} = 6$

The correct answer is option A.

70. **Topic:** Interpreting linear functions

The correct answer is B

$$F = \dfrac{9}{5}C + 32$$

$$\dfrac{9}{5}C = F - 32$$

$$C = \dfrac{5}{9}(F - 32)$$

Thus, difference between two Celsius readings based on two Fahrenheit readings

$$= C_1 - C_2 = \dfrac{5}{9}((F_1 - 32) - (F_2 - 32)) = \dfrac{5}{9}(F_1 - F_2)$$

Change in Fahrenheit scale = 36°

Thus, difference in Celsius scale =

$$\dfrac{5}{9}(F_1 - F_2) = \dfrac{5}{9} \times 36 = 20^\circ$$

The correct answer is option B.

71. **Topic:** Graphing linear equations

The correct answer is C

Equation of the line:

$$\dfrac{y-2}{x+3} = \dfrac{n-2}{7+3}$$

$$\dfrac{y-2}{x-3} = \dfrac{n-2}{10}$$

$$y = \dfrac{n-2}{10}(x+3) + 2$$

$$y = \left(\dfrac{n-2}{10}\right)x + \dfrac{3(n-2)}{10} + 2$$

$$y = \left(\dfrac{n-2}{10}\right)x + \dfrac{3n}{10} - \dfrac{6}{10} + 2$$

$$y = \left(\dfrac{n-1}{6}\right)x + \left(\dfrac{3n}{10} + 1.4\right)$$

Thus, the Y–intercept = $k=(0.3n+1.4)$

The correct answer is Option C.

72. **Topic:** Linear function (word problems)

The correct answer is D

Harry gets a salary of $350 and saves $M from it.

Thus, Harry is left with $(350–M)

If he spends $A on each member, and there are 8 members, then total amount spent must be equal to $(8A)

$8A=(350–M)$

Or,

$$A = \dfrac{350 - M}{8} = 43.75 - 0.125M$$

73. **Topic:** Linear inequality and equation (word problems)

    The correct answer is D

    Ratio of the number of students in section A and B is 2:3.

    Also, the average weight of the students of section A is 2 lbs less than that of the students of section B.

    Let the average weight of the students of section B be x lbs.

    Thus, the average weight of the students of section $A = (x–2)$ lbs.

    Thus, overall average weight of all 50 students =

    $$\frac{2(x-2)+3x}{2+3} = \frac{5x-4}{5}$$

    Thus, $\dfrac{5x-4}{5} = 40 => x = 40.8$

    Thus, the average weight of the students of section $B = 40.8$ lbs.

    Hence, the answer is D.

74. **Topic:** Linear function (word problems)

    The correct answer is C

    For the first 3 hours, the Amount charged is 50

    For more than 3 hours, the number of chargeable hours at the rate of 10, should be $(H–3)$

    Thus, the Amount collected should be

    $50 + (H-3) \times 10 = 10H + 20$

    The correct answer is option C.

75. **Topic:** Systems of linear inequalities (word problems)

    The correct answer is A

    Let the number of wrong answers $= w => 4 \leq w \leq 8$

    Number of correct answers $= (N-w)$

    Thus, total score:

    $$S = 3.5(N - w) - 0.45w = 3.5N - 3.95w$$

    Minimum score happens when

    $$w = 8 : S = 3.5N - 3.95x8 = 3.5N - 31.6$$

    Maximum score happens when

    $$w = 4 : S = 3.5N - 3.95x4 = 3.5N - 15.8$$

    $$3.5N - 31.6 \leq S \leq 3.5N - 15.8$$

    The correct answer is option A.

76. **Topic:** Linear function (word problems)

    The correct answer is D

    Let the linear function be: $D(p)=kp+l$, where k and l are constants

    At $p = 45, D = 1000 => 1000 = 45k + 1$

    After \$5 increase, new demand decreases by 5

    If $p = 50, D = 995 => 995 = 50k + 1$

    Subtracting the 2 equations:

    $$5k = -5 => k = -1$$

    $$l = 1045$$

    Thus: $D(p) = -p + 1045$

    Only Option D, on simplification, leads to the same function.

    Alternative:

    At $p = 45$, the Demand must be 1000.

    Only option that satisfies this condition is Option (D)

    Hence the answer is Option D.

77. **Topic:** Linear function (word problems)

    The correct answer is B

    Number of squares initially = 13 ×14 = 182

    After Bob draws the additional squares, the grid has (13+3)=16 rows

    There are (14+n) squares in each row

    Thus, the total number of squares = 16(14+n)=224+16n

    Thus, increase in the number of squares = (224+16n)–182=42+16n

78. **Topic:** Systems of linear inequalities (word problems)

    The correct answer is B

    The man travels n times per month.

    Normal travel: Total cost = $($nx$)$

    With the pass: Total cost = $\{P+(x-r)n\}$

    Thus, the pass will be profitable if:

    $$P + (x - r)n < nx$$

    $$P < n\{x - (x - r)\}$$

    $$P < rn => n > \frac{P}{r}$$

    The correct answer is option B.

79. **Topic:** Solving systems of linear equations

    The correct answer is B

    $$2a - 3b = a + 2b$$

    $$=> a = 5b$$

    $$a : b = 5 : 1$$

    The correct answer is option B.

80. **Topic:** Linear inequalities and equations (word problems)

    The correct answer is C

    The standard cost of installing w windows and d doors is 230w+320d+180.

    A 12% discount is 0.12(230w+320d+180).

    To get the bill for John's project we subtract the discount from standard cost,

    which is 0.88(230w+320d+180).

    The correct answer is option C.

81. **Topic:** Systems of Linear Inequalities (word problems)

    The correct answer is 100

    The value of A that creates no solution is 100, because this is the value of A that makes the system of linear inequalities the same with different inequality signs. If A is 100, the second inequality turns into $200h + 100b > 1000$, which simplifies to $2h + b > 10$.

    This is the same as the original equation but with a less than instead of a greater than. If this was the case, there would be no solution that could make 2h+b less than 10 and greater than 10 at the same time, creating no solution.

82. **Topic:** Graphing Linear Equations (word problems)

    The correct answer is 10.22

    To find the y intercept, either plug in 0 for x or turn the equation into slope intercept form. I will show the first strategy.

    Plugging 0 in for x gets the following equation: $(y - 3.5) = -2.4(0 - 2.8)$. Simplifying becomes $y - 3.5 = -2.4(-2.8)$. Continue to combine like terms and simplify to get y=10.22.

    So the y intercept is 10.22.

83. **Topic:** Linear function (word problems)

The correct answer is 563

As Abe reads 23 pages every morning, thus after 'M' mornings he should have read '$23M$' pages

Also, as Abe reads 31 pages every evening, after 'E' evenings he should have read '$31E$' pages

So, the total pages read by Abe by that time should be given by $N = 23M + 31E$

After exactly 11 mornings have passed, $M=11$ and $E=10$, we get $N = 253 + 310 = 563$

The correct answer is 563.

MULTIPLE CHOICE QUESTIONS

84

Sam works as a janitor and needs to stack chairs in the gym. The first chair is 25 inches tall. After stacking 4 chairs, including the first one, the height of the stack is now 34 inches tall. What equation represents this equation, with y being total height in inches and x being total number of chairs?

A) $y = 25x$

B) $y = 3x + 22$

C) $y = 3x + 25$

D) $\dfrac{y}{34} = 25$

A B C D
○ ○ ○ ○

85

Twelve friends raised some funds among themselves for a dinner party. Ten of them contributed $80 each while the other two contributed $80 and $120 more than the average of all twelve friends. What was the average contribution of all the friends taken together?

A) $220

B) $180

C) $100

D) $80

A B C D
○ ○ ○ ○

86

The distance, d, in feet, covered by a ball in the nth second after being dropped from the top of a building is given by $d = 6n + 1$. What is the total distance, in feet, covered by the ball in the first 5 seconds?

A) 27

B) 31

C) 65

D) 95

A B C D
○ ○ ○ ○

87

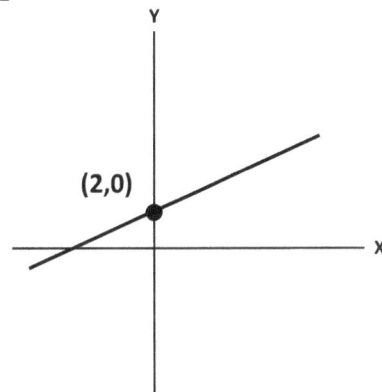

The graph above depicts a straight line having the equation $y = mx + n$. What can be said about the line given by the equation $y = nx + m$?

A) The line passes through the 1st, 2nd and 3rd quadrants

B) The line passes through the 1st, 2nd and 4th quadrants

C) The line passes through the 1st, 3rd and 4th quadrants

D) The line passes through the 2nd, 3rd and 4th quadrants

A B C D
○ ○ ○ ○

88

Chad decides to save at least $105 over a period of 15 days. Initially, for the first n days, he saves $3 every day; for the next $2n$ days, he saves 75 cents more per day than what he was saving initially. If, for the remaining days, he saves $$s$ per day, which of the following gives the correct relation between n and s?

A) $s > 3.5\left(\dfrac{10-n}{5-n}\right)$

B) $s \geq 3.5\left(\dfrac{10-n}{5-n}\right)$

C) $s \leq 3.5\left(\dfrac{10-n}{5-n}\right)$

D) $s < 3.5\left(\dfrac{10-n}{5-n}\right)$

A B C D
○ ○ ○ ○

89

The number of inventory items, n, in a factory, at the end of each month starting from January in 2016, was given by the relation: $n=60+15m$, where m represents the number of months completed after January in that year. If 80 items were procured in each month for the inventory, what is the total number of items used from the inventory till end of March in that year? Assume that there was no inventory carried forward from the previous year.

A) 65

B) 85

C) 130

D) 150

A B C D
○ ○ ○ ○

90

The cost of 3 chocolates and 2 candies is $14 and the cost of 1 chocolate and 3 candies is $14. What is the maximum of candies Ron can buy for $42 if he buys candies and chocolates both.

A) 11

B) 10

C) 8

D) 6

A B C D
○ ○ ○ ○

91

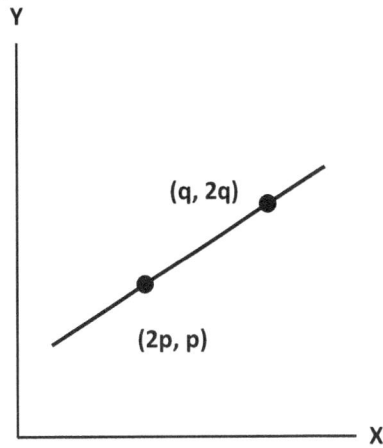

The graph above depicts a straight line.

If $q > 2p$, which of the following options could be the slope of the line shown?

A) $\dfrac{1}{2}$

B) 1

C) 2

D) $\dfrac{7}{2}$

A B C D
○ ○ ○ ○

GRID-IN

92

If the solution to the following system of equations is (A,B), what is A+B?

$$\frac{8x^3 + 4x^2}{2x^2} + 4y = 10$$

$$4y^2 - 6y = 2x + \frac{(6y)^2}{9}$$

93

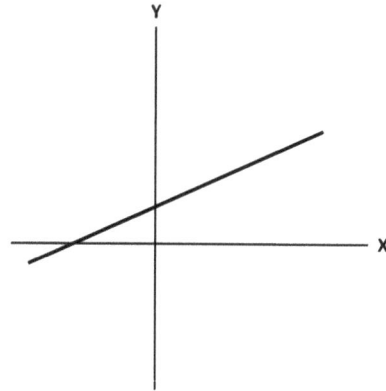

The graph below depicts the straight line $y = \frac{x}{2} + 3$. If the line is reflected about the X axis and the equation of the new line is $y = mx + n$, what is the value of $|m + n|$?

84. Topic: Linear Function (word problems)

The correct answer is B

The equation that dictates this scenario is B)$y=3x+22$. When 3 extra chairs were added, the stack grew by $34-25=9$ inches. Each stacked chair increases the height by 3, therefore $3x$ in the equation. You also need to account for the initial chair, which is 25 inches.

But, if you choose C) you would be double counting the first chair by counting it in the $3x$ term and the +25 term. Therefore, the equation becomes $y=3x-3+22$, which is Answer Choice B.

85. Topic: Linear inequality and equation (word problems)

The correct answer is C

Let the average contribution of all 12 friends be $x

Thus, total contributions of all 12 friends = $12x$.

Average of 10 friends is $80.

Thus, total contributions of these 10 friends = $80 × 10=$800.

Also, contributions from the last two friends are $(x+80)$ and $(x+120)$.

Thus, we have:

$=800+(x+80)+(x+120)=>12x=1000+2x=>x=100$.

Thus, average contribution of all the friends taken together = $100.

Hence, the answer is C.

86. Topic: Interpreting linear functions

The correct answer is D

Distance covered in the 1st second: $d=6×1+1=7$

Distance covered in the 2nd second: $d=6×2+1=13$

Distance covered in the 3rd second: $d=6×3+1=19$

Distance covered in the 4th second: $d=6×4+1=25$

Distance covered in the 5th second: $d=6×5+1=31$

Thus, total distance $=7+13+19+25+31=95$ feet.

The correct answer is option D.

87. Topic: Graphing linear equations

The correct answer is A

From the diagram it is clear that the line $y=mx+n$ is a flat line, the slope is less than 1.

Thus, the value of $0<m<1$

Also, the Y–intercept is 2, i.e. $n=2$

Thus, in the line $y=nx+m$, the slope is $n=2$, the Y–intercept is a positive fraction.

Thus, the line would be as shown:

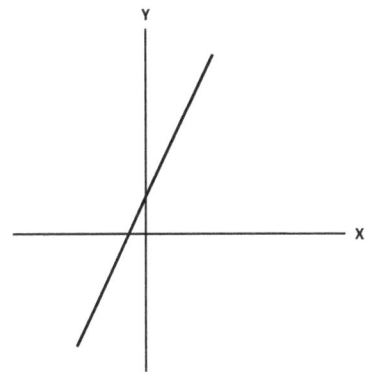

The Quadrants go in order from the top right corner to the bottom right corner in a C shape. Thus, this line goes through all quadrants except quadrant 4.

The correct answer is option A.

88. Topic: Systems of linear inequalities (word problems)

The correct answer is B

Amount saved in the first n days = $\$(3n)$

Amount saved in the next $(2n)$ days = $\$(3.75 \times 2n) = \$(7.5n)$

Days remaining = $15 - n - 2n = 15 - 3n$

Thus:

$$3n + 7.5n + s(15 - 3n) \geq 15 - 3n$$

$$10.5n + 15s - 3ns \geq 105 => 21n + 30s - 6ns \geq 210$$

$$7n + 10s - 2ns \geq 70 => s(10 - 2n) \geq 70 - 7n$$

$$s \geq \frac{7(10 - n)}{2(5 - n)} => s \geq 3.5 \left(\frac{10 - n}{5 - n} \right)$$

The correct answer is option B.

89. Topic: Interpreting linear functions

The correct answer is D

For January: $m = 0$

Thus, number of items = 60

Since 80 items were procured in January, $80 - 60 = 20$ items were used up in January.

For February: $m = 1$

Thus, number of items = $60 + 15 = 75$ => Number of additional items = $75 - 60 = 15$

Since 80 items were procured in February, $80 - 15 = 65$ items were used up in February.

For March: $m = 2$

Thus, number of items = $60 + 15 \times 2 = 90$ => Number of additional items = $90 - 75 = 15$

Since 80 items were procured in March, $80 - 15 = 65$ items were used up in March.

Thus, total items used up = $20 + 65 + 65 = 150$

The correct answer is option D.

90. Topic: Linear function (word problems)

The correct answer is B

Let the cost of 1 chocolate, and 1 candy be $\$x$ and $\$y$, respectively.

Thus:

$$3x + 2y = 14 \ldots(i)$$

$$x + 3y = 14 \ldots(ii)$$

Multiplying (ii) by -3 and adding with (i):

$$-7y = -28 \ldots(iii)$$

Hence, $y = 4$.

Substituting $y = 4$ to (ii): $x + 12 = 14 => x = 2$.

Thus, for $\$42$ Ron can by a maximum 10 candies and 1 chocolate.

The correct answer is option B.

91. Topic: Graphing linear equations

The correct answer is D

Slope of the line = $m = \dfrac{(2q - p)}{(q - 2p)}$

Since both points are in the first quadrant, $p > 0$ and $q > 0$

Since $q > 2p$, let $q = 2p + k$, where $k > 0$

Thus, slope m=

$$\frac{2(2p + k - p)}{(2p + k) - 2p} = \frac{3p + 2k}{k} = 3 \left(\frac{p}{k} \right) + 2$$

Thus, the slope is greater than 2.

The correct answer is option D.

92. Topic: Solving Linear Equations and Inequalities (word problems)

The correct answer is 2

Simplify the first equation by dividing the first two terms in the numerator by the denominator to get $4x+2+4y=10$.

Combine like terms to get $4x+4y=8$. Now combine like terms on the second equation and reduce.

First distribute the squared to the $6y$, to get $36y^2$. Then divide by 9 to get $4y^2$. Cancel the $4y^2$ out on both sides and obtain $-6y=2x$. Then divide by 2 to get $x=-3y$.

Substitute $x=-3y$ into the first equation to get $4(-3y)+4y=8$. Simplify and combine like terms to get $-8y=8$, then divide by -8 to get $y=-1$. Plug y into the equation $x=-3y$ to get $x=-3(-1)=3$. So $x=3$ and $y=-1$.

Add them together to get $A+B$, which is $3+(-1)$. The solution is 2.

93. Topic: Graphing linear equations

The correct answer is 3.5

Since the equation of the line: $y = \dfrac{x}{2} + 3$

a reflection over the x-axis will give the equation $y = \dfrac{-x}{2} - 3$. This means m = $\dfrac{-1}{2}$ and n = -3. so

$$\left| \dfrac{-1}{2} - 3 \right| = \left| -3.5 \right| = 3.5$$

The solution is 3.5.

This page is intentionally left blank

Chapter 3
Passport to Advanced Math

MULTIPLE CHOICE QUESTIONS

1

Which expression is equivalent to

$$2x^2 + 3x + 1$$

A) $(2x+1)(2x+1)$

B) $(x+2)(x+1)$

C) $(x-2)(x-1)$

D) $(2x+1)(x+1)$

A B C D
○ ○ ○ ○

2

Let $\emptyset$ be an operation on x and y defined as $x \emptyset y = \dfrac{x^{-2} + y^{-2}}{x^{-1} + y^{-1}}$. Find the value of $(1 \emptyset 1) \emptyset 3$?

A) 0.83

B) 1.00

C) 2.50

D) 2.67

A B C D
○ ○ ○ ○

3

Let ! be an operation on p and q defined as $p!q = p^2 + 4pq + q^4$. If $-1!x = -3,$ what is the value of $x!(x+1)$?

A) – 11

B) 1

C) 2

D) 61

A B C D
○ ○ ○ ○

4

What is the positive value of x that satisfies the equation: $\dfrac{6}{x+1} = \dfrac{3}{x-1} - 1$?

A) 1

B) 2

C) 3

D) 4

A B C D
○ ○ ○ ○

5

If $f(x) = \dfrac{a^x - 1}{a^x + 1}$, choose the correct statement.

i. $f(-x) = f(x)$

ii. $f(-x) = -f(x)$

iii. $f(2x) = 2f(x)$

A) Only I

B) Only II

C) Only III

D) Both II and III

A B C D
○ ○ ○ ○

6

$f(x)=2|x|+x$. Which of the options is the correct value of $f(-2)+f(-4)$?

A) $f(-3)$

B) $f(-1)$

C) $f(0)$

D) $f(2)$

A B C D
○ ○ ○ ○

7

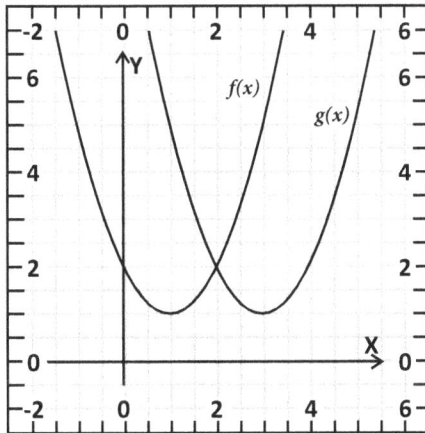

The graphs of $f(x)$ and $g(x)$ are shown below. Which option is true?

A) $g(x)=f(x-2)$

B) $g(x)=f(x)+1$

C) $g(x)=f(x-1)$

D) $g(x)=f(x)-2$

A B C D
○ ○ ○ ○

8

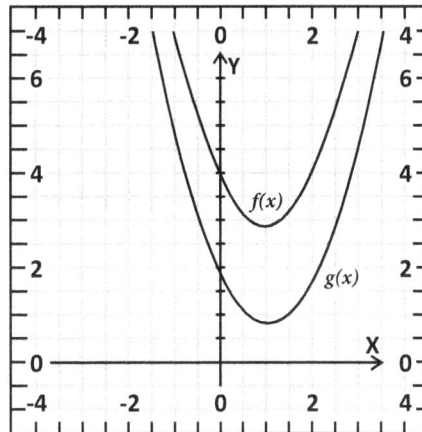

The graphs of $f(x)$ and $g(x)$ are shown below. Which option is true?

A) $f(x)=g(x+2)$

B) $f(x)=g(x)+2$

C) $f(x)=g(x-2)$

D) $f(x)=g(x)-2$

A B C D
○ ○ ○ ○

9

If $2x = a - \dfrac{1}{a}$, where $a > 0$, what is the value of $\sqrt{(x^2+1)} + x$?

A) 1

B) $\dfrac{1}{a}$

C) a

D) $\dfrac{1}{2}\left(a + \dfrac{1}{a}\right)$

A B C D
○ ○ ○ ○

10

If $h(x) = 2^{kx-1}$, what is the value of $\dfrac{h(a)\,h(b)}{h(a+b)}$?

A) 4

B) 2

C) 1

D) 0.5

A B C D
○ ○ ○ ○

11

If $f(x) = x^3 - kx^2 + 2x$ and $f(-x) = -f(x)$, the value of k is _____

A) – 2

B) 0

C) 1

D) 2

A B C D
○ ○ ○ ○

GRID-IN

12

If $x+3=10$, what is $x^2 + 3x$?

13

If $f(x)=8x^2-10$, what is the absolute value of x when $f(x)=62$?

14

The product of three consecutive positive integers is 8 times the sum of the three numbers. What is the sum of the three integers?

15

If $f(x) = |x-2| + x^2 - 1$ and

$g(x) + f(x) = x^2 + 3,$ find the maximum value of $g(x)$.

1. **Topic:** Solving Quadratic Equations

The correct answer is D

If you FOIL the answer choice, you will obtain $2x^2 + 1x + 2x + 1,$ which simplifies to $2x^2 + 3x + 1,$ which is our original expression.

2. **Topic:** Functions

The correct answer is A

$$x\phi y = \frac{x^{-2} + y^{-2}}{x^{-1} + y^{-1}} = \frac{\left(\dfrac{1}{x^2} + \dfrac{1}{y^2}\right)}{\left(\dfrac{1}{x} + \dfrac{1}{y}\right)} = \frac{x^2 + y^2}{xy(x+y)}$$

Thus, we have:

$$(1\phi1)\phi3 = \left(\frac{1^2 + 1^2}{1 \times 1 \times (1+1)}\right)\phi3 = 1\phi3 =>$$

$$\frac{1^2 + 3^2}{1 \times 3 \times (1+3)} = \frac{10}{12} = \frac{5}{6} = 0.83$$

Hence, the correct answer is A.

3. **Topic:** Functions

The correct answer is D

$$x!1 = -3 =>$$

$$x^2 - 4x + 1 = -3 =>$$

$$x^2 - 4x + 4 = 0$$

$$(x-2)^2 = 0 => x = 2$$

Thus,

$$x!(x+1) = 2!3 =$$
$$2^2 - 4 \times 2 \times 3 + 3^4 =$$
$$4 - 21 + 81 = 61$$

4. **Topic:** Solving quadratic equations

The correct answer is B

Simplifying the equation, we have:

$$\frac{6}{x+1} = \frac{3}{x-1} - 1 =>$$

$$\frac{6}{x+1} - \frac{3}{x-1} = -1 =>$$

$$\frac{6(x-1) - 3(x+1)}{(x+1)(x-1)} = -1$$

$$\frac{3x-9}{x^2-1} = -1 =>$$

$$3x - 9 = 1 - x^2 + 3x - 10 = 0 =>$$

$$x^2 + 5x - 2x - 10 = 0$$

$$(x+5)(x-2) = 0 => x = -5 \text{ or } 2$$

Thus, the positive value of x is 2.

Hence, the correct answer is B.

5. **Topic:** Functions

The correct answer is B

$$f(-x) = \frac{a^{-x} - 1}{a^{-x} + 1} = \frac{\dfrac{1}{a^x} - 1}{\dfrac{1}{a^x} + 1} =>$$

$$\frac{1 - a^x}{1 + a^x} = -\frac{a^x - 1}{a^x + 1} = -f(x).$$

Hence, statement I is not true, and statement II is true.

Again, $f(2x) = \dfrac{a^{2x} - 1}{a^{2x} + 1}$

While $2f(x) = 2\left(\dfrac{a^x - 1}{a^x + 1}\right) = \dfrac{2a^x - 2}{a^x + 1}$

Thus, $f(2x) \neq 2f(x)$

Hence, statement III is not true.

Hence, the correct answer is B.

6. **Topic:** Functions

The correct answer is D

$f(x)=2|x|+x$.

Thus, $f(-2)=2|-2|+(-2)=2 \times 2-2=2$.

Also, $f(-4)=2|-4|+(-4)=2 \times 4-4=4$.

Thus, $f(-2)+f(-4)=2+4=6$.

Hence, we need to choose that option whose value is 6.

Going by the options, we get:

Option (A): $f(-3)=2|-3|+(-3)=6-3=3 \neq 6$.

Option (B): $f(-1)=2|-1|+(-1)=2-1=1 \neq 6$.

Option (C): $f(0)=2|0|+(0)=0 \neq 6$.

Hence, option (D) must be the answer. Let us verify:

Option (D): $f(2)=2|2|+(2)=4+2=6$.

Hence, the correct answer is D.

7. **Topic:** Nonlinear equation graphs

The correct answer is A

It appears that the graph of $f(x)$ has been shifted right to get the graph of $g(x)$.

Let us pick a few values of y and check the values of x for each of $f(x)$ and $g(x)$.

At $y=1$: $x=1$ for $f(x)$ while we have $x=3$ for $g(x)$.

At $y=2$: $x=0$ or 2 for $f(x)$ while we have $x=2$ or 4 for $g(x)$.

At $y=5$: $x=-1$ or 3 for $f(x)$ while we have $x=1$ or 5 for $g(x)$.

Thus, we see that for the same y values, the values of x in $g(x)$ are two more than that of $f(x)$.

Thus, we can say that $g(x)=f(x-2)$.

Say $x=3$: $g(x)=g(3)=1$ and $f(x-2)=f(1)=1=>g(3)=f(1)$.

Thus, the correct answer is A.

8. **Topic:** Nonlinear equation graphs

The correct answer is B

It appears that the graph of $g(x)$ has been shifted up to get the graph of $f(x)$.

Let us pick a few values of x and check the values of y for each of $f(x)$ and $g(x)$.

At $x=0$: $y=2$ for $g(x)$ while we have $y=4$ for $f(x)$.

At $x=1$: $y=1$ for $g(x)$ while we have $y=3$ for $f(x)$.

At $x=3$: $y=5$ for $g(x)$ while we have $y=7$ for $f(x)$.

Thus, we see that for the same x values, the values of y in $f(x)$ are two more than that of $g(x)$.

Thus, we can say that $f(x)=g(x)+2$.

Say $x=1$: $f(x)=f(1)=3$ and $g(x)=g(1)=1=>f(1)=g(1)+2$.

Thus, the correct answer is B.

9. **Topic:** Structure in expressions

The correct answer is C

We have:

$$x = \frac{1}{2}\left(a - \frac{1}{a}\right)$$

$$x^2 + 1 = \left\{\frac{1}{2}\left(a - \frac{1}{a}\right)\right\}^2 + 1$$

$$= \frac{1}{4}\left(a^2 + \frac{1}{a^2} + 2\right)$$

$$= \frac{1}{4}\left(a + \frac{1}{a}\right)^2$$

$$\sqrt{(x^2 + 1)} = \frac{1}{2}\left(a + \frac{1}{a}\right)$$

$$\sqrt{(x^2 + 1)} + x = \frac{1}{2}\left(a + \frac{1}{a}\right) + \frac{1}{2}\left(a - \frac{1}{a}\right) = a$$

The correct answer is option C.

10. Topic: Functions

The correct answer is D

$$\frac{h(a)h(b)}{h(a+b)} = \frac{(2^{ka-1}2^{kb-1})}{2^{k(a+b)-1}} =>$$

$$\frac{2^{ka-1+kb-1}}{2^{k(a+b)-1}} = \frac{2^{k(a+b)-2}}{2^{k(a+b)-1}} =>$$

$$2^{k(a+b)-2-(k(a+b)-1)} =>$$

$$2^{-1} = \frac{1}{2} = 0.5$$

Hence, the correct answer is D.

11. Topic: Functions

The correct answer is B

$$f(-x) = (-x)^3 - k(-x)^2 + 2(-x) =>$$

$$-x^3 - kx^2 - 2x$$

Since

$$f(-x) = -f(x) => -x^3 - kx^2 - 2x =>$$

$$-(x^3 - kx^2 + 2x) => 2kx^2 = 0 => k = 0$$

(Note: We should not conclude that $x=0$ since according to the question, $f(-x)=-f(x)$ for all x in general).

Hence, the correct answer is B.

12. Topic: Isolating Quantities

The correct answer is 70

If $x+3=10$, $x=7$. Then plug in 7 into the expression we are trying to solve for and obtain $7^2+3(7)$. Simplify to get $49+21=70$.

Hence, the correct answer is 70.

13. Topic: Misc

The correct answer is 3

To solve, replace $f(x)$ with 62. You then get $62 = 8x^2 - 10$. Move the 10 over to get $72 = 8x^2$. Divide by 8 to get $9 = x^2$. Then x is either 3 or –3 when you take the square root. The absolute value of the answer is therefore 3.

14. Topic: Solving quadratic equations

The correct answer is 15

Let the three integers be $x-1$, x, $x+1$.

Thus, we have:

$$(x-1)x(x+1) = 8((x-1) + x + (x+1)) =>$$

$$x(x^2 - 1) = 24x$$

$$x^2 - 1 = 24 => x^2 = 25 => x = \pm5$$

Since the numbers are positive, we take $x=5$.

Thus, the sum of the three numbers =

$$(x-1) + x + (x+1) = 3x = 3 \times 5 = 15.$$

Hence, the correct answer is 15.

15. Topic: Functions

The correct answer is 4

We have:

$$g(x) = x^2 + 3 - f(x) =>$$

$$x^2 + 3 - (|x-2| + x^2 - 1) =>$$

$$x^2 + 3 - |x-2| - x^2 + 1$$

$$g(x) = 4 - |x-2|$$

$g(x)$ will be maximum when $|x-2|$ is minimum. This would happen at $x=2$ and the corresponding maximum value of $g(x)$ is 4.

MULTIPLE CHOICE QUESTIONS

What is the solution to the following equation?

$$\sqrt{10x + 14} = 2x + 4$$

i. $x = -\dfrac{1}{2}$

ii. $x = -1$

iii. $x = \dfrac{1}{2}$

iv. $x = 2$

A) i and ii

B) i and iv

C) ii and iii

D) All of the above

A B C D
○ ○ ○ ○

17

What is the value of B if the equation
$x^2 + Bx + 4 = 0$ has solutions of $x=1$ and $x=4$?

A) 5

B) –5

C) 1

D) –4

A B C D
○ ○ ○ ○

18

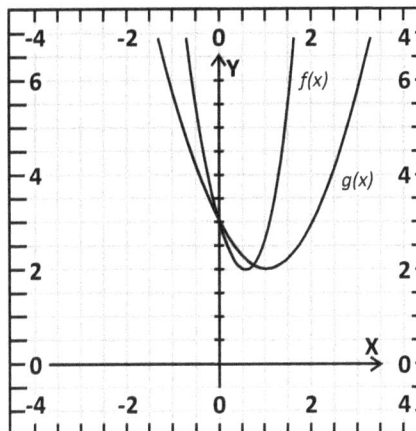

The graphs of $f(x)$ and $g(x)$ are shown below.
Which option is true?

A) $f(x)=g(x+1)$

B) $f(x)=g(x)+1$

C) $f(x)=2g(x)$

D) $f(x)=g(2x)$

A B C D
○ ○ ○ ○

19

What is the value of x that satisfies the equation:

$$\sqrt{x-3} = \sqrt{2x+2} - 2?$$

A) 7

B) 4

C) 9

D) 12

A B C D
○ ○ ○ ○

20

$$f(x) = \frac{x-k}{5} \text{ and } g(x) = 5x + 7.$$

If $f(g(x)) = g(f(x))$, what is the value of k?

A) 2

B) 4

C) 5

D) 7

A B C D
○ ○ ○ ○

21

If $f(x + 2) = x + 7$ and $g(f(x)) = 2x$, find the value of $g(5)$.

A) 0

B) 1

C) 3

D) 5

A B C D
○ ○ ○ ○

22

If $f(x) = ax^2 + bx + c$ and

$f(x + 1) = f(x) + x + 1$, then the value of

$(a + b)$ is ___

A) – 2

B) – 1

C) 0

D) 1

A B C D
○ ○ ○ ○

23

In the formula $s = ut - \frac{a}{2}t$, which of the following is NOT the correct expression of a in terms of s, u and t?

A) $2u - \frac{2s}{t}$

B) $\frac{2(ut - s)}{t}$

C) $\frac{u - st}{2t}$

D) $\frac{1}{t}(2ut - 2s)$

A B C D
○ ○ ○ ○

24

Let $\forall$ be an operation on a defined as $\forall a = (a^2 - 3a - 4)$. If $\forall k$ also equals $(k–4)$, find the positive value of k.

A) –5

B) 2

C) 4

D) 1

A B C D
○ ○ ○ ○

25

What is the value of $\frac{\sqrt{x+13}}{x} x\sqrt{x}$ if $x = 36$?

A) 36

B) 42

C) 49

D) 294

A B C D
○ ○ ○ ○

GRID-IN

26

Use the following rational expression to answer the question.

$$y = \frac{3x - 6}{2x + 10}$$

The horizontal asymptote is $y=A$, where A is a constant. The horizontal asymptote occurs when the function has a y value equal to 0.

The vertical asymptote is $x=B$, where B is a constant. The vertical asymptote occurs when the function has an undefined y value, meaning that the denominator is 0.

What is the value of $A-B$?

27

What is the x value of the solution to the system of linear equations?

$$y = 4x + 1$$

$$2x + 3y = 19$$

28

The function $f(x)$ is defined as follows:

$f(x) = x^2 - 1$ if $x \le 3$

$f(x) = 2x + 2$ if $3 < x \le 9$

$f(x) = 4x - 8$ if $x > 9$

What is the value of k if $f(f(f(3))) = (k+1)^2$ where k is a positive integer?

29

Find the sum of the possible integer values of m:

$$2m + n = 10$$

$$m(n - 1) = 9$$

30

How many solutions exist for the equation $|x - 1|^2 + 4x = 0$?

31

If $x - y = 2$ and $x^2 - y^2 = 9,$ what is the value of $(x^3 - y^3 - xy^2 - x^2y)$?

16. Topic: Radicals and Rational Exponents

The correct answer is A

To solve this problem, you first need to square both sides to get rid of the radical. $10x + 14 = (2x + 4)^2$ Now FOIL (distribute) the right–hand side to obtain $10x + 14 = 4x^2 + 16x + 16$. Now, move over all of the terms to the right side to get $0 = 4x^2 + 6x + 2$. Divide by 2 to get an easier equation to factor. $0 = 2x^2 + 3x + 1$. Then factor to get $0 = (2x + 1)(x + 1)$. Then set each of the parentheses equal to 0 to get

$$x = \frac{-1}{2} \text{ and } x = -1.$$

17. Topic: Solving Quadratic Equations

The correct answer is B

If the solutions are 1 and 4, the equation can be written as $(x - 1)(x - 4) = 0$. When you distribute the parentheses, you obtain $x^2 - 4x - 1x + 4 = 0$. Combining like terms gives you $x^2 - 5x + 4 = 0$. Compare this to the original equation to see that $B = -5$.

18. Topic: Nonlinear equation graphs

The correct answer is D

It appears that $f(x)$ has been made narrower compared to $g(x)$ keeping y values same.

Let us pick a few values of y and check the values of x for each of $f(x)$ and $g(x)$.

At $y=2$: $x=1$ for $g(x)$ while we have $x=0.5$ for $f(x)$.

At $y=3$: $x=0$ for both $g(x)$ and $f(x)$.

At $y=6$: $x=3$ for $g(x)$ while we have $x=1.5$ for $f(x)$.

Thus, we see that for the same y values, the values of x in $f(x)$ are half of that of $g(x)$.

Also, the minimum values of both $f(x)$ and $g(x)$ are the same.

Thus, the graph of $f(x)$ is narrower than the graph of $g(x)$ by a factor of two.

Thus, we can say that $f(x)=g(2x)$.

Say $x=1$: $f(x)=f(1)=3$ and $g(2x)=g(2)=3=>f(1)=g(2)$.

Thus, the correct answer is D.

19. Topic: Solving quadratic equations

The correct answer is A

Squaring both sides of the given equation, we have:

$$\left(\sqrt{x-3}\right)^2 = \left(\sqrt{2x+2} - 2\right)^2 =>$$

$$x - 3 = 2x + 2 - 4\sqrt{2x+2} + 4 =>$$

$$4\sqrt{2x+2} = x + 9$$

Squaring both sides of the above equation:

$$16(2x + 2) = (x + 9)^2 =>$$

$$32x + 32 = x^2 + 18x + 81 =>$$

$$x^2 - 14x + 49 = 0$$

$$(x - 7)^2 = 0 => x = 7$$

Hence, the correct answer is A.

20. **Topic:** Functions

The correct answer is D

$$f(g(x)) = \frac{g(x) - k}{5} = \frac{(5x + 7) - k}{5} =>$$

$$\frac{5x + 7 - k}{5}$$

$$g(f(x)) = 5(f(x)) + 7 =>$$

$$5x\frac{(x - k)}{5} + 7 =>$$

$$x - k + 7$$

Since

$$f(g(x)) = g(f(x)) =>$$

$$\frac{5x + 7 - k}{5} = x - k + 7 =>$$

$$5x + 7 - k = 5x - 5k + 35$$

$$4k = 28 => k = 7$$

Hence, the correct answer is D.

Alternative:

We know that $f(g(x)) = g(f(x))$ is true only when one function is the inverse of the other i.e. $f(x) = g^{-1}(x)$ (in fact, $f(g(x)) = g(f(x)) = x$).

Let us find the inverse of $g(x)$:

We have: $y = 5x + 7 =>$

$$5x = y - 7 =>$$

$$x = \frac{y - 7}{5} \quad .$$

Interchanging x and y:

$$y = \frac{x - 7}{2} => g^{-1}(x) = \frac{x - 7}{5} \quad .$$

Thus, we have $g^{-1}(x) = \frac{x - 7}{5} = f(x) = \frac{x - k}{5}$.

Comparing $g^{-1}(x)$ and $f(x)$, we get: k=7.

Hence, the correct answer is D.

21. **Topic:** Functions

The correct answer is A

$$f(x + 2) = x + 7 = (x + 2) + 5.$$

Thus, we can say that: $f(x) = x + 5$.

$$g(f(x)) = g(x + 5) =>$$

$$2x = 2(x + 5) - 10 =>$$

$$g(x + 5) = 2(x + 5) - 10$$

Thus, we can say that: $g(x) = 2x - 10$.

Hence, $g(5) = 2(5) - 10 = 0$.

Hence, the correct answer is A.

22. **Topic:** Functions

The correct answer is D

$$f(x + 1) = f(x) + x + 1 =>$$

$$a(x + 1)^2 + b(x + 1) + c =>$$

$$ax^2 + bx + c + x + 1$$

$$a((x + 1)^2 - x^2) + b((x + 1) - x) = (x + 1)$$

$$a(2x + 1) = b = x + 1.$$

The above is an identity, hence would be true for all values of x.

Since we need $a + b$, we substitute $x = 0$ in the above identity so that we get $2x + 1 = 1$.

Thus, we have:

$$a(2 \times 0 + 1) + b = 0 + 1 => a + b = 1$$

Hence, the correct answer is D.

23. Topic: Isolating quantities

The correct answer is C

$$s = ut - \frac{a}{2}t$$

$$\frac{a}{2}t = ut - s$$

$$a = \frac{2(ut - s)}{t}$$

$$a = 2u - \frac{2s}{t}$$

$$a = \frac{1}{t}(2ut - 2s)$$

The correct answer is option C.

24. Topic: Functions

The correct answer is C

According to the definition for the symbol ∀, we have

$$\forall k = (k^2 - 3k - 4).$$

Thus,

$$k^2 - 3k - 4 = k - 4 =>$$

$$k^2 - 4k = 0 => k(k - 4) = 0 =>$$

$$k = 0 \; or \; 4$$

Thus, the positive value of k is 4.

Hence, the correct answer is C.

25. Topic: Radicals and Rational Exponents

The correct answer is B.

Since $x = 36$ we can evaluate

$$\frac{\sqrt{x+13}}{x}x\sqrt{x}; \frac{\sqrt{x+13}}{x}x\sqrt{x} = \frac{\sqrt{36+13}}{36}36\sqrt{36}$$

$$= \frac{\sqrt{49}}{36}(36)\sqrt{36} = \sqrt{49}\cdot\sqrt{36} = 7\cdot6 = 42.$$

Choices A, C, and D are incorrect and reflect arithmetic errors in simplifying expressions.

26. Topic: Rational Expressions and Polynomials

The correct answer is 7

The horizontal asymptote can be found by setting the numerator equal to 0. This is because we want the whole function to equal zero, so if we set the numerator equal to zero we will obtain a function value of 0. So, $3x-6=0$, $x=2$. Therefore, $A=2$. The vertical asymptote can be found by setting the denominator equal to 0. So, $2x+10=0$. Then, $x=-5$. Therefore, the vertical asymptote is at $x=-5$, and $B=-5$. The value of $A-B$ is therefore $2-(-5)=7$. The solution is 7.

27. Topic: Linear and Quadratic Systems

The correct answer is $\frac{8}{7}$

Use substitution to replace the y in the second equation with $4x+1$. The second equation then becomes $2x+3(4x+1)=19$. After distributing, the equation becomes $2x+12x+3=19$. Combining like terms you get $14x=16$. Divide by 14 and simplify to get a solution of $\frac{8}{7}$.

28. **Topic:** Functions

The correct answer is 7

$f(3) = 3^2 - 1 = 8$

(since $f(x) = x^2 - 1$ if $x \leq 3$)

Thus, $f(f(3)) = f(8) = 2 \times 8 + 2 = 18$

(since $f(x) = 2x + 2$ if $3 < x \leq 9$)

Thus, $f(f(f(3))) = f(18) = 4 \times 18 - 8 = 64$

(since $f(x) = 4x - 4$ if $x > 9$)

Thus, we have $f(f(f(3))) = 64 = (k+1)^2$

$k + 1 = 8$ (we do not take $k + 1 = -8$ since k is positive)

$k = 7$.

Hence, the correct answer is 7.

29. **Topic:** Quadratic equations

The correct answer is 3

We have:

$2m+n=10$ … (i)

$m(n-1)=9$ … (ii)

From (i): $n=10-2m$

Substituting the above in (ii):

$m(n-1) = 9 \Rightarrow$

$m((10-2m)-1) = 9$

$m(9-2m) = 9 \Rightarrow$

$9m - 2m^2 = 9 \Rightarrow$

$2m^2 - 9m + 9 = 0$

$2m^2 - 6m - 3m + 9 = 0 \Rightarrow$

$2m(m-3) - 3(m-3) = 0$

$(m-3)(2m-3) = 0 \Rightarrow$

$m = 3$ or $\dfrac{3}{2}$

Since m is an integer, there is only one value of m possible.

Thus, sum of all integer values of m is 3.

Hence, the correct answer is 3.

30. **Topic:** Solving quadratic equations

The correct answer is 1

We have: $|x-1|^2+4x=0$.

Case I: If $x-1<0 => |x-1|=-(x-1)$.

Case II: If $x-1>0 => |x-1|=(x-1)$.

Thus, in either case, $|x-1|^2=(x-1)^2=x^2-2x+1$.

Hence, we have:

$x^2-2x+1+4x=0 => x^2+2x+1=0 => (x+1)^2=0 => x=-1$.

Thus, there is only one solution for x.

Hence, the correct answer is 1.

31. **Topic:** Structure in expressions

The correct answer is 18

We have: $x^3 - y^3 - xy^2 - x^2y$

$$= x^3 - x^2y - xy^2 + y^3$$
$$= x^2(x-y) - y^2(x-y)$$
$$= (x-y)(x^2-y^2)$$
$$= 2 \times 9 = 18$$

MULTIPLE CHOICE QUESTIONS

32

Using the tables given, what is the value of $f(g(m(-1)))$?

x	-1	0	1
$f(x)$	0	2	-12
$g(x)$	1	1	-1
$m(x)$	0	-1	1

A) −1

B) 0

C) 1

D) −12

A B C D
○ ○ ○ ○

33

What is the equation of the line that intersects the following graph at its maxima and its y intercept?

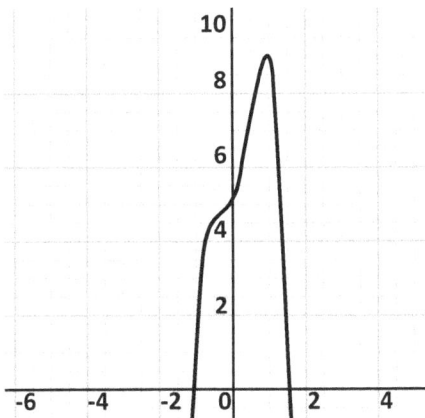

A) $y = 5x + 4$

B) $y = -\dfrac{1}{4}x + 5$

C) $y = 4x + 5$

D) There is no line that intersects both the y intercept and the maxima of the graph.

A B C D
○ ○ ○ ○

Let $\cong$ be an operation on a and b defined as $a \cong b = ab + b^2$. If $p \cong q = 0$ where p and q are non–zero integers, which of the following options is true?

A) $p+q=1$

B) $p+2q=0$

C) $p+3q=2p$

D) $p-2q=-3q$

A B C D
○ ○ ○ ○

35

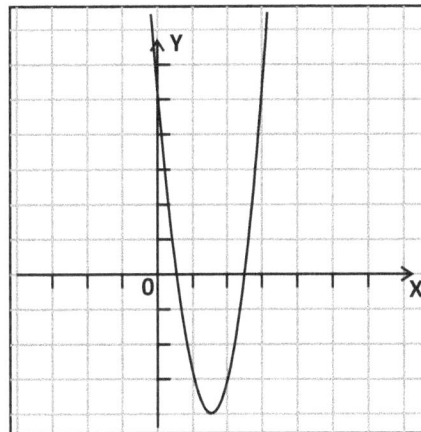

The graph of a quadratic expression $ax^2 + bx + c$ is shown above. Which of the following is correct?

A) $a>0$, $b>0$, $c<0$

B) $a<0$, $b>0$, $c>0$

C) $a<0$, $b<0$, $c<0$

D) $a>0$, $b<0$, $c>0$

A B C D
○ ○ ○ ○

GRID-IN

36

What is the value of $|A-B|$ that gives you a solution $x=3$ and $x=2$ for the following quadratic equation?

$$Ax^2 - 5x + B = 0$$

37

What is the absolute value of the minimum solution to the following equation:

$$\frac{(2x+5)(x-3)-19}{x+4} = 3x-6$$

38

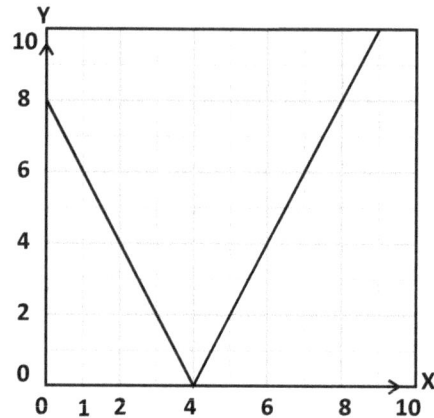

The graph of $y=f(x)$ is shown above. If $f(k)=6$, then what is the minimum value of m so that $f(m)=k$?

32. Topic: Functions

The correct answer is D

In order to find the solution, you must use the concept of composite functions. First, start at the inner function and find $m(-1)$.

Based on the table, $m(-1)=0$. Then find $g(0)$. Based on the table, $g(0)=1$. Then find $f(1)$. Based on the table, $f(1)=-12$.

Therefore, the answer is D, -12.

33. Topic: Misc

The correct answer is C

The y intercept is $(0, 5)$ and the maxima is $(1, 9)$. To find the slope of the equation of the line you find the change in y and then divide it by the change in x. The change in y is $9 - 5 = 4$ and the change in x is $1 - 0 = 1$. The slope is therefore $\frac{4}{1}$ or 4.

The y intercept is $(0, 5)$, so the equation becomes $y = 4x + 5$, Choice C.

34. Topic: Functions

The correct answer is D

We have:

$$p \cong q = 0 => pq + q^2 = 0 =>$$

$$q(p + q) = 0 => p + q = 0.$$

Thus, options A, and B are not true.

Option C:

$$p + 3q = p + q + 2q = 0 + 2q = 2q.$$

Hence, option C is not true.

Option D:

$$p - 2q = p + q - 3q = 0 - 3q = -3q.$$

Hence, option D is true.

Hence, the correct answer is D.

35. Topic: Polynomial factors and graphs

The correct answer is D

From the graph above, when $x=0$, the value of y i.e. $f(0)$ is positive since the graph intersects the Y–axis above the origin.

Substituting $x=0$ in $f(x)$, we get: $f(0)=0+0+c=c$. Thus, the value of c must be positive.

We can see that the graph is open upwards. Hence, the value of a must be positive.

Since both roots are positive in the above graph, the sum of roots is also positive.

We know that the sum of the roots of the quadratic function $f(x) = ax^2 + bx + c$ is given by $\frac{-b}{a}$.

Thus, we can say that $\frac{-b}{a}$ is positive, hence, $\frac{b}{a}$ is negative.

Since we know that a is positive, b must be negative.

Thus, we have $a > 0, b < 0, c > 0$.

Hence, the correct option is D

36. Topic: Solving Quadratic Equations

The correct answer is 5

To find the solution, plug in the values given:

When you plug in $x = 3$, you obtain the following simplified equation: $9A - 15 + B = 0$

When you plug in $x = 2$, you obtain the following simplified equation: $4A - 10 + B = 0$

Now use strategies of systems of linear equations to solve. Then, use elimination (subtract the second equation from the first).

When you subtract the second equation from the first, you get $5A - 5 = 0$, so solving for A you get 1.

Now plug in A to get B. $9(1) - 15 + B = 0$. B is therefore 6.

The value of $|A + B| = |1 - 6| = |-5| = 5$. The solution is 5.

37. Topic: Radicals and Rational Exponents

The correct answer is 5

Multiply both sides by $x + 4$ to eliminate the denominator. The equation then becomes $(2x + 5)(x - 3) - 19 = (3x - 6)(x + 4)$. Then FOIL and combine like terms to get $2x^2 - x - 15 - 19 = 3x^2 + 6x - 24$. Then subtract everything to the right side to get the left side equal to 0. The equation then becomes $0 = x^2 + 7x + 10$. Factoring the equation get you the following: $0 = (x + 2)(x + 5)$, and the solutions are -5 and -2. The minimum solution is then -5. The absolute value of this is 5. Therefore, the answer is 5.

38. Topic: Functions

The correct answer is 0.5.

From the graph, we can see that $f(1) = 6$ and $f(7) = 6$. Since we need to find the value of m so that $f(m) = k$, $f(m)$ could equal 1 or 7. We can draw a horizontal line through both $y = 1$ and $y = 7$ and read the lowest x-value of the point where the line intersects the graph of $f(x)$.

We can see that the lowest x-value occurs at $y = 7$, where x is between 0 and 1. We can see that if we move two units along the y-axis, we move one unit along the x-axis.

Thus, if we move one unit along the y-axis, we would move one unit along the x-axis.

Thus, the lowest possible value of m is 0.5 (the other possible values are 3.5, 4.5, and 7.5). Hence, the correct answer is 0.5.

MULTIPLE CHOICE QUESTIONS

39

For what values of x is $g(x) = x^2 + 3x + 2$ equal to $g(x) = 10x - 4$?

A) −1 and −6

B) 1 and 2

C) 1 and 6

D) 1 and −6

A B C D
○ ○ ○ ○

40

The following equation represents the amount of bacteria grown in a lab over time, t, measured in days. After 3 days, how many bacteria are present?

$$B(t) = 100(2.3)^t$$

A) 121.67

B) 230

C) 1216.7

D) 690

A B C D
○ ○ ○ ○

41

Which of the following equations corresponds to the following graph

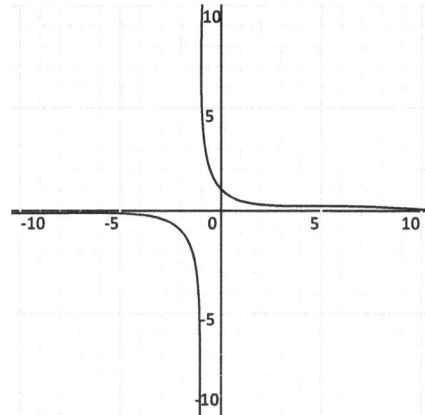

A) $F(x) = 2x^2 + 3x + 5$

B) $F(x) = -x + 8$

C) $F(x) = \dfrac{1}{x+1}$

D) $F(x) = e^x$

A B C D
○ ○ ○ ○

42

If $4m^2 + 28m = 40,$ what does

$2m^2 + 14m - 10$ equal?

A) 0

B) 10

C) 20

D) –10

A B C D
○ ○ ○ ○

43

Maria has a goldfish pond in her backyard. When she started the pond, she only had 5 goldfish. Since then, the number of goldfish has grown exponentially. Which of the following graphs below matches the situation presented?

A)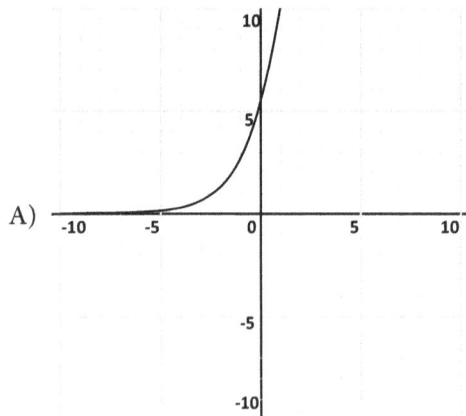

B)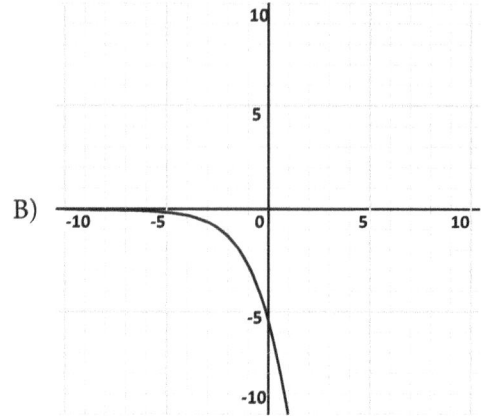

C)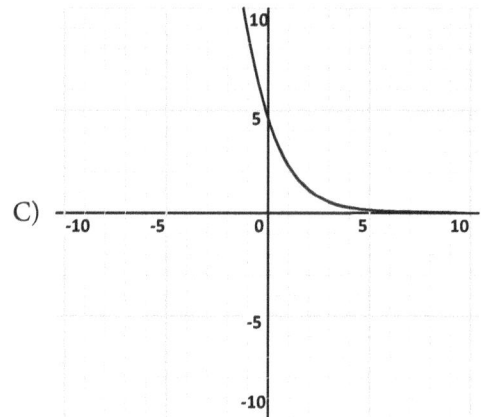

D)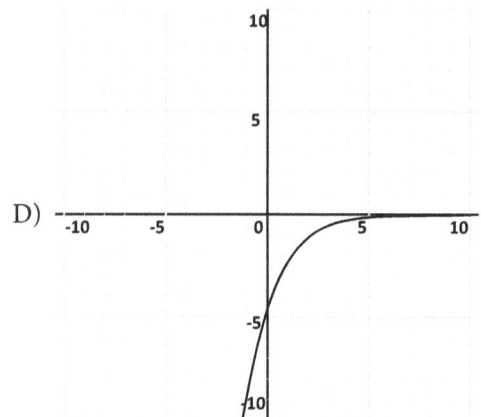

A B C D
○ ○ ○ ○

44

Use the following equations to answer the question.

$$m(x) = 2x + 5$$

$$y(x) = (m(x) - 5)^2$$

Which expression below is equivalent to $y(x)$?

A) $y(x) = 4x^2$

B) $y(x) = 4x^2 - 5$

C) $y(x) = 2x + 7$

D) $y(x) = 2x$

A B C D
○ ○ ○ ○

45

Which of the graphs matches the following equation, where A, B, C, and D are all positive constants?

$$y = Ax^4 + Bx^3 + Cx^2 + D$$

A)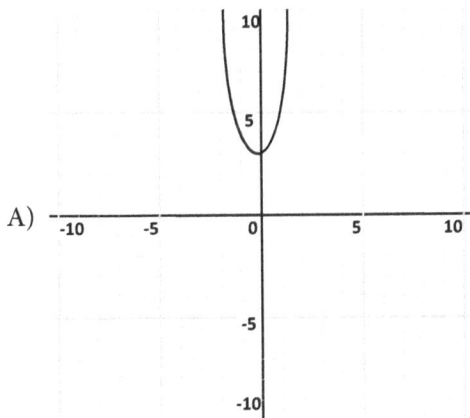

B)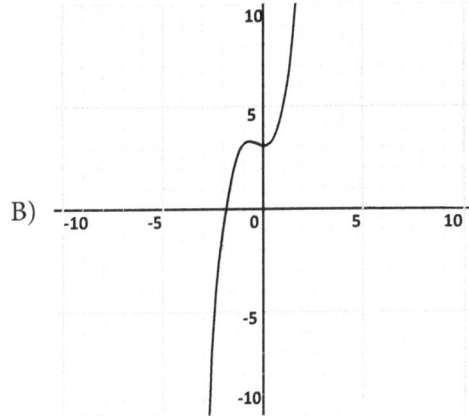

C)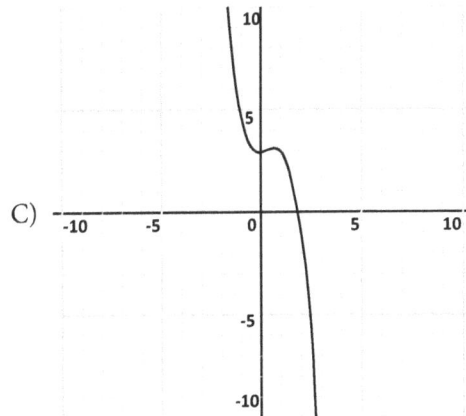

D)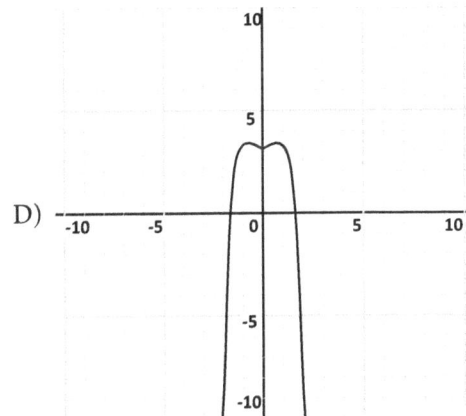

A B C D
○ ○ ○ ○

46

What are the values of the x intercepts of the following graph?

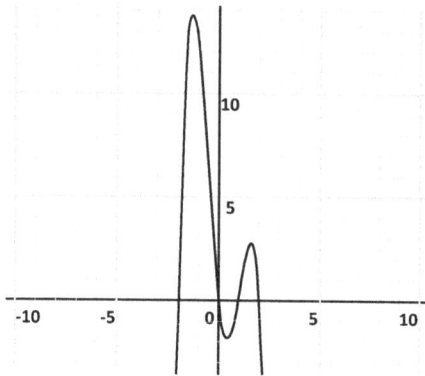

i. (3, 0)   ii. (2, 0)

iii. (−2, 0)   iv. (0, 0)

v. (1, 0)   vi. (5, 0)

A) ii, iii, iv

B) ii, iii, iv, v

C) i, ii, vi

D) iv, v, vi

A B C D
○ ○ ○ ○

47

The following equation represents the height off of the ground (in meters) of a pigeon as it flies from a telephone pole to the ground. The variable t represents the time (in seconds) of the pigeon's flight.

$$F(t) = -2t^2 + 3t + 16$$

What does the value $F(0)=16$ represent?

A) At 16 seconds, the bird reaches the ground.

B) The bird starts at a height of 16 meters.

C) After 2 seconds, the bird has traveled 16 meters.

D) The bird can travel 16 meters per second

A B C D
○ ○ ○ ○

48

After multiplying by 2, each of the following numbers becomes a perfect square EXCEPT

A) 72

B) 162

C) 392

D) 500

A B C D
○ ○ ○ ○

49

Let n be the value of the least integer $(0 < n < 5)$ so that $3^{2^n} + 4$ is not prime. What is the value of the remainder when $3^{2^n} + 4$ is divided by n?

A) 1

B) 2

C) 3

D) 4

A B C D
○ ○ ○ ○

50

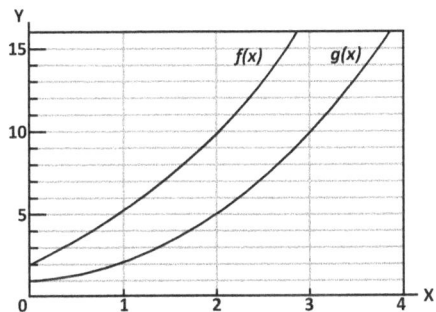

The graphs of $f(x)$ and $g(x)$ are shown below. Which option is true?

A) $f(x) = (x+2)^2$

B) $f(x) = x^2 + 1$

C) $g(x) = x^2$

D) $g(x) = x^2 + 1$

A B C D
○ ○ ○ ○

51

In a series, the first term is k. Each term thereafter is three times the preceding term. The sum of the first six terms is 728. What is the sum of the first three terms of the series?

A) 2

B) 13

C) 26

D) 80

A B C D
○ ○ ○ ○

52

If $f(x) = 8 - x^2$ where $-3 < x < 3,$ what is the range of values of $f(x)$?

A) $0 < y < 7$

B) $-1 \le y \le 8$

C) $8 < y < 17$

D) $-1 < y \le 8$

A B C D
○ ○ ○ ○

53

If $a^6 b^3 = 4816$ and $\dfrac{a^{10}}{b} = 301,$ what is the value of $\dfrac{b^2}{a^2}$?

A) 301

B) 64

C) 16

D) 4

A B C D
○ ○ ○ ○

GRID-IN

54

The number of units sold, N, of a product follows the relation $N=120-C$, where C is the selling price per unit. The cost to setup the manufacturing facility is $150 and the cost per unit is $5. If all units are sold, what should be the least selling price, in dollars, per unit to have a profit of $400?

$$f(x) = x^2 + 16$$

For what value of k is $f(2k+1) = 2f(k)+1$ if k is a positive integer?

At how many points does the line $y = 2x - 1$ intersect the circle $(x-4)^2 + (y-6)^2 = 2$?

39. Topic: Solving Quadratic Equations

The correct answer is C

In order to find the solution values of x, we must set both equations equal. So, $x^2 + 3x + 2 = 10x - 4$. In order to factor we need to set the entire function equal to zero and move everything to one side. In order to do this, subtract $10x$ and add 4 to the other side. The equation then becomes $x^2 - 7x + 6 = 0$. Then factor. Factoring should look like this: $(x - 6)(x - 1) = 0$. Then, set each set of parentheses equal to zero to get $x - 6 = 0$ and $x - 1 = 0$. The solutions are then 6 and 1, which is answer choice C.

40. Topic: Quadratic and Exponential Word Problem

The correct answer is C

In order to find the number of bacteria, you need to plug in 3 into t in the equation. The resulting equation becomes $B(3) = 100(2.3)^3$. Plug this into your calculator.

The answer is then Choice C, 1216.7 bacteria.

41. Topic: Rational Expressions and Polynomials

The correct answer is C

$$F(x) = \left(\frac{1}{x+1}\right)$$

The graph depicted shows a rational equation with a vertical asymptote at $x = -1$, which corresponds to the equation chosen in the answer. A vertical asymptote represents a domain restriction where the function goes to either +infinity or –infinity. A vertical asymptote appears when at an x value where the denominator will become zero. Because we cannot divide by 0, our domain is restricted and the asymptote prevents our function from having values at this restricted domain.

Another way to approach this problem is to plug the functions into a graphing calculator and graph, or calculate a list of $F(x)$ values when plugging in x values.

42. Topic: Structure in expression

The correct answer is B.

In order to find the solution, first divide the given equation by 2 to get $2m^2 + 14m = 20$ Then, substitute 20 in for $2m^2 + 14m$ in the expression that we need to find. Now we have 20–10, which is 10.

43. Topic: Nonlinear Equation Graphs

The correct answer is A

The solution is A, because this is exponential growth with a growth factor greater than 1. B and D do not make sense because the values would never be negative since it represents the number of goldfish in a pond. C is incorrect because it represents exponential decay.

44. Topic: Functions

The correct answer is A

In order to find an equivalent expression to $y(x)$, plug in $m(x)$ where indicated to get $y(x) = (2x + 5 - 5)^2$, which simplifies to $y(x) = (2x)^2$, which further simplifies to $4x^2$. The solution is then Choice A.

45. Topic: Rational Expressions and Polynomials

The correct answer is A

This is because the polynomial has all positive coefficients and the highest order polynomial is even, make the end behaviors at –x and +x both to positive infinity.

46. Topic: Misc

The correct answer is B

There are X intercepts at $x=-2$, 0, 1, and 2. X–intercepts are found by locating the intersection of the x axis and the function's graph.

47. Topic: Interpreting Nonlinear Expressions

The correct answer is B

When the $t=0$ seconds, the pigeon is at a height of 16 meters. This means that the start of the pigeon's flight begins at a height of 16 meters.

48. Topic: Radicals and rational exponents

The correct answer is D

We need to find the number which when multiplied by 2 becomes a perfect square. Thus, we need to break the numbers in their prime form and check if the exponent of each prime is an even number (*since perfect squares must have even exponents of each prime factor*). Working with options, we have:

A): $72 \times 2 = 2^4 \times 3^2$

Since the exponents are even, the resulting number will be a perfect square.

B): $162 \times 2 = 3^4 \times 2^2$

Since the exponents are even, the resulting number will be a perfect square.

C): $392 \times 2 = 2^4 \times 7^2$

Since the exponents are even, the resulting number will be a perfect square.

D): $500 \times 2 = 2^3 \times 5^3$

Since the exponents are not even, the resulting number will not be a perfect square.

Hence, the answer should be D.

Hence, the answer is D.

49. Topic: Radicals and rational exponents

The correct answer is A

We need to try out a few values of n and check which value of n satisfies.

Since $0<n<5$ and we need the least value of n, we should try the values of n from 1 onwards (*and not from 4 backwards*).

With $n = 1 : 3^{2^n} + 4 = 3^2 + 4 = 13$ is prime.

$n = 2 : 3^{2^n} + 4 = 3^4 + 4 = 85$ is not a prime number.

Hence, the value of $n=2$ and the corresponding value of $3^{2^n} + 4 = 85$.

Thus, when $3^{2^n} + 4$ is divided by n, i.e. 85 is divided by 2, the remainder comes as 1.

Hence, the answer is A.

50. Topic: Polynomial factors and graphs

The correct answer is D

Options A and B deal with $f(x)$.

A set of points satisfying $f(x)$ can be given as: $\{(1, 5), (2, 10)\}$.

Option A: We put $x=1$ which gives us $f(x) = 3^2 = 9$ which does not satisfy the point $(1, 5)$.

Option B: We put $x=1$ which gives u $f(x) = 1^2 + 1 = 2s$ which does not satisfy the point $(1, 5)$.

Options C and D deal with $g(x)$.

A set of points satisfying $g(x)$ can be given as: $\{(1, 2), (2, 5), (3, 10)\}$.

Option (C): We put $x=1$ which gives us $g(x) = 1^2 = 1$ which does not satisfy the point $(1, 2)$.

Option (D): We put $x=1$ which gives us $g(x) = 1^2 + 1 = 2$ which satisfies the point $(1, 2)$.

Thus, checking the options, we can see that option D satisfies the above set of points.

Hence, the correct answer is D.

51. Topic: Quadratic and exponential (word problems)

The correct answer is C

The first 5 terms of the above series are:

$k, 3k, 3^2 k, 3^3 k, 3^4 k$ and $3^5 k$

i.e. $k, 3k, 9k, 27k, 81k$ and $243k$.

Thus, we have:
$k + 3k + 9k + 27k + 81k + 243k = 364k$

Thus, $364k = 728 => k = \dfrac{728}{364} = 2$

Thus, the sum of the first three terms =
$k + 3k + 9k = 13k = 13 \times 2 = 26$

Hence, the correct answer is C.

52. Topic: Functions

The correct answer is D

Since
$-3 < x < 3 => 0 \le x^2 < 9 =>$

$-9 < -x^2 \le 0$

We have, $y = f(x) = 8 - x^2$

Thus,
$-9 + 8 < 8 - x^2 \le 0 + 8 =>$

$-1 < 8 - x^2 \le 8 => -1 < f(x) \le 8$

Hence, the range of the function is given by:
$-1 < y \le 8$

Hence, the correct answer is D.

53. Topic: Radicals and rational exponents

The correct answer is D

We have:

$a^6 b^3 = 4816 \ldots$ (i) and

$\dfrac{a^{10}}{b} = 301 \ldots$ (ii)

Dividing (i) by (ii):

$\dfrac{a^6 b^3}{\dfrac{a^{10}}{b}} = \dfrac{4816}{301} =>$

$\left(a^6 b^3\right) \times \left(\dfrac{b}{a^{10}}\right) = 16 =>$

$\dfrac{b^4}{a^4} = 16$

Taking square root on both sides:

$\dfrac{b^2}{a^2} = \sqrt{16} = 4.$

Hence, the answer is D.

54. Topic: Linear and quadratic systems

The correct answer is 10

For N units sold at $\$C$, total selling price =

$\$(CN) = \$C(120 - C)$

Total cost =
$\$(150 + 5N) = \$(150 + 5(120 - C)) =>$

$\$(750 - 5C)$

Selling price=Cost price+$\$400$

$C(120 - C) = 750 - 5C + 400$

$C^2 - 125C + 1150 = 0$

$C^2 - 115C - 10C + 1150 = 0$

$(C - 115)(C - 10) = 0$

$C = 10 \; or \; 115$

Thus, the minimum selling price = \$10.

55. Topic: Functions

The correct answer is 2

$f(2k + 1) = (2k + 1)^2 + 16 =>$

$4k^2 + 4k + 17$

$2f(k) + 1 = 2(k^2 + 16) + 1 = 2k^2 + 33$

Thus, we have:

$4k^2 + 4k + 17 = 2k^2 + 33 =>$

$2k^2 + 4k - 16 = 0 =>$

$k^2 + 2k - 8 = 0$

$(k - 2)(k + 4) = 0 =>$

$k = 2 \; or \; -4$

Since k is positive, we have $k=2$.

Hence, the correct answer is 2.

56. Topic: Linear and quadratic systems

The correct answer is 2

We have:
$(x - 4)^2 + (y - 6)^2 = 2 \; and \; y = 2x - 1$

$(x - 4)^2 + (2x - 1 - 6)^2 = 2$

$(x - 4)^2 + (2x - 7)^2 = 2$

$x^2 - 8x + 16 + 4x^2 - 28x + 49 = 2$

$5x^2 - 36x + 63 = 0$

$5x^2 - 21x - 15x + 63 = 0$

$x(5x - 21) - 3(5x - 21) = 0$

$(x - 3)(5x - 21) = 0$

$x = 3 \; or \; \dfrac{21}{5}$

Alternatively, one can use the quadratic–root formula to determine the roots.

Thus, there are 2 points of intersection.

The correct answer is 2.

MULTIPLE CHOICE QUESTIONS

57

Which of the following sets of quadratic equations has no solution?

A) $y = 4x^2 + 1$

$y = -x^2 - 1$

B) $y = -4x^2 + 1$

$y = -x^2 - 1$

C) $y = -4x^2 + 1$

$y = x^2 - 1$

D) $y = \dfrac{-1}{2}x^2 + 1$

$y = 5x^2 - 1$

A B C D
○ ○ ○ ○

58

The following systems of equations represent the speed $S(t)$ and $F(t)$ of two racecars as they are speeding up. At what time (t) do they have the same speed?

$$S(t) = -2t^2 + 3t + 30$$

$$F(t) = 3t^2 - 4t - 10$$

A) $\dfrac{7 - \sqrt{849}}{10}$ seconds

B) $\dfrac{7 + \sqrt{849}}{10}$ seconds

C) $\dfrac{7}{10}$ seconds

D) 0 seconds

A B C D
○ ○ ○ ○

59

Using the graphs of $f(x)$ and $g(x)$ shown below, what is the value of $g(f(0))$?

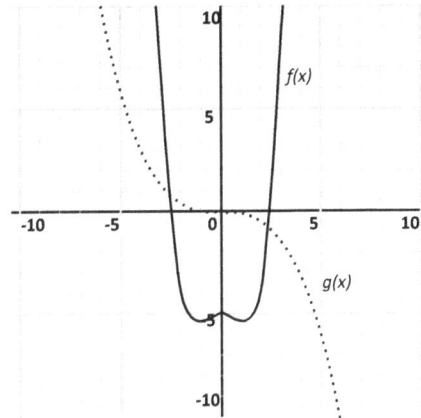

A) 0

B) −5

C) 6

D) 4.5

A B C D
○ ○ ○ ○

60

Let $\leftrightarrow$ be an operation on p and q defined as $p \leftrightarrow q = (2^p - q)$. If $p \leftrightarrow 12 = p$, then find the value of p.

A) 2

B) 4

C) 8

D) 12

A B C D
○ ○ ○ ○

61

If $\dfrac{2x+3}{(x+1)(x+2)} = \dfrac{A}{x+1} + \dfrac{B}{x+2}$ for all real

values of $x(\neq -1, -2)$, what is the value of

$(A + B)$?

A) 1

B) 2

C) 3

D) 4

A B C D
○ ○ ○ ○

62

It is observed that the number of ants living in a colony increase by 25% every week. After four weeks of observation, total ants were found to be 6250. How many ants were found when the observation was first made?

A) 1250

B) 2560

C) 3125

D) 3250

A B C D
○ ○ ○ ○

GRID-IN

63

Your neighbor Jim is building a dog pen in his backyard. You are unsure of the exact dimensions but know that the length of the rectangular pen is two times greater than 5 more than the width. If the area of the pen is 48 square feet, what is the value of L–W?

64

Use the following rational expression to answer the question.

$$y = \frac{0.5x - 6.5}{1.2x - 10}$$

When will the function have a y value equal to 0?

65

How many times does the equation $y=4$ intersect the following polynomial equation shown in the graph?

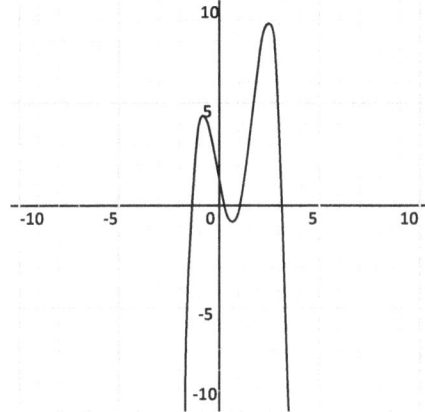

66

Find the value of x when $y=3$ in the following equation:

$$\frac{\sqrt{2x+4}}{\sqrt{3x-2}} = \frac{1}{3}y^2$$

67

The carnival comes to Rileyville every year. The carnival gets new rollercoasters each year and attracts more and more customers each year they come. They model the attendance at their carnivals by the following exponential function:

$$A(y) = 25 \times 3^y$$

Where y is the number of years since 2000 and $A(y)$ is the total attendance at the carnival. In how many years after 2000 is the attendance at the carnival 18,225?

68

A man puts \$P in a bank which offers r% interest compounded annually. After 2 years, the amount of money in the bank is \$M. What is the value of r if M=\$1728 and P=1200?

69

If $9^x - 2 \cdot 3^x - 3 = 0$, what is the value of x?

70

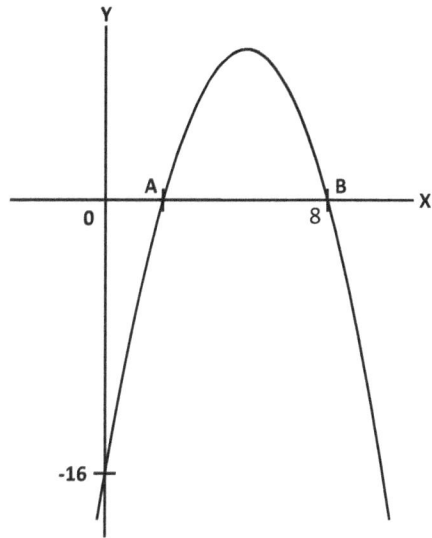

The graph of $f(x) = -x^2 + ax + b$ is shown below. What is the area of the square constructed with side AB?

71

What is the y coordinate of the vertex for the parabola defined by the function $y = 2x^2 - 8x + 11$?

57. **Topic:** Linear and Quadratic Systems

    The correct answer is A

    The answer choice A is correct. The first equation has a positive, upward forming parabola with a minimum value of (0, 1). The second equation has a negative, downward forming parabola with a maximum value of (−1, 0). Therefore, these two quadratic equations will never intersect, and there is no solution to the system of quadratic equations.

58. **Topic:** Linear and Quadratic Systems

    The correct answer is B

    Set $S(t)$ equal to $F(t)$ to get the time that the speeds are equal. Therefore, $-2t^2 + 3t + 30 = 3t^2 - 4t - 10$. Then, move everything to the right hand side to obtain $0 = 5t^2 - 7t - 40$.

    Use the quadratic formula to solve for t:

    $$t = \frac{-b \pm \sqrt{b^2 - 4ac}}{2a} =>$$

    $$\frac{7 \pm \sqrt{49 + 5 \times 4 \times 40}}{10} =>$$

    $$\frac{7 \pm \sqrt{849}}{10}$$

    Because the time must be positive, the answer is therefore

    $$t = \frac{7 + \sqrt{849}}{10} \text{ seconds.}$$

59. **Topic:** Functions

    The correct answer is C

    First evaluate $F(0)$, which is −5.

    Then find $G(-5)$, which is 6.

    Therefore the correct answer is 6.

60. **Topic:** Functions

    The correct answer is B

    We have: $p \leftrightarrow 12 = p$

    Going by the option:

    Option (A):

    $p \leftrightarrow 12 = p =>$

    $2^p - 12 = p =>$

    $2^2 - 12 = 2 =>$

    which is not true.

    Option (B):

    $p \leftrightarrow 12 = p =>$

    $2^p - 12 = p =>$

    $2^4 - 12 = 4 =>$

    which is true.

    Hence, (B) must be the correct option (we can verify the other options as not correct).

    Option (C):

    $p \leftrightarrow 12 = p =>$

    $2^p - 12 = p =>$

    $2^8 - 12 = 8 =>$

    which is not true.

    Option (D):

    $p \leftrightarrow 12 = p =>$

    $2^p - 12 = p =>$

    $2^{12} - 12 = 12 =>$

    which is not true.

    Hence, the correct answer is B.

61. Topic: Structure in expressions

The correct answer is B

$2x+3=A(x+2)+B(x+1)$

$2x+3=(A+B)x+(2A+B)$

Since the above is true for all values of x, it is an identity.

$A+B=2$

The correct answer is option B.

62. Topic: Quadratic and exponential (word problems)

The correct answer is B

Let the number of ants initially be N.

The number of ants increases by 25% every week.

Thus, after one week, the number of ants would be:

$$N + 25\% \ of \ N = N\left(1+\frac{25}{100}\right) =>$$

$$N\left(1+\frac{1}{4}\right) = \frac{5N}{4}$$

The number of ants at the end of every week is shown in the table below:

Time duration	Number of ants
1 Week	$\frac{5}{4} \times N = \frac{5N}{4}$
2 Weeks	$\frac{5}{4} \times \frac{5N}{4} = \frac{25N}{16}$
3 Weeks	$\frac{5}{4} \times \frac{25N}{16} = \frac{125N}{64}$
4 Weeks	$\frac{5}{4} \times \frac{125N}{64} = \frac{625N}{256}$

Thus, we have:

$$\frac{625N}{256} = 6250 =>$$

$$N = 6250 \times \frac{256}{625} = 2560$$

Hence, the correct answer is B.

63. Topic: Quadratic and Exponential (Word Problems)

The correct answer is 13

To find the dimensions of the pen, you need to set up a quadratic formula. The equation of area of a rectangle is *length* x *width* = *Area*. We know *Area* = 48, and *length* = 2 x (*width*+5). Using *W* for *width* and *L* for *length*, we can then rewrite the equation to become 48=2(*W*+5)(*W*). Distributing, dividing by 2, and moving values over gets you to $0 = W^2 + 5W - 24$. Using factoring, you obtain 0=(*W*+8)(*W*–3). So, the solutions of width are –8 and 3 feet. Since width cannot be negative, use the 3 feet solution. Now, to find length, plug into *L*=2(*W*+5). So, *L*=2(3+5)=16. The value of *L*–*W* is therefore 16–3=13.

64. Topic: Rational Expressions and Polynomials

The correct answer is 13

The y value of the function will equal zero when numerator equals 0. So, 0.5*x*–6.5=0, 0.5*x*=6.5, and *x*=13. To make sure that the function does not equal $\frac{0}{0}$, check the denominator to make sure it is nonzero. Plugging *x*=13 into the denominator will give the following expression: 1.2(13)–10, which is equal to 5.6. The denominator is nonzero, and the numerator is zero, creating a zero y value for this function.

Thus, x=13 is the correct answer

65. Topic: Polynomial Factors and Graphs

The correct answer is 4

The equation $y=4$ intersects the graph shown at $(-1, 4)$, $(-0.618, 4)$, $(1.618, 4)$, and $(3, 4)$. This solution can be found by graphing $y=4$ and counting the number of intersections. The solution is 4 intersections.

66. Topic: Isolating Quantities

The correct answer is 0.88

Plug in y in the equation and obtain 3 on the right–hand side. Multiply the left side's denominator of $\sqrt{3x-2}$ to the right side by using cross multiplication. Then you have the equation $\sqrt{2x+4} = 3\sqrt{3x-2}$. Square both sides to get $2x+4 = 9(3x-2)$. Then distribute and combine like terms. You then obtain the equation $22 = 25x$. Solving for x, you get $x = 0.88$.

67. Topic: Quadratic and Exponential (*Word Problems*)

The correct answer is 6

In order to find this, plug 18225 in for $A(y)$. You then get $18225 = 25 \times 3^y$. Divide both sides by 25 to get 729. Now you have $729 = 3^y$. Take the log of both sides to get $\log(729) = y \times \log(3)$ Divide by $\log(3)$ to obtain a y value of 6. Alternatively, you can notice that $729 = 3^6$. Therefore, the answer is 6.

68. Topic: Isolating quantities

The correct answer is 20

Amount after 2 years =

$$\$\left\{ P\left(1 + \frac{r}{100}\right)^2 \right\}$$

$$M = P\left(1 + \frac{r}{100}\right)^2$$

$$\left(1 + \frac{r}{100}\right)^2 = \frac{M}{P}$$

$$1 + \frac{r}{100} = \left(\frac{M}{P}\right)^{\left(\frac{1}{2}\right)}$$

$$\frac{r}{100} = \left(\frac{M}{P}\right)^{\left(\frac{1}{2}\right)} - 1$$

$$r = 100\left\{ \left(\frac{M}{P}\right)^{\left(\frac{1}{2}\right)} - 1 \right\}$$

$$r = 100\left\{ \left(\frac{1728}{1200}\right)^{\left(\frac{1}{2}\right)} - 1 \right\}$$

$$r = 20$$

69. Topic: Rational expressions and polynomials

The correct answer is 1

Let us assume $3^x = k$

Thus, $9^x = (3^x)^2 = k^2$

Hence, our equation becomes:

$k^2 - 2k - 3 = 0$

$k^2 - 3k + k - 3 = 0$

$k(k-3) + 1(k-3) = 0$

$(k+1)(k-3) = 0$

$k = -1$ or 3

Thus, we have: $3^x = -1$ or $3^x = 3$

Since 3^x is always positive, we can conclude that

$3^x = 3$

$x = 1$

Hence, the correct answer is 1

70. Topic: Polynomial factors and graphs

The correct answer is 36

The graph represents $f(x) = -x^2 + ax + b$.

The Y–intercept is $-16 \Rightarrow b = -16 \Rightarrow$ Product of

roots $= \dfrac{b}{-1} = 16$

Since one of the roots is 8 (X–intercept), the

other root is $\dfrac{16}{8} = 2$. Thus, coordinates of point

A are $(2, 0)$.

Thus, the length of AB = 8 – 2 = 6

Thus, area of the square = $6^2 = 36$.

71. Topic: Polynomial factors and graphs

The correct answer is 3.

Vertex form of a quadratic function is $f(x) = a(x - h)^2 + k$ where $h = \dfrac{-b}{2a}$ and $k = f(h)$.

Here, a and b are represented $y = ax^2 + bx + c$.

In the function $f(x) = 2x^2 - 8x + 11, a = 2, b = -8$

therefore the vertex is $h = \dfrac{-(-8)}{2(2)} = \dfrac{8}{4} = 2$ and

$k = f(2) = 2(2)^2 - 8(2) + 11 = 3$.

The vertex is $(2, 3)$ and the y coordinate is 3.

MULTIPLE CHOICE QUESTIONS

72

Which of the following equations have one of the same x intercepts?

i. $y = (x-2)(x+5)$

ii. $y = 2x^2 + 3x + 1$

iii. $y = 2x^2 - x - 1$

iv. $y = 4x^2 + 7x - 15$

v. $y = -x^2 - 3x + 10$

A) i & ii

B) iii & iv

C) i & v

D) ii & iv

A B C D
○ ○ ○ ○

73

Which of the following answer choices is equivalent to the following equation?

$$F(x) = \left(\frac{\sqrt[5]{x}}{x^{-\frac{2}{3}}} \right)^{-7}$$

A) $F(x) = \dfrac{1}{x^{\frac{91}{15}}}$

B) $F(x) = \dfrac{1}{x^{\frac{17}{15}}}$

C) $F(x) = x^{\frac{15}{91}}$

D) None of these solutions are equivalent to the original equation.

A B C D
○ ○ ○ ○

74

For a skydiver jumping from a plane, the distance, in meters, from the ground is calculated by the following function: $P(t) = -4.9t^2 + 2.1t + 80$, where t is the time since the diver jumped. What is the value of $P(7)-P(10)$ and what does this mean?

A) $P(10)-P(7)=145.4$. This means that for three seconds, between t=7 seconds and t=10 seconds, the skydiver moved 145 meters downwards.

B) $P(10)-P(7)=-243.6$. This means that for three seconds, between t=7 seconds and t=10 seconds, the skydiver moved 243.6 meters downwards.

C) $P(10)-P(7)= -3$. This means that there is a change of –3 meters from t=7 seconds to t=10 seconds.

D) $P(10)-P(7)= 42$. This means that 42 seconds has passed in this interval.

A B C D
○ ○ ○ ○

75

If $x+y=10$, what does

$3x^3 + 6x^2y + 6y^2x + 3y^3 - 50$ equal?

A) 1000

B) 100

C) 2950

D) 1050

A B C D
○ ○ ○ ○

76

If $M(x) = (F(x + 2))^2$ and $F(x) = \sqrt{0.25x}$,
What is the value of $M(3)$?

A) $M(3) = \sqrt{0.75}$

B) $M(3) = \sqrt{0.75} + 2$

C) $M(3) = 1.25$

D) $M(3) = \sqrt{2.5}$

A B C D
○ ○ ○ ○

77

How many two–digit numbers exist such that
the difference of the squares of its digits is 24?

A) 2

B) 4

C) 6

D) 8

A B C D
○ ○ ○ ○

78

Joe throws a ball upwards from a height of
12 feet from ground level. The height of the
ball above the ground after time t seconds
from when the ball was thrown is given by the
expression $h(t) = -t^2 + at + b$. The ball comes
back to the ground after 8 seconds. What is the
value of $(a + b)$?

A) 6.5

B) 12.0

C) 18.5

D) 19.0

A B C D
○ ○ ○ ○

79

If $(x - 3)^2 < 25$ and $(y - 5)^2 < 4$, what is sum
of the maximum and minimum possible values

of $\dfrac{x}{y}$ given that x and y are integers?

A) 2.67

B) 2.00

C) 1.50

D) 1.20

A B C D
○ ○ ○ ○

80

For all non–negative numbers x, let
$f(x) = x^3 - 8$ and $g(x) = x - 2$. For how
many integer values of x is $f(x)=g(x)$?

A) 0

B) 1

C) 2

D) 3

A B C D
○ ○ ○ ○

GRID-IN

81

The following function contains the point

$$\left(3, \frac{32}{125}\right)$$

$$y = K\left(\frac{2}{5}\right)^x$$

Where x is the independent variable, y is the
dependent variable, and K is an unknown
positive number. What is the value of K?

82

What is a possible value of B if $(x + A)^2 = -6B + A^2$ and the following equations are also true: $(x + A)^2 = 10$ and $A = 2B$ Note, A and B are constants.

72. Topic: Polynomial Factors and Graphs

The correct answer is C

The x intercept of i. is $x=2$ and $x=-5$.

In order to find this, you can set each of the parentheses equal to 0.

This becomes $x-2=0$ and $x+5=0$, which has solutions of $x=-5$. In equation v, you can factor the expression to become $(-x-5)(x-2)$, which gives you solutions of $x=-5$ and $x=2$.

73. Topic: Radicals and Rational Exponents

The correct answer is A

To find the equivalent expression, the original expression must be simplified. First, simplifying the numerator with the denominator inside the parentheses. Do this by subtracting the exponents from each other. $\sqrt[5]{x}$ become $x^{\frac{1}{5}}$

Then, do $\dfrac{1}{5}-\left(\dfrac{-2}{3}\right)$.

Combine the fractions by using a common denominator of 15. This creates the expression $\dfrac{13}{15}$

Now, multiply -7 by $\dfrac{13}{15}$ because when an exponent is raised to another exponent, you multiply.

This gives you $\dfrac{-91}{15}$.

Put the term in the denominator to eliminate the negative exponent, and you obtain

$$F(x) = \dfrac{1}{x^{\frac{91}{15}}}$$

74. Topic: Interpreting Nonlinear Expressions

The correct answer is B

$P(7)=-4.9(49)+2.1(7)+80 =-145.4$ and

$P(10)=-4.9(100)+2.1(10)+80=-389$

So $P(10)-P(7)=-389-(-145.4)=-243.6$.

This means that in 3 seconds, from 7 to 10 seconds, the skydiver traveled 243.6 meters downward toward the ground.

Therefore, B is the correct answer

75. Topic: Isolating Quantities

The correct answer is C

You must recognize that the expression we are trying to find is $3(x + y)^3 - 50$, due to the binomial expansion of $(x + y)^3$ as $x^3 + 2x^2y + 2xy^2 + y^3$, which, when multiplied by 3, is $3x^3 + 6x^2y + 6xy^2 + 3y^3$. Substitute in 10 for $x + y$ and you get $3(1000)-50$, which is 2950.

76. Topic: Functions

The correct answer is C

First, define $M(x)$ in terms of x by plugging in the composite function into $F(x)$. $F(x+2)$ will become $\sqrt{0.25(x+2)}$ which simplifies to $\sqrt{0.25x + 0.5}$ .Now, square this function as directed in the composite function statement. $\left(\sqrt{0.25x + 0.5}\right)^2 = 0.25x + 0.5$. This is equal to $M(x)$. So, $M(x) = 0.25x + 0.5$. Plug in 3 for x to solve for $M(3)$. $M(3) = 0.25 \times 3 + 0.5$ Therefore, $M(s) = 0.75 + 0.5 = 1.25$. Therefore, the answer is C.

77. Topic: Quadratic and exponential (word problems)

The correct answer is B

Let the two–digit number be $N=10x+y$ where x and y are the digits.

We know that $1 \le x \le 9$ and $0 \le y \le 9$.

Thus, we have:

$x^2 - y^2 = 24$ or $y^2 - x^2 = 24$

Let us work with the first condition:
$x^2 - y^2 = 24$:

$x^2 - y^2 = 24 => (x+y)(x-y) = 24$

Thus, we need to break 24 in two factors, one of which will be $x+y$ and the other will be $x-y$.

Now, x and y must be integers.

In order for this to happen, either $x+y$ and $x-y$ should both be even, or both be odd (if one is even and the o138ther is odd, on adding them, we will get $2x$ which will be odd which is not possible for an integer).

Since 24 is even, we cannot have both its factors as odd. Thus, both $x+y$ and $x-y$ must be even (*while assigning values to $x+y$ and $x-y$, we must keep in mind that $x+y>x-y$*).

Thus, possible values of $x+y$ and $x-y$ are listed below:

$x+y$	$x-y$	x^*	y^{**}	$N=$ $10x+y$
12	2	7	5	75
6	4	5	1	51

*: add x+y and x-y and divide the result by 2
**: subtract x-y from x+y and divide the result by 2

Thus, there are two values of N possible, 75 and 51.

For the second case, i.e. $y^2 - x^2 = 24$, we will get the reverse numbers i.e. 57 and 15.

Thus, there are 4 possible numbers.

Hence, the correct answer is B.

78. Topic: Quadratic and exponential (word problems)

The correct answer is C

$h(t) = -t^2 + at + b$

At $t=0$, height of the ball above the ground level is 12 feet.

Thus, $h(0) = 12 => b = 12$

Thus, $h(t) = -t^2 + at + 12$

Again, at $t=8$, height of the ball above the ground level is zero.

Thus,

$h(8) = 0 => -64 + 8a + 12 = 0 => a = \dfrac{52}{8} = 6.5$

Thus, $h(t) = -t^2 + 6.5t + 12$

Thus, $a + b = 6.5 + 12 = 18.5$

Hence, the correct answer is C.

79. Topic: Solving quadratic equations

The correct answer is C

We have:

$(x-3)^2 < 25 =>$

$-5 < (x-3) < 5 =>$

$-2 < x < 8$

$(y-5)^2 \le 4 =>$

$-2 < (y-5) < 2 =>$

$3 < y < 7$

The value of $\dfrac{x}{y}$ will be maximum when both x and y are of the same sign with magnitude of x as maximum and the magnitude of y as minimum.

Thus, we take

$x = 7$ and $y = 4 => \dfrac{x}{y} = \dfrac{7}{4} = 1.75$

(since x is less than 8 and is an integer, we take x as 7 as the maximum value; similarly, since y is more than 3 and is an integer, we take y as 4 as the minimum value).

The value of $\dfrac{x}{y}$ will be maximum when x and y are of opposite signs with magnitude of x as maximum and the magnitude of y as minimum (since y is always positive, we must take x as negative).

Thus, we take

$$x = 7 \text{ and } y = 4 => \frac{x}{y} = \frac{7}{4} = 1.75$$

Hence, the sum of the maximum and minimum possible values of $\dfrac{x}{y}$ equals $1.75 + (-0.25) = 1.50$.

Hence, the correct answer is C.

80. **Topic:** Linear and quadratic systems

The correct answer is B

$$f(x) = x^3 - 8$$

$$x^3 - 8 = x - 2$$

We have:

$$f(x) = g(x)$$

$$(x-2)(x^2 + 2x + 4) - (x - 2) = 0$$

$$(x-2)(x^2 + 2x + 4) = 0$$

$$x = 2 \text{ or } x^2 + 2x + 4 = 0$$

(*which has imaginary solutions*)

Thus, there is 1 possible value of x.

The correct answer is option B.

81. **Topic:** Nonlinear Equation Graphs

The correct answer is 4

Plug 3 into the equation for x and $\dfrac{32}{125}$ into the equation for y.

You obtain $\dfrac{32}{125} = K\left(\dfrac{2}{5}\right)^3 \cdot \left(\dfrac{2}{5}\right)^3 = \dfrac{8}{125}$

Therefore, the equation becomes $\dfrac{32}{125} = K\left(\dfrac{8}{125}\right)$.

Solve for K by multiplying both sides by $\dfrac{125}{8}$.

$K=4$.

82. **Topic:** Structure in expression

The correct answer is $\dfrac{5}{2}$ or -1.

Substitute in $(x+A)^2 = 10$ and $A=2B$ to get $10 = -6B + (2B)^2$. Distribute the exponent to get $10 = -6B + 4B^2$. Use factoring to solve $(2B-5)$ $(B+1) = 0$, so B can either be $\dfrac{5}{2}$ or -1.

This page is intentionally left blank

Chapter 4
Problem Solving and Data Analysis

MULTIPLE CHOICE QUESTIONS

1

For a hiking trail Mike uses a map such that $\frac{1}{2}$ inch represents 1 mile. Mike has measured the length of the trail as 18 inches. How many miles is the trail length?

A) 18 miles

B) 9 miles

C) 36 miles

D) 24 miles

A B C D
○ ○ ○ ○

2

Item	Price (dollars)
Grapes	3
Broom	12
Olive oil	15
Socks	4
Eggs	5
Napkins	4
Chocolate	6

The Table above shows the item Jane bought from a convenient store and their prices. What is the median price of the items Jane bought?

A) 7

B) 6

C) 5

D) 4

A B C D
○ ○ ○ ○

3

In a three–digit number ABC, where A, B and C represent digits from 0 to 9, the value of the digit A equals the cube of the digit C. How many such three–digit numbers ABC exist?

A) 5

B) 10

C) 20

D) 30

A B C D
○ ○ ○ ○

4

A sequence is shown below:

$1, 4, -2, 1 \ldots$

The first term is 1. The second term is obtained by multiplying the first term with 4, the third term is obtained by dividing the second term by (-2), and the fourth term is obtained by adding 3 to the third term. The same above cycle then repeats for the 5th, 6th and 7th terms and so on. What is the sum of the first 22 terms of the above sequence?

A) 8

B) 21

C) 22

D) 32

A B C D
○ ○ ○ ○

5

$P=\{1,2,3,4\ldots20\}$.

How many integers n can be selected from the set P such that $(n^2 + n^3)$ is a perfect square?

A) 2

B) 3

C) 4

D) 5

A B C D
○ ○ ○ ○

6

The average of seven distinct positive integers is 8. What is the greatest possible value of one of the integers?

A) 9

B) 11

C) 35

D) 45

A B C D
○ ○ ○ ○

7

On Children's day celebrations, gifts were distributed among the children of the locality. There was a total of 96 pens and 72 pencils to be given away as gifts. What could be the total number of pens and pencils given to each child if maximum number of children received the gifts and every child received the same number of gifts? *Note: All the gifts were identical.*

A) 3

B) 4

C) 7

D) 12

A B C D
○ ○ ○ ○

GRID-IN

8

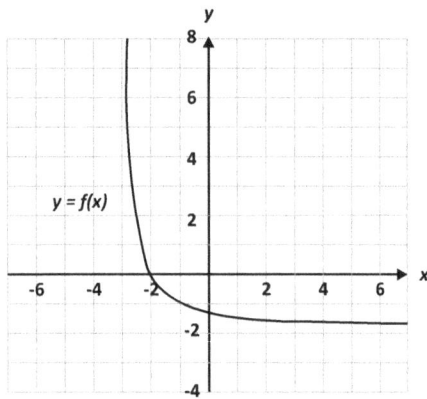

The graph of $y=f(x)$ is shown in the *xy-plane*. What is the value of $f(-2)$?

9

A crate contains *green* and *red* apples in the ratio 7 : 11. When *ten green* apples and *ten red* apples are removed from the crate, the ratio becomes 9 : 17. How many *red apples* were originally in the bag?

10

A survey was made on the breed of dogs kept by pets in different families in a city and the results were tabulated as shown below:

Breed of dogs	Number of families
Rottweiler	125
Labrador	213
German shepherd	97
Spitz	163
Doberman	n

If the median number of dogs was 163, what is the minimum possible value of n?

11

In the International Oxford School, all students play at least one of the two games rugby and baseball. 40% of all students play both rugby and baseball. If 20% of the students who play baseball do not play rugby, then what is the percentage of all students who play baseball?

12

$A=\{-1,2,3,5\}$ $B=\{-2,3,4\}$

We define a product of numbers from sets above, $P=ab$, in which a is a number form A and b is a number from B. What is the probability that product P will be positive and less than 11?

1. **Topic:** Units

   The correct answer is C

   Since 1/2 inch represents 1 mile, it follows that the trail length is 2(18)=36 miles.

   Hence, the correct answer is C.

2. **Topic:** Center, spread, and shape of distributions.

   The correct answer is C

   First, we order the values from the table: 3, 4, 4, 5, 6, 12, 15.

   Since there are 7 values, the median is the fourth value, 5.

   The correct answer is option C.

3. **Topic:** Data inferences

   The correct answer is C

   We know that $A=C^3$.

   Possible values of (A,C) which would satisfy the relation above are (1,1) and (8,2) (Here, $A \neq 0$ since we need a three–digit number. Also, since the value of A has to be a single digit, $C \neq 3$ or higher values).

   For both the cases above, B can assume any value from 0 to 9, i.e. there are 10 possibilities.

   Thus, we can have the following numbers:

   101,111,121,...191 i.e. 10 possibilities, and 802,812,822,...892 i.e. 10 possibilities i.e. 10+10=20 possibilities.

   Hence, the answer is C.

4. **Topic:** Misc.

   The correct answer is C

   The above sequence starts with 1 and the fourth term also becomes 1.

   Thus, the same three terms 1, 4 and –2 would repeat.

   The sum of the above three terms =

   $1 + 4 + (-2) = 3$.

   Thus, each set of the above three terms adds up to 3.

   In the first 22 terms, the above set of three terms would be repeated 7 times (since the quotient of the division of 22 by 3 is 7).

   Each of the above 7 groups would add up to 3.

   Hence, the sum of the terms of the above 7 groups = $3 \times 7 = 21$.

   The 22nd term is equivalent to the first term of the 8th group i.e. the first term of the sequence = 1.

   Hence, the sum of the first 22 terms = 21 + 1 = 22.

   Hence, the correct answer is C.

5. **Topic:** Relationships between variables

   The correct answer is B

   We have: $n^2 + n^3 = n^2(n+1)$

   Thus, in order that $(n^2 + n^3)$ be a perfect square, $(n+1)$ must be a perfect square as well (since n^2 is already a perfect square).

   Thus, from the set $P=\{1,2,3,4...20\}$, we need to select those values of n such that $(n+1)$ becomes a perfect square. This is possible only for n=3,8, and 15 (since 3+1=4, 8+1=9, and 15+1=16, which are all perfect squares).

   Hence, we can select 3 such integers.

   Hence, the answer is B.

6. **Topic:** Center, spread and shape of distributions

The correct answer is C

Since the average of seven integers is 8, their sum = 7 × 8 = 56.

Since we need to maximize one of the integers, we need to minimize the other six integers.

The minimum possible value of a positive integer is 1.

Since the integers are distinct and minimum in value, we choose the six integers to be 1, 2, 3, 4, 5 and 6.

The sum of the above six integers = 21.

Hence, the last number = 56 – 21 = 35.

Thus, the greatest possible value of one of the seven integers is 35.

Hence, the correct answer is C.

7. **Topic:** Misc.

The correct answer is C

We know that each gift set is identical.

Thus, the maximum number of children among whom the gifts could be distributed would be the greatest common factor of 96 and 72 i.e. 24.

Thus, each gift set should have $\frac{96}{24} = 4$ pens and

$\frac{72}{24} = 3$ pencils i.e. a total of 4+3=7 items.

Hence, the answer is C.

8. **Topic:** Key features of graphs

The correct answer is 0

We see on the graph that $f(-2)= 0$.

9. **Topic:** Ratios, rates, and proportions

The correct answer is 28.

Let the initial number of green and red apples be $7k$ and $11k$ respectively.

Again, let the final number of green and red apples be $9l$ and $17l$ respectively.

Since an equal number of green and red apples are removed, the difference between the number of green and red apples should remain the same.

Thus: $11k–7k=17l–9l=>4k=8l=>k=2l$.

Thus, the initial number of green and red apples are $7k=14l$ and $11k=22l$ respectively.

Thus, reduction in the number of green and red apples = $14l–9l=5l$ and $22l–17l=5l$ respectively.

Hence, we have $5l=10=>l=2$.

Thus, the initial number of red apples = $14l=14 \times 2=28$.

Hence, the correct answer is 28.

10. **Topic:** Center, spread and shape of distributions

The correct answer is 163

Since 163 is the median value, there must be equal number of terms less than or more than 163.

We already have 97 and 125 less than 163. So, n must be more than or equal to 163.

Hence, the minimum value of n is 163.

Hence, the correct answer is 163.

11. Topic: Data inferences

The correct answer is 50

The different regions are shown in the Venn diagram below:

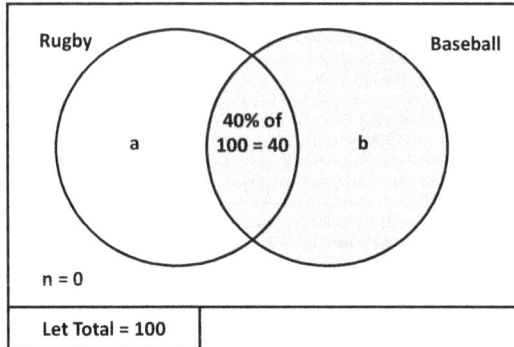

Since all students play at least one of the two games rugby and baseball, we have n=0.

We know that 20% of the students who play baseball do not play rugby.

$$\frac{20}{100} \times (40 + b) = b =>$$

$$8 + \frac{b}{5} = b => b = 10$$

Thus:

Thus, total number of students who play baseball = 10 + 40 = 50.

Thus, percentage of students who play baseball =

$$\frac{50}{100} \times 100 = 50\%$$

Hence, the correct answer is 50.

12. Topic: Misc

The correct answer is $\frac{1}{3}$

We find all possible values of product $P=ab$:

$(-1)\ (-2)=2, (-1)\ 3=-3, (-1)\ 4=-4$

$2\ (-2)=-4, 2\ (3)=6, 2\ (4)=8$

$3\ (-2)=-6, 3\ (3)=9, 3\ (4)=12$

$5\ (-2)=-10, 5\ (3)=15, 5\ (4)=20$

There are 12 products, 7 of which are positive, and 4 of the positive are less than 11.

Thus, the probability that P is positive and less than 11 is $\frac{4}{12}$ which is $\frac{1}{3}$.

MULTIPLE CHOICE QUESTIONS

13

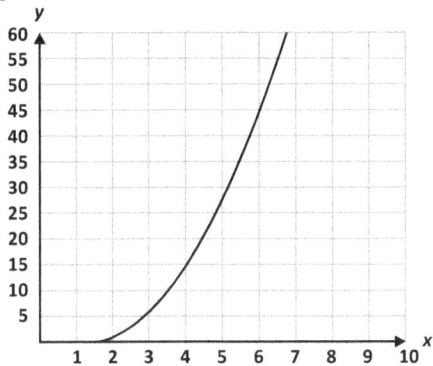

What is the approximate slope of the function on the graph above between $x=4$ and $x=6$?

A) 15

B) 22

C) –10

D) 12

A B C D
○ ○ ○ ○

14

A researcher surveyed a random sample of people in City A about how often they dine out. Using the sample data, the researcher estimated that 12.3% of people in City A dine out 3 or more times per week, with a margin error of 2.5%.

Which of the following is the most appropriate conclusion about all people in City A, based on the information above?

A) The researcher is 14.8% sure that the most part of people in City A dine out 3 and more times per week.

B) At least 9.8%, but not more than 14.8% of people in City A dine out exactly 3 times per week.

C) It is likely that the percentage of people in City A who dine out 3 or more times per week is between 9.8% and 14.8%.

D) It is likely that more than 14.8% of people dine out more than 3 times per week.

A B C D
○ ○ ○ ○

15

An administration of City X wanted to convert a green area into a parking lot and decided to assess the opinions of all city residents about this conversion. 750 city residents, who have jobs around this place, were asked about their opinion. The survey showed that the most part of sampled people supported converting. Which of the following is true about the survey?

A) The result shows that the most part of all city residents support converting.

B) The survey sample has not enough people to be representative.

C) For a valid survey it should include all city residents.

D) The survey sample is not representative.

A B C D
○ ○ ○ ○

16

A retail chain has 32 stores in 12 different states. A marketing office of this chain wants to know percent of returning customers at each store. Which of the following sampling methods can work the best to estimate the proportion of all customers who shop at the store two and more times?

A) Selecting one of the 32 stores at random and then surveying every customer who makes a purchase at that store during one working day.

B) Selecting one of the 32 stores at random and then surveying all customers who visit that store during one working day.

C) Selecting 20 customers at each store during one working day at random and then surveying each selected customer.

D) Surveying each customer who spends $100 or more at each store during one working day.

A B C D
○ ○ ○ ○

17

Andrew was asked by his friend to count all the numbers from 1 to 90 that are divisible by two and three but not by five. Andrew made a mistake in the process and counted the result as 10. What is the difference between the actual result and the result that Andrew got?

A) 2

B) 4

C) 6

D) 10

A B C D
○ ○ ○ ○

18

Which of the following can be a possible value of the average of 8 consecutive odd natural numbers?

A) 21

B) 27

C) 32

D) 37

A B C D
○ ○ ○ ○

19

During the Inter–School Debate championship, students of the 9th grade of Illinois Public School had to be divided in groups. It was found that if they were divided into groups of four, one student was left out. If they were divided into groups of six, then too, one student was left out. What was the minimum number of students in the grade such that they can be perfectly divided in groups of five?

A) 15

B) 20

C) 25

D) 30

A B C D
○ ○ ○ ○

20

A sequence is shown below:

1, 4, – 4 …

The first term is 1. Each even numbered term is 3 more than the previous term and each odd numbered term after the first is (– 1) times the previous term. What is the sum of the first 32 terms of the above sequence?

A) – 1

B) 0

C) 1

D) 3

A B C D
○ ○ ○ ○

21

The mean of five positive integers is 5. The mode of the 5 numbers is 8. What is the maximum possible value of the lowest term?

A) 1

B) 2

C) 3

D) 4

A B C D
○ ○ ○ ○

22

Out of 35 students in section *A* of the 7th grade of Manhattan Public School, 10 students like baseball, 20 students like basketball and 10 students like rugby. 3 students like baseball and basketball, 4 students like basketball and rugby, and 6 students like baseball and rugby. If 2 students like all three games, how many students do not like any of the above three games?

A) 5

B) 6

C) 8

D) 9

A B C D
○ ○ ○ ○

23

The Farm–Fresh fruit store in California stocks Apples, Peaches and Lychees. While ordering fruits for its store, the owner wanted the fruits in particular ratios as depicted in the table below:

Fruits	Required Ratio
Apples : Peaches	4 : 9
Apples : Lychees	3 : 8

What is the ratio of Peaches to Lychees?

A) $\dfrac{6}{1}$

B) $\dfrac{3}{4}$

C) $\dfrac{4}{27}$

D) $\dfrac{27}{32}$

A B C D
○ ○ ○ ○

24

In the final examinations for 9th grade students of New York Public School, 3 students failed in Mathematics, Science and History; 4 students failed in Mathematics and History; 5 students failed in Science and History; 4 students failed in Mathematics and Science; 10 students failed in Mathematics; 12 students failed in History and 8 students failed in Science.

How many students passed all 3 exams if there were 42 students?

A) 15

B) 19

C) 22

D) 20

A B C D
○ ○ ○ ○

GRID-IN

25

There are 500 employees in a company and 44% of them are female. If 25% of male employees play soccer, how many male workers play soccer?

26

Airfares in Relation to the Flight Distance

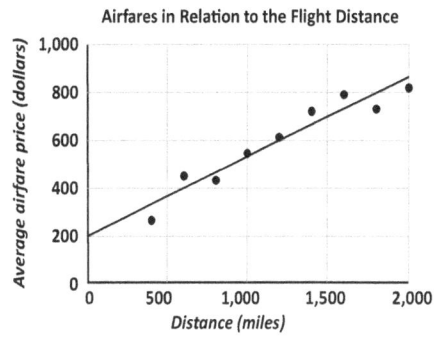

The scatterplot above depicts average airfare prices in relation to the flight distance, in miles. The line of best fit for the data is also shown. According to the line of best fit, what is the predicted increase in average price for every 100 miles?

13. **Topic:** Key features of graphs

    The correct answer is A

    We see that at $x=4$, $y=15$ and at $x=6$, $y=45$.

    Hence, we find the slope: $\dfrac{45-15}{6-4}=15$.

    The correct answer is option A.

14. **Topic:** Data Inferences.

    The correct answer is C

    The researcher is certain that the percentage of people in City A who dine out 3 or more times per week is between 12.3%−2.5%=9.8% and 12.3%+2.5%=14.8%.

    The correct answer is option C.

15. **Topic:** Data collection and conclusions.

    The correct answer is D

    The survey is not representative since the survey sample is not random. Only people who work around this area were asked.

    Choice A is incorrect. We cannot make any conclusion about all citizens since the survey sample is not random.

    Choice B is incorrect. The number of people is sufficient.

    Choice C. For valid surveys we do not need all citizens in a sample, but we should choose them at random.

    The correct answer is option D.

16. **Topic:** Data collection and conclusions.

    The correct answer is C

    Selecting 20 customers at each store during one working day at random and surveying them gives a representative sample of data.

    Choice A is incorrect. Surveying customers at one store does not give representative data about all other stores. Moreover, surveying only those customers who make purchases does not give information about all population.

    Choice B is incorrect. Surveying customers at one store does not give representative data about all other stores.

    Choice D is incorrect. The customers are not chosen at random, hence the sample data is not representative.

    The correct answer is option C.

17. **Topic:** Misc.

    The correct answer is A

    We have to find the numbers from 1 to 90 divisible by 2 and 3 but not by 5. We know that 90 is a multiple of the LCM of 2,3,5 i.e. 30.

    All integers from 1 to 90 can be categorized according to multiples of 2,3,5, as shown in the tree diagram below:

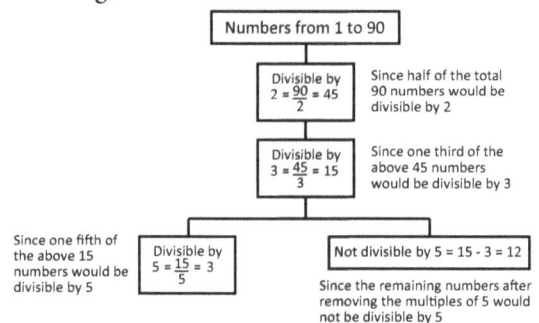

    Hence, there are 12 numbers from 1 to 90 which are divisible by 2 and 3 but not divisible by 5.

    Thus, the difference between the actual result and the result that Andrew had obtained = 12−10=2.

    Hence, the answer is A.

18. **Topic:** Center, spread and shape of distributions

The correct answer is C

The mean of 8 consecutive odd integers (i.e. integers having a constant gap between each other) must be the average of the middle two terms i.e. the 4th and 5th terms. Since the 4th and 5th terms are both consecutive odd integers, their average must be an even number.

Hence, the only option possible is 32 (In that case, the numbers are 25, 27, 29, 31, 33, 35, 37, and 39).

Hence, the correct answer is C.

19. **Topic:** Relationships between variables

The correct answer is C

Let the number of students in the 9th grade be x.

Since when divided in groups of four or six, one student was left over, we can say that the number of students must be one more than a multiple of the LCM of 4 and 6 i.e. 12.

Thus, $x=12k+1$, where k is some positive integer.

Now, we know that x is divisible by 5.

Thus, the smallest value of x comes when we put $k=2$ (by hit and trial, we can see that $k=1$ does not satisfy, so we check with $k=2$).

Thus, $x=12\times2+1=25$.

Hence, the minimum number of students in that grade was 25.

Hence, the answer is C.

20. **Topic:** Relationships between variables

The correct answer is B

The first few terms are shown below:

$t_1=1$

$t_2=1+3=4$

$t_3=4\times(-1)=-4$

$t_4=-4+3=-1$

$t_5=-1\times(-1)=1$

$t_6=1+3=4$

$t_7=4\times(-1)=-4$

$t_8=-4+3=-1$

Thus, we see that the same four terms 1, 4, – 4, and – 1 keep repeating.

The sum of the above four terms is

$1 + 4 + (– 4) + (– 1) = 0$.

Since for every four terms the sum becomes zero, the sum of the first 32 terms (32 is a multiple of 4) is also zero.

Hence, the correct answer is B.

21. **Topic:** Center, spread and shape of distributions

    The correct answer is B

    Since the mean of 5 integers is 5, the sum of the integers = $5 \times 5 = 25$.

    There is a single mode of 8.

    Thus, 8 must be present more than once.

    Now, 8 cannot be present more than thrice as four times 8 becomes 32 which exceeds the total of the five positive integers.

    If 8 is present thrice, then we have the sum as

    $3 \times 8 = 24$.

    Thus, the other two positive integers would add up to $25 - 24 = 1$; which is not possible.

    Thus, 8 must be present exactly twice, and they add up to $2 \times 8 = 16$.

    Thus, the other three integers add up to 9.

    These three integers cannot be 3 each as then the mode would no longer be 8 and would become 3 instead.

    Thus, the sum of those three integers can be made 9 in the following ways (we cannot repeat the same number even twice; else the set of integers will no longer have a single mode):

    i) 2, 3, 4: Here, the minimum term is 2.

    ii) 1, 3, 5: Here, the minimum term is 1.

    iii) 1, 2, 6: Here, the minimum term is 1.

    Since we need the maximum possible value of the lowest term, we take it as 2 (since $2 > 1$).

    Hence, the correct answer is B.

22. **Topic:** Data inferences

    The correct answer is B

    The different regions are shown in the Venn diagram below:

    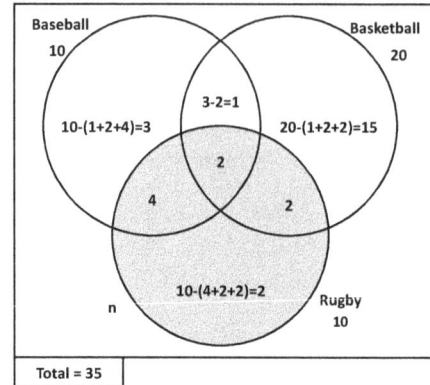

    Thus, the number of students who do not like any of the three games is:

    $n = 35 - (3 + 1 + 15 + 4 + 2 + 2 + 2) = 35 - 29 = 6$.

    Hence, the correct answer is B.

23. **Topic:** Ratios, rates, and proportions

    The correct answer is D

    We have the following information:

    $$\frac{Apples}{Peaches} = \frac{4}{9}$$

    $$\frac{Apples}{Lychees} = \frac{3}{8}$$

    Now, we rearrange the ratios so that all common terms cancel out leaving Peaches and Lychees.

    Hence, we have:

    $$\frac{Peaches}{Lychees} = \frac{9}{4} \times \frac{3}{8} = \frac{27}{32}$$

    Hence, the answer is D.

24. Topic: Data inferences

The correct answer is C.

The different regions are shown in the Venn diagram below:

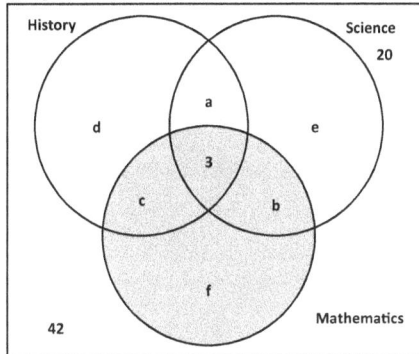

The students who failed History and Science = a= 5−3 =2.

The students who failed History and Mathematics = c= 4−3 =1.

The students who failed Mathematics and Science = b= 4−3 =1.

The students who failed History = d= 12−3−2−1 =6.

The students who failed Mathematics = f= 10−3−1−1 =5.

The students who failed Science = e= 8−3−2−1 =2.

Thus, the number of students who passed all exams = 42−3−2−1−1−6−5−2=42−20=22.

Hence, the correct answer is C.

25. Topic: Percents.

The correct answer is 70.

The number of male employees is

500(1−0.44)=280.

We know that 25% male workers play soccer, hence 280(0.25)=70 male workers play soccer.

26. Topic: Scatterplots

The correct answer is $33\frac{1}{3}$.

According to the scatterplot, the line of best fit passes through the points (0,200) and (1500,700), hence we can find the slope:

$$\frac{700-200}{1500-0}=\frac{1}{3}$$

This means the line of best fit predicts a $\frac{1}{3}$ dollar increase in average price for every 1 mile increase in distance.

Thus, we find that the line of best fit predicts a $33\frac{1}{3}$ dollar increase in average price for every 100 miles.

MULTIPLE CHOICE QUESTIONS

27

	Can ride a bicycle	Cannot ride a bicycle	Total
Boys	18		
Girls		12	
			64

The table above shows how many students at preliminary school can or cannot ride a bicycle.

If $\dfrac{3}{4}$ students can ride a bicycle, what is the probability that a randomly selected student is a boy who cannot ride a bicycle?

A) $\dfrac{1}{4}$

B) $\dfrac{1}{16}$

C) $\dfrac{3}{8}$

D) $\dfrac{5}{12}$

A B C D
○ ○ ○ ○

28

John and Robert buy a postcard every time when they travel. In January John and Robert had 8 postcards each. Since January, John's postcards grew by 2 postcards every 3 months and Robert's postcards grew by 20% of the increased number after every 3 months. Which of the following is the best estimate for the number of postcards which John and Robert will have 6 months later?

A) 23

B) 14

C) 15

D) 29

A B C D
○ ○ ○ ○

29

R is the sum of squares of 50 consecutive even integers starting with 2, and S is the sum of squares of 50 consecutive integers starting with 1. S is what percentage less than R?

A) 25%

B) 33%

C) 50%

D) 75%

A B C D
○ ○ ○ ○

30

In the 10th grade of Brooklyn Public School, the ratio of the number of boys to the number of girls was 3 : 5. Among the students, some had taken up literature as a specialization while the rest had taken up science.

The ratio of the number of literature students to science students was 5 : 7. If it is known that one–third the number of boys had taken up science as a specialization, what fraction of the girls had literature as their specialization?

A) $\dfrac{4}{15}$

B) $\dfrac{2}{5}$

C) $\dfrac{3}{5}$

D) $\dfrac{2}{3}$

A B C D
○ ○ ○ ○

31

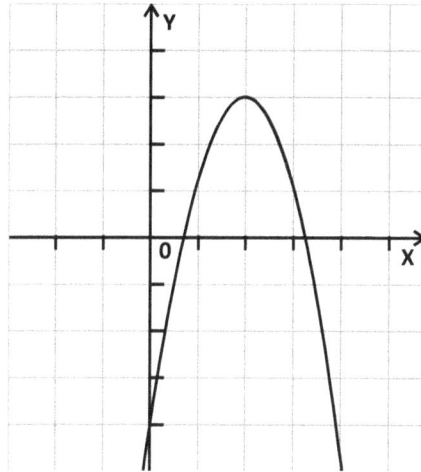

Which of the following can be the correct expression for the graph of the quadratic shown above?

A) $y = x^2 - 6x + 8$

B) $y = -x^2 - 6x - 8$

C) $y = -x^2 + 6x - 8$

D) $y = -x^2 + 6x + 8$

A B C D
○ ○ ○ ○

32

The Boulevard Hotel has a peculiar way of numbering its rooms. The first room on each floor is numbered as the product of all floor numbers below it starting from floor number one (the ground floor is not counted).

For example, the first room on the fourth floor would be numbered as 1×2×3=6.

All successive room numbers would be numbered three more than the previous room number.

Thus, on the fourth floor, rooms are numbered as 6,6+3=9,6+(2×3)=12,6+(3×3)=15, etc. If it is known that there are six rooms on each floor, how many room numbers on the fifteenth floor are prime numbers?

A) 0

B) 2

C) 4

D) 5

A B C D
○ ○ ○ ○

33

AB and *CA* are two–digit numbers which satisfy the multiplication:

$$\begin{array}{r} A\ B \\ \times\ \ C\ A \\ \hline 1\ B\ C\ A \end{array}$$

If *A*,*B*,*C* are distinct integers from 2 to 5, what is the value of *A+B+C*?

A) 2

B) 3

C) 5

D) 10

A B C D
○ ○ ○ ○

GRID-IN

34

A bookstore is selling books and DVD discs. In the first 2 hours after opening there were sold 4 books and 1 DVD. After that the number of sold books is growing by 25% on the changing figure every hour, and the number of sold DVD discs is growing by 2 every hour. What is the best estimate for the difference between sold books and DVDs after 2 hours?

35

20, 15, 10, 35, 40, x

If the mean of the six numbers above is 23, what is the value of x?

36

Let P be a set of 21 integers from –10 to 10, i.e. P={–10,–9,–8,–7…7,8,9,10}. In how many ways can one select 2 integers from the above set such that their sum comes to minus one?

27. **Topic:** Table data

    The correct answer is B

    $\frac{3}{4}$ of 64 students can ride a bicycle,

    it is $\frac{3}{4} \times 64 = 48$ students.

    Hence the number of boys who can ride a bicycle is 64–(48+ 12)=4.

    Thus, the probability that a randomly chosen student is a boy who cannot ride a bicycle is

    $\frac{4}{64} = \frac{1}{16}$

    The correct answer is option B.

28. **Topic:** Linear and exponential growth

    The correct answer is A

    After 6 months John has 8+2(2)=12 postcards.

    And Robert has $8(1.2^2) = 8(1.44) = 11.52$, hence 11 postcards.

    Hence, together they have 12+11=23 postcards.

    The correct answer is option A.

29. **Topic:** Data inferences

    The correct answer is D

    Let us write the terms of the series R:
    $R = 2^2 + 4^2 + 6^2 + ...100^2$ (since we are looking at 50 consecutive even numbers, it would start with 2 and end in 100).

    So, $R = 2^2(1^2 + 2^2 + 3^2 + ...50^2) = 4k$, where $k = 1^2 + 2^2 + 3^2 + ...50^2$.

    Let us also write the terms of the series $S: S = 1^2 + 2^2 + 3^2 + ...50^2$ (since we are looking at 50 consecutive numbers, it would start with 1 and end in 50).

    So, $S = k$, where $k = 1^2 + 2^2 + 3^2 + ...50^2$.

    Thus, we see that $R = 4k$ and $S = k$.

    Hence, the required percentage =

    $\frac{4k - k}{4k} \times 100 = \frac{3}{4} \times 100 = 75\%$

    Hence, the answer is D.

30. Topic: Ratios, rates, and proportions

The correct answer is A

We can see that the total students in the 10th grade are classified in two ways:

First, we have Boys : Girls = 3:5.

Second, we have Literature : Science = 5:7.

According to the first classification, the total comes to 3+5=8 while according to the second, the total comes to 5+7=12.

Since the total in both cases should be the same, we assume the total to be the LCM of 8 and 12 i.e. 24 for our convenience.

Thus, if the total number of students in the 10th grade is 24:

Number of boys = $\dfrac{3}{3+5} \times 24 = 9$ and number

of girls = $\dfrac{5}{3+5} \times 24 = 15$

Again, number of literature students

$\dfrac{5}{5+7} \times 24 = 10$ and number of science students

$= \dfrac{7}{5+7} \times 24 = 14$

We also know that one–third the number of boys

i.e. $\dfrac{1}{3} \times 9 = 3$ boys have taken up science.

Thus, the remaining science students i.e. 14–3=11 students must have been girls.

Thus, the remaining girls i.e. 15–11=4 girls must have taken up literature.

Thus, the fraction of girls who had literature as

their specialization = $\dfrac{4}{15}$.

Hence, the answer is A.

31. Topic: Key features of graphs

The correct answer is C

The graph of the equation $y = ax^2 + bx + c$, is an upside–down parabola if $a<0$

Also, the Y intercept in the graph (the point where $x=0$) is negative $=>c<0$

Since both roots are positive, the sum of the

roots is also positive $=> -\dfrac{b}{a} > 0$

$\dfrac{b}{a} < 0$

Since $a<0$, we have: $b>0$

The correct answer is option C.

32. Topic: Data inferences

The correct answer is A

From the given information, we can say that the first room on the fifteenth floor would be: $1\times2\times3\times4\times5\times\ldots\times14=N$ (say).

Thus, successive room numbers would be: $N,(N+3),(N+6),(N+9),(N+12)$ and $(N+15)$.

We can see that N is a multiple of all integers from 1 to 14. Thus, N is a multiple of 3,6,9 and 12.

Again, since N is a multiple of both 3 and 5, it is also a multiple of 15.

Thus, $(N+3)$ is not prime since it is divisible by 3.

Similarly, $(N+6)$ is not prime since it is divisible by 6.

$(N+9)$ is not prime since it is divisible by 9.

$(N+12)$ is not prime since it is divisible by 12.

Finally, $(N+15)$ is not prime since it is divisible by 15.

Thus, none of the numbers are primes.

33. **Topic:** Data inferences

The correct answer is D

We know that the digits are distinct, and their values are from 2 to 5. Hence, A and B can be 2,3,4 or 5.

We can see that the only option that can give us the last A in multiplication $B \times A$ is $A=5$ and $B=3$.

Thus, C can only be either 2 or 4 (since all digits are distinct).

If $C=2$, we get $(53)(25) = 1325$ which is exactly $1BCA$.

If $C=4$, we get $(53)(45) = 2385$ which is not equal to $1BCA$.

Thus, $A+B+C=5+3+2=10$.

Hence, the answer is D.

34. **Topic:** Linear and exponential growth

The correct answer is 1

After 2 hours the store sold $4(1.25^2)=6.25$, hence 6 books,

and $1+2(2)=5$ DVDs.

Then the difference is $6-5 = 1$.

35. **Topic:** Center, spread, and shape of distributions.

The correct answer is 18

The sum of the six numbers: $23(6)=138$.

The value of x: $138-(20+15+10+35+40)=18$.

36. **Topic:** Data inferences

The correct answer is 10

We need to choose two numbers that add up to -1.

The possible ways of selecting two numbers which add up to -1 are: $(-10,9)$; $(-9,8)$; $(-8,7)$; $(-7,6)$; $(-6,5)$; $(-5,4)$; $(-4,3)$; $(-3,2)$; $(-2,1)$ and $(-1,0)$.

Thus, there are 10 possible cases.

Hence, the answer is 10.

MULTIPLE CHOICE QUESTIONS

37

Ellen's room is shown in the following diagram. What is the area of Ellen's room in square inches?

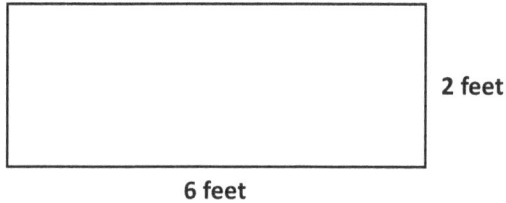

2 feet

6 feet

A) 12 square inches

B) 72 square inches

C) 1728 square inches

D) 144 square inches

A B C D
○ ○ ○ ○

38

If $\dfrac{3x}{5} = \dfrac{x+7}{4}$, what is the value of x?

A) 35

B) 7

C) 5

D) 4

A B C D
○ ○ ○ ○

39

The price of a smartphone is $522 after 24% discount and 4% additional tax to the discounted price.

What was the original price of the smartphone before discount and tax?

A) $686.80

B) $659.90

C) $725

D) $628

A B C D
○ ○ ○ ○

40

Rachel made 1 liter of lemonade. She gave two 8–ounce glasses of lemonade to her friends.

How many ounces of lemonade does Rachel have?

(1 ounce = 0.028 liter)

A) 17.5 ounces

B) 16.75 ounces

C) 18.32 ounces

D) 19.71 ounces

A B C D
○ ○ ○ ○

41

	Attend art classes	Do not attend art classes
Boys	16	42
Boys	26	28

At school 112 students were asked about their gender and if they attend art classes. The results are introduced in the table above. What percent of students do not attend art classes?

A) 37.5%

B) 48%

C) 62.5%

D) 54.5%

A B C D
○ ○ ○ ○

42

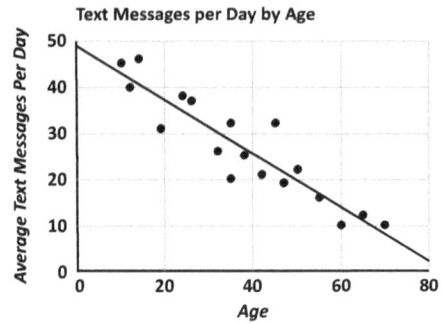

Text Messages per Day by Age

According to the line of best fit in the scatter plot above, which of the following best approximate the age when people send 30 text messages per day?

A) 32

B) 28

C) 38

D) 30

A B C D
○ ○ ○ ○

43

Jane wanted to boil water. When Jane put water on stove, its temperature was 70°F. After 5 minutes Jane reduced heat. Which of the following graphs in the mT–plane could best represent the temperature, T, in degrees Fahrenheit, m minutes after Jane put water on the stove?

A)

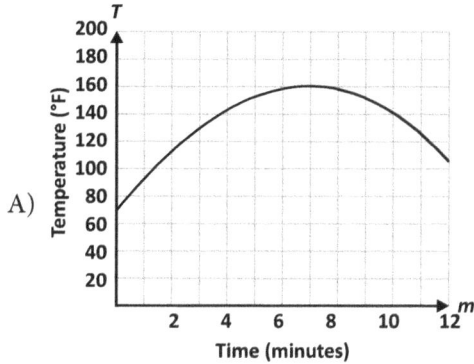

B)

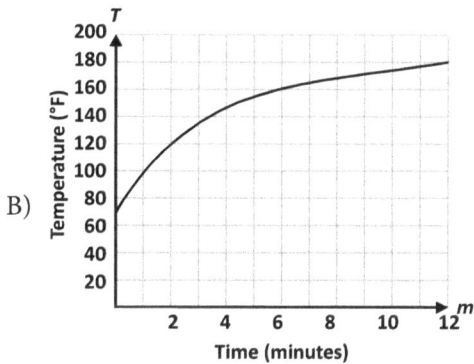

C)

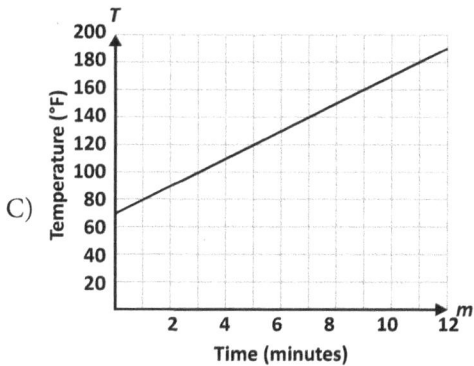

D)

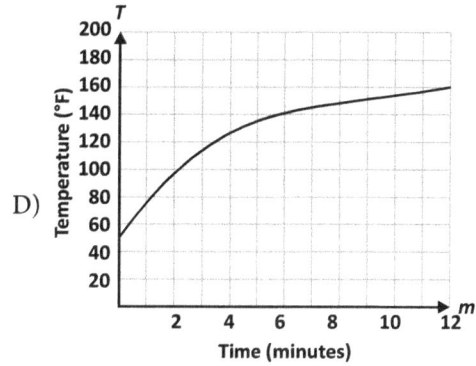

A B C D
○ ○ ○ ○

44

The following equation represents the population growth of ants: $P(t) = 70(16)^t$, where $P(t)$ is the population after t weeks. Which of the following best describes the relation between the population of ants, $P(t)$, and the number of weeks that have passed, t?

A) The relationship is exponential since the population is getting 70 times larger than the previous week.

B) The relationship is linear since the population is getting 16 more ants each week.

C) The relationship is exponential since the population is getting 16 times larger than the previous week.

D) The relationship is linear since the population is getting 70 more ants each week.

A B C D
○ ○ ○ ○

45

32 dentists in City *X* are randomly selected for a survey. 12 of them report working on Sundays. If there are 120 dentists in this city, what is an estimate of the total number of dentists that they work on Sundays?

A) 35

B) 24

C) 52

D) 45

A B C D
○ ○ ○ ○

46

Item	Price (dollars)
Grapes	3
Broom	12
Olive oil	15
Socks	4
Eggs	5
Napkins	4
Chocolate	6

The Table above shows the item Jane bought from a convenient store and their prices. What is the mean price of the items Jane bought?

A) 7

B) 5

C) 8

D) 6

A B C D
○ ○ ○ ○

47

New medicine against migraine was tested. For this study people with repeated migraine symptoms were divided into two groups: one group got old medicine and the other one got new one for 3 weeks. Before the studies all people did not use any treatment against migraine.

After 3 weeks scientists compared results and concluded that people who took the new medicine had 65% less migraine symptoms after treatment and people who took the old medicine had 37% less symptoms after treatment. Based on the results of this study, which of the following conclusions are valid?

A) Taking the new medicine reliefs 65% more symptoms of migraine than the old one.

B) It is hardly possible that the new medicine helps better than the old one, since none of the treatments shows 100% symptoms relief.

C) Taking the new medicine shows better results in migraine treatment than the old one during the study period.

D) Since the study was only 3 weeks long, we cannot compare the effects of two given treatments.

A B C D
○ ○ ○ ○

48

Consider the set of integers

$P = \{1, 2, 3, 4 \ldots 51\}$.

Let us define *A* as the average of the odd integers in *P* and *B* as the average of the even integers in *P*. What is the value of $A - B$?

A) – 1

B) 0

C) 1

D) 2

A B C D
○ ○ ○ ○

49

At the Orient Store clearance sale, articles are sold at a price resulting in 10% loss for the store owner. The store owner decides to double the existing selling price of each article. What is his current percentage profit if it is known that all articles have the same price?

A) 100

B) 90

C) 85

D) 80

A B C D
○ ○ ○ ○

▼

Use the graph below for questions 50-52

The graph below gives the production and consumption of crude oil in certain countries of the world.

Figures below the names of the countries indicate crude reserves in million tonnes. Shortfall / (excess) between production and consumption is met by imports / (exports).

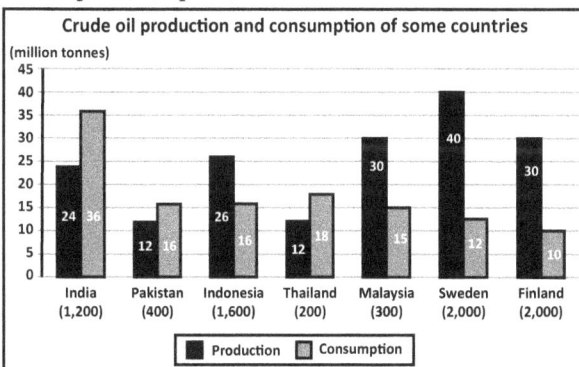

Crude oil production and consumption of some countries

50

Which country has the maximum percentage difference between its production and consumption?

A) Malaysia

B) Sweden

C) Finland

D) Indonesia

A B C D
○ ○ ○ ○

51

Which country has shown a nearly constant TV share for the 5 years?

A) Hong Kong

B) Malaysia

C) Singapore

D) China

A B C D
○ ○ ○ ○

52

By what "percentage points" has the share of TV sets in Hong Kong grown from 1993 to 1997?

A) 7

B) 15

C) 16

D) 21

A B C D
○ ○ ○ ○

▲

53

John has a large collection of coins with him. The coins are split between of one–dollar coins, quarters, and dimes (one quarter is equivalent to one–fourth of a dollar and one dime is equivalent to one–tenth of a dollar). If the ratio of the number of one dollar coins to quarters to dimes is 3 : 8 : 10 and they are exactly $210, how many quarters does John have?

A) 35

B) 80

C) 105

D) 280

A B C D
○ ○ ○ ○

GRID-IN

54

The dog toy company Tater Tot Toys tests the durability of the toys by giving them to the owner's pet Toto. The company gives Toto 10 toys to try, and within a day Toto rips 4 apart. Because Toto ripped 4 toys apart, the company labels these toys as "non–durable". If the company sells 450 of the toys, how many of them should they expect to be "non–durable" if the sample given to Toto was representative of all of the toys at the company?

55

Tree Growth

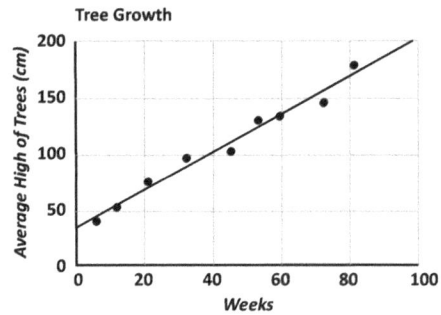

New trees were planted in the park area. The scatterplot above shows the average high of new trees by weeks along with a line of best fit, which has equation $y = 1.7x + 34$. According to the line of best fit, what is the average height of trees in the 43th week?

56

A representative sample of people who spend vacation in County *X* reveals that 32.5% of the people in the sample travel 2 or 3 days. If there are 12640 people spending their vacation in County *X* every week, approximately how many of them travel 2 or 3 days?

57

The odds in favor of Ann clearing a driving test is 1 : 4. The odds in favor of Brad clearing the same driving test is 5 : 4. What is the probability that at least one of them would clear the test?

37. Topic: Units

The correct answer is C

First, convert each of the dimensions into units of inches. The conversion needed is 1 ft=12 inches. Therefore, 6 feet=72 inches and 2 feet=24 inches. To get the area, you then multiply 72x24 and obtain 1728. Therefore, the answer is C.

38. Topic: Ratios, rates, and proportions.

The correct answer is C

$$\frac{3x}{5} = \frac{x+7}{4} => 12x = 5x + 35 =>$$

$$7x = 35 => x = 5.$$

Hence, the correct answer is C.

39. Topic: Percents

The correct answer is B

Let x be the original price of the smartphone before discount and tax.

The price of the smartphone after discount is $x-0.24x= 0.76x$.

The price of the smartphone after 4% of tax is $0.76x(1+0.04)=0.791x$.

Then we have the equation:

$0.791x = 522 => x =659.9$

Hence, the correct answer is B.

40. Topic: Units

The correct answer is D

After Rachel gave two 8–ounce glasses of lemonade to her friends, she has 1–2(8).028=0.552 liter of lemonade.

Let us convert 0.552 liter to ounce:

$$\frac{0.552}{0.028} = 19.71 \text{ ounces.}$$

Hence, the correct answer is D.

41. Topic: Table data

The correct answer is C

The total number of students who do not attend art classes is 42+28=70.

The percent of students who do not attend art classes is $\frac{70}{112}100\% = 62.5\%$

The correct answer is option C.

42. Topic: Scatterplots

The correct answer is A

According to the graph, the horizontal line that represents 30 messages per day intersects the line of best fit at a point where the vertical coordinate is between 30 and 40, and closer to 30 than 40. Thus, of the choice given, 32 is the best approximation of the ages when people send 30 messages per day on average.

The correct answer is option A.

43. Topic: Key features of graphs

The correct answer is B

We know that the initial water temperature was 70^0 F, hence the graph has to start at point (0,70). We see that the graph D does not satisfy this condition.

We also see that on graph B, the slope of the curve decreases at point $x=5$, which corresponds to Jane reduced heat.

On graph A the temperature starts decreasing after 6 minutes, that is wrong.

On graph C temperature increases with a constant slope, that does not reflect that fact that Jane decreased the heat, hence, this is wrong.

The correct answer is option B.

44. **Topic:** Linear and exponential growth

    The correct answer is C

t	P(t)
0	70
1	1120
2	17920

    From the table, we see that the population is getting 16 times more than the previous week.

    The correct answer is option C.

45. **Topic:** Data Inferences.

    The correct answer is D

    Sample proportion: $\dfrac{12}{32}$

    Estimate: $\dfrac{12}{32}120 = 45$

    The correct answer is option D.

46. **Topic:** Center, spread, and shape of distributions.

    The correct answer is A

    Mean $= \dfrac{3 + 12 + 15 + 4 + 5 + 4 + 6}{7} = 7$

    The correct answer is option A.

47. **Topic:** Data collection and conclusions.

    The correct answer is C

    Based on the study results we can conclude that the new medicine shows better results than the old one during this study.

    Choice *A* is incorrect because the new medicine reduces symptoms by 65% compared to symptoms before the treatment started.

    Choice *B* is incorrect. Although none of the medications showed 100% symptoms relief, we can see that the new reduced more symptoms than the old one.

    Choice *D* is incorrect. We can make conclusions about the effectiveness of treatment based on 3 weeks studies.

    The correct answer is option C.

48. **Topic:** Center, spread and shape of distributions

    The correct answer is B

    A is the average of 1, 3, 5, 7 … 51.

    Since the numbers are consecutive odd integers, the average can be simply obtained as

    $= \dfrac{first\ term\ +\ last\ term}{2} = \dfrac{1 + 51}{2} = 26$

    Hence, *A* = 26.

    B is the average of 2, 4, 6 … 50.

    Since the numbers are consecutive even integers, the average can be simply obtained as

    $= \dfrac{first\ term\ +\ last\ term}{2} = \dfrac{2 + 50}{2} = 26$

    Hence, *B* = 26.

    Thus, *A*–*B*=0.

    Hence, the answer is B.

49. Topic: Percents

The correct answer is D

Let the cost price of each article be $100 (since this is a percentage–based question, the choice of the initial value has no effect on the final answer).

Thus, the initial selling price of each article = $(100–10% of 100)=$90.

Thus, new selling price = $90 × 2=$180.

Hence, profit = $(180–100)=$80.

Thus, percentage profit =

$$\frac{\text{Profit}}{\text{Cost price}} \times 100 = \frac{80}{100} \times 100 = 80\%$$

Hence, the answer is D.

50. Topic: Data collection and conclusions

The correct answer is B

$$\text{Malaysia} = \frac{30-15}{15} \times 100 = 100\%$$

$$\text{Sweden} = \frac{40-12}{12} \times 100 = 233.3\%$$

$$\text{Finland} = \frac{30-10}{10} \times 100 = 200\%$$

$$\text{Indonesia} = \frac{26-16}{16} \times 100 = 62.5\%$$

51. Topic: Data collection and conclusions

The correct answer is B

We can observe from the graph that Malaysia has more or less a constant TV share for 5 years. In three of its years, the share is constant at 32% (1994 – 1996).

In all the other countries, there have been fluctuations in the TV share percent values.

In Thailand too, the percent share values have not fluctuated by much. However, on comparing Malaysia and Thailand, it is clear that the share values of Malaysia have been more 'constant'.

52. Topic: Data collection and conclusions

The correct answer is A

The "percent points" simply refer to the difference between percent values.

Thus, from 1993 to 1997, the percent share has increased from 43% to 50%, i.e. an increase of 7 percent points.

(*Note: We do not know the change in population for Hong Kong from 1993 to 1997. Hence, the actual percent change cannot be determined.*)

53. Topic: Ratios, rates, and proportions

The correct answer is D

The ratio of number of one–dollar coins to quarters to dimes with John = 3:8:10.

Thus, let the number of one–dollar coins, quarters and dimes with John be $3k, 8k$, and $10k$ respectively, where k is some constant.

Let us calculate the total amount with John in dollars.

Thus: $3k$ one–dollar coins amount to $3k$.

$8k$ quarters amount to $\$\dfrac{8k}{4} = \$2k$

$10k$ dimes amount to $\$\dfrac{10k}{10} = \$k$

Thus, total amount with John = $\$(3k + 2k + k) = \$6k$

Hence, we have: $6k = 210 \Rightarrow k = 35$.

Thus, the number of quarters with him
$= 8k = 8 \times 35 = 280$

Hence, the answer is D.

54. Topic: Data Inferences.

The correct answer is 180.

If 4 out of every 10 are non–durable, we can use this sample size to infer about the larger population of dog toys. We can multiply the fraction of non–durable sample toys by the total population to get the number of non–durable in the batch of 450. The expression then becomes

$\frac{4}{10} \times 450,$ which equals 180.

55. Topic: Scatterplots

The correct answer is 107.1cm.

Since the line of best fit has equation $y=1.7x+34$, where x is the week and y is an average trees' high, then we substitute $x=43$ and get the average high in the 43th week: $y=1.7(43)+34=107.1$cm.

56. Topic: Data Inferences.

The correct answer is 4108.

Sample proportion: 32.5%=0.325.

Estimate: 12640 (0.325)=4108.

57. Topic: Data inferences

The correct answer is $\frac{5}{9} = 0.55$

Probability that Ann clears the driving test =

$\frac{1}{1+4} = \frac{1}{5}$

Thus, probability that Ann does not clear the

driving test = $1 - \frac{1}{5} = \frac{4}{5}$

Probability that Brad clears the driving test =

$\frac{4}{4+5} = \frac{4}{9}$

Thus, probability that Brad does not clear the

driving test = $1 - \frac{4}{9} = \frac{5}{9}$

Thus, probability that neither of them clears the

driving test = $\frac{4}{5} \times \frac{5}{9} = \frac{4}{9}$

Thus, probability that at least one of them clears

the driving test = $1 - \frac{4}{9} = \frac{5}{9}$

Hence, the correct answer is $\frac{5}{9} = 0.55$

MULTIPLE CHOICE QUESTIONS

58

There are 450 students in East Middle School. If 37 of those students take French, what percent of students takes French?

A) 0.082%

B) 8.2%

C) 82%

D) 12.16%

A B C D
○ ○ ○ ○

59

The following graph represents the number of hours worked on a job on the x axis, and the amount paid to work on the job. What does the line of best fit represent?

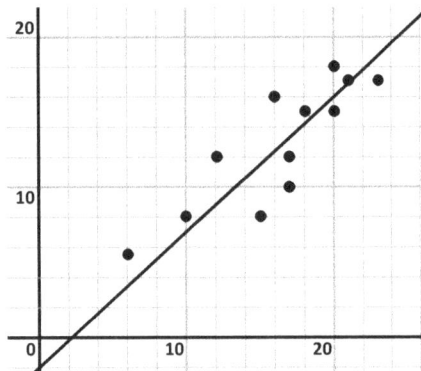

A) The line of best fit represents the average total amount the worker was paid per job.

B) The line of best fit represents the average number of hours the worker worked.

C) The line of best fit represents the average hourly wage the worker received

D) The line of best fit is meaningless in this example because the number of hours worked, and the amount paid are unrelated.

A B C D
○ ○ ○ ○

60

A price of a package of 6 cans of soda is $7.50. The same soda is sold at $1.50 per can. If Kelly bought two packages of soda rather than 12 cans of soda individually, the amount she saved on 12 cans of soda is what percent of the amount she paid?

A) 15%

B) 20%

C) 25%

D) 30%

A B C D
○ ○ ○ ○

61

Movie preferences	Male	Female
Adventure	23	12
Drama	6	42
Crime	20	10
Comedy	36	25
Historical	38	17

The table above summarizes the book preferences of 229 customers at a bookstore.

If one of the customers is selected randomly, what is the probability that the person prefers crime or historical books?

A) 0.253

B) 0.465

C) 0.175

D) 0.371

A B C D
○ ○ ○ ○

62

Desert area has been increasing by 9% every 2 years. The total desert area at the beginning of 2008 was approximately 12 500 000 square miles. If A is the area of desert t years after 2008, which of the following equations gives the area of desert over time?

A) $A = 1250000(1.09)^{2t}$

B) $A = 1250000(1.09)^{\frac{t}{2}}$

C) $A = 1250000(0.91)^{\frac{t}{2}}$

D) $A = 1250000 + 0.91(2t)$

A B C D
○ ○ ○ ○

63

If a,b,c,d are four distinct numbers such that: $a+c=2d$ and $b+d=2c$, which of the following is the correct expression for the average of the four numbers?

A) $c + d$

B) $\dfrac{3a + c}{4}$

C) $\dfrac{a + 2c}{2}$

D) $\dfrac{b + 3d}{4}$

A B C D
○ ○ ○ ○

64

The graph below gives the production and consumption of crude oil in certain countries of the world. Answer the following questions based on the graph below:

Figures below the names of the countries indicate crude reserves in million tonnes.

Shortfall / (excess) between production and consumption is met by imports / (exports).

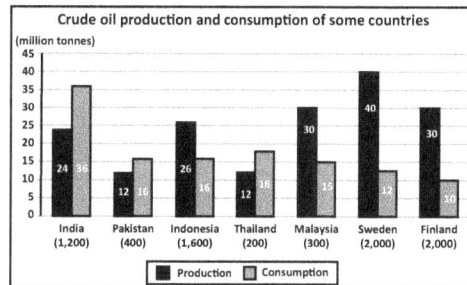

If Sweden produces 5% of world crude oil produce, then what is the percentage share of India in the world crude oil production?

A) 1.5%

B) 3.0%

C) 3.5%

D) 4.0%

A B C D
○ ○ ○ ○

65

The Strand Book Store in New York recently purchased 60 copies of Fahrenheit 451 at an average price of $250 per book. The store sold 75% of the books at $300 each and sold the remaining books to a book dealer for a lump sum of $2000. What was the net profit or loss of the store?

A) $500 profit

B) $450 profit

C) Neither profit nor loss

D) $500 loss

A B C D
○ ○ ○ ○

66

The graph shows the percentage of population owning TV sets in various countries.

TV share in Asia Pacific, in percent

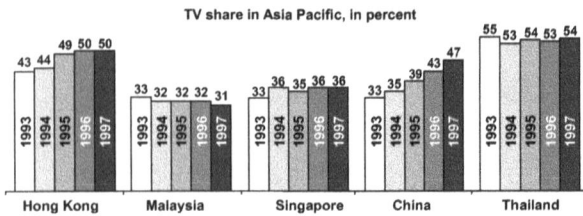

Which of the following countries has shown the highest percent decline in the percent share of TV sets from 1993 to 1997?

A) Hong Kong

B) Thailand

C) Singapore

D) Malaysia

A B C D
○ ○ ○ ○

67

A group of people were surveyed to choose one of the two TV shows they preferred more: Sherlock Holmes and Friends. Of the total 30 people who put forward their choice, 18 chose Sherlock Holmes and 20 chose Friends. Each person had to choose one of the two shows mentioned above. Choose the correct statement(s):

I.   8 people liked both shows.

II. 22 people preferred one show over the other.

III. 12 people liked only one of the two shows.

A) Only I

B) Only II

C) Only III

D) Both I and II

A B C D
○ ○ ○ ○

68

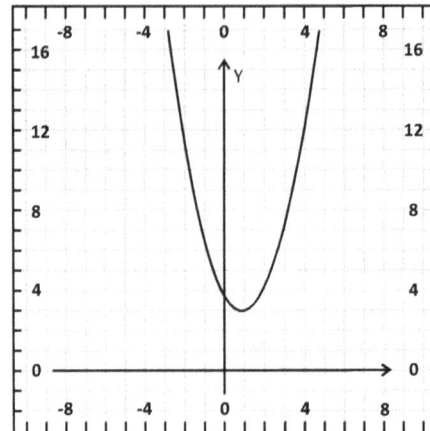

Which of the following forms of the equation below directly gives the coordinates of the vertex of the graph of the quadratic expression shown above?

A) $y = (x-1)(x-4)$

B) $y = x^2 + 4$

C) $y = (x-1)^2 + 3$

D) $y = 2(x-1)^2 + 3$

A B C D
○ ○ ○ ○

69

What is the probability that '4' will appear exactly thrice on rolling a normal dice four times?

A) $\dfrac{1}{324}$

B) $\dfrac{5}{1296}$

C) $\dfrac{1}{216}$

D) $\dfrac{5}{324}$

A B C D
○ ○ ○ ○

GRID-IN

70

Team Dolphins and Team Bears played hockey last season. How much larger was the median of the Bear's number of goals compared to the Dolphin's number of goals?

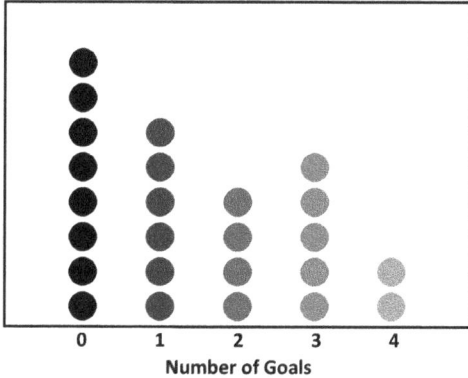

Team Dolphins

Number of Goals

Team Bears

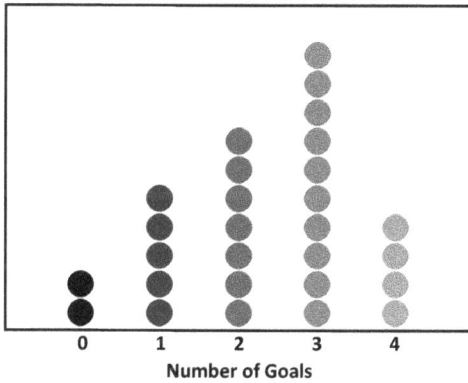

Number of Goals

71

	Can ride a bicycle	Cannot ride a bicycle	Total
Boys			32
Girls	16	12	28

The table above shows how many students at preliminary school can or cannot ride a bicycle. If $\frac{2}{3}$ students can ride a bicycle, how many boys cannot ride a bicycle?

72

A man travels at a speed of 12 miles/hr. How long, in minutes, to the nearest integer, would he take to cover a distance of 3750 yards?

(1 mile=5280 yards)

73

What is the number of ways a four–member debate team be selected from six boys and five girls so that at least one girl is always present in the team?

74

In the recently conducted TAS examination, 15% of the candidates got selected from the total number of candidates who wrote the exam. In another exam, the TCA, half the number of TAS candidates appeared and 20% of the candidates got selected. If the number of candidates selected in these two exams combined were 18000, how many candidates actually appeared for the TAS (in thousands)?

75

If the relation between A and B is known to be of the form: $B = k \times n^A$, what is the value of $(k + n)$?

The following data was observed between the variables A and B:

A	B
3	24
4	48
5	96

58. **Topic:** Percents

    The correct answer is B

    To find the percent of students that take French, take the number of students taking French, and divide that by the total number of students, then multiply by 100%. 37/450=0.082. Then you need to multiply by 100% to get 8.2%.

59. **Topic:** Scatterplots

    The correct answer is C

    The answer is C. The line of best fit represents the average linear fit of the data. It takes all of the data points into account to use a linear relationship to relate the two variables. The slope of the linear fit represents the average change in y over the change in x, which in this case is the average pay per hour. Therefore, C is correct.

60. **Topic:** Percents

    The correct answer is B

    The price of 2 packages of soda is 7.50 (2) =15.

    The price of 12 cans of soda is 1.50(12) = 18.

    Kelly saved 18−15 = 3 dollars.

    Her saving is $\dfrac{3}{15}$ = 0.20, which is 20% of the amount of money that she spent on 2 packages of soda.

    Hence, the correct answer is B.

61. **Topic:** Table Data

    The correct answer is D

    First, we find how many people prefer crime or historical books: 20+10+38+17=85.

    Then the probability is 85/229=0.371.

    The correct answer is option D.

62. **Topic:** Linear and exponential growth

    The correct answer is B

    The area is growing at a nonconstant rate, hence this is an exponential growth, choices A, B, or C.

    The area is growing by 9%, every 2 years, hence

    $$A = 12\,500\,000\,(0.91)^{\frac{t}{2}}.$$

    The correct answer is option B.

63. **Topic:** Data inferences

    The correct answer is D

    We have: a+c=2d and b+d=2c.

    The average of the four numbers =
    $$\dfrac{a+b+c+d}{4}$$

    Thus, going by options:

    1) $a + b + c + d = (a + c) + (b + d) = 2d + 2c$

    i.e. $\dfrac{a+b+c+d}{4} = \dfrac{2d+2c}{4} = \dfrac{c+d}{2}$

    Hence, A is incorrect.

    2) $a + b + c + d = a + c + (b + d) =$

    $a + c + 2c = a + 3c$

    i.e. $\dfrac{a+b+c+d}{4} = \dfrac{a+3c}{4}$

    Hence, (B) and (C) are incorrect.

    3) $a + b + c + d = (a + c) + b + d =$

    $2d + b + d = b + 3d$

    i.e. $\dfrac{a+b+c+d}{4} = \dfrac{b+3d}{4}$

    Hence, D is correct.

    Therefore, the correct answer is D.

64. **Topic:** Data collection and conclusions

The correct answer is B

Production of crude oil in Sweden = 40 million tonnes

Production of crude oil in India = 24 million

Thus, we have:

40 million tonnes = 5% of world crude oil produce

8 million tonnes = 1% of world crude oil produce

24 million = 3% of world crude oil produce

65. **Topic:** Percents

The correct answer is A

Total cost incurred by the store = $250×60=$15000.

Sales proceeds generated by selling 75% or $\dfrac{75}{100}$ ×60 i.e. 45 books = $300×45=$13500.

Sales proceeds generated by selling the remaining books = $2000.

Hence, total sales proceeds = $(13500+2000)=$15500.

Hence, net profit = (Net sales proceeds – Net cost incurred) = $(15500–15000)=$500.

Hence, the answer is A.

66. **Topic:** Data collection and conclusions

The correct answer is D

The percent share has declined only for Malaysia and Thailand from 1993 to 1997.

Malaysia: Percent decline in the percent share of TV sets = $\dfrac{33-31}{33} \times 100 = 6.06\%$

Thailand: Percent decline in the percent share of TV sets = $\dfrac{55-54}{55} \times 100 = 1.82\%$

Thus, Malaysia has the highest percent decline in the percent share of TV sets from 1993 to 1997.

67. **Topic:** Data inferences

The correct answer is D

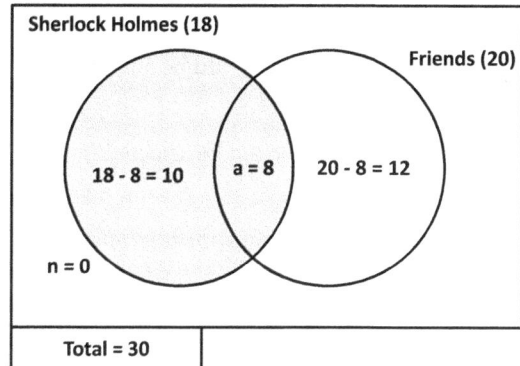

We have: 30=18+20–a=>a=8

Thus, 8 people liked both shows.

Also, 10 people preferred Sherlock Holmes over Friends and 12 people preferred Friends over Sherlock Holmes.

Thus, 10 + 12 = 22 people preferred one show over the other.

Also, 22 people liked only one show.

Thus, statements *I* and *II* are correct.

Hence, the correct answer is D.

68. **Topic:** Key features of graphs

The correct answer is C

We know that the equation of a quadratic when expressed in the form $y = a(x - k)^2 + l$, gives the coordinates of the vertex as (*k,l*).

Thus, the possible answers are options B, C and D.

From the graph, we can see that at *x*=0, *y*=4 and at *x*=1, *y*=3.

Only option C satisfies the same.

The correct answer is option C.

69. Topic: Data inferences

The correct answer is D

The number '4' has to appear thrice.

The fourth number should be a number other than four.

The fourth number can be selected in $_5C_1 = 5$ ways.

The four numbers can appear in any order. The number of such ways $_4C_1 = \dfrac{4!}{3!} = 4$

Thus, the number of favorable cases = $5 \times 4 = 20$.

Number of total cases when a dice is rolled four times = $6 \times 6 \times 6 \times 6 = 1296$.

Hence, required probability = $\dfrac{20}{1296} = \dfrac{5}{324}$

Hence, the correct answer is D.

70. Topic: Center, Spread, and Shape of Distributions

The correct answer is 1.5

The median of the Bear's was 2.5. The median of the Dolphins was 1. The Bear's median was 2.5–1=1.5 larger than the Dolphin's median number of goals.

71. Topic: Table data

The correct answer is 8

There are 32+28=60 students in total and $\dfrac{2}{3}$ can ride a bicycle, which is $\dfrac{2}{3}$ 60=40 students.

Since we know that 16 girls can ride a bicycle, we conclude that 40–16=24 boys also can ride a bicycle.

There are 32 boys, hence 32–24=8 boys cannot ride a bicycle.

72. Topic: Units

The correct answer is 4

Distance = 3750 yards = $\dfrac{3750}{5280} = 0.71$ miles

Thus, time = $\dfrac{0.71}{12} = 0.059$ hours = 0.059×60=3.55 minutes, i.e. 4 minutes (to the nearest integer).

73. The correct answer is 315

Total number of ways in which four members can be selected from 6 + 5 = 11 members = $C_4^{11} = \dfrac{11!}{4!7!} = 330$

This includes the cases where no girls are present in the team. We need to remove these cases.

Total number of ways of selecting four members from only boys = $C_4^6 = \dfrac{6!}{4!2!} = 15$.

Thus, the number of ways in which at least one girl will be present in the team = 330 – 15 = 315.

Hence, the correct answer is 315.

74. Topic: Percents

The correct answer is 72

Let the number of candidates who appeared for the TAS be 100 and the number of candidates who appeared for the TCA be 50 (since half the number of candidates appeared in the TCA as compared to the TAS).

Thus, number of candidates selected in the TAS = 15% of 100=15, and the number of candidates selected in the TCA = 20% of 50=10.

Thus, total number of candidates who were selected = 15+10=25.

However, we know that these 25 are actually equal to 18000.

We need to find the actual number of students who appeared in TAS i.e. the actual number of students corresponding to 100.

Since $25 \equiv 18000$, we have

$$100 \equiv \frac{18000}{25} \times 100 = 72000$$

i.e. 72 thousands.

Hence, the answer is 72.

75. Topic: Linear and exponential growth

The correct answer is 5

Plugging in the values from the table in the equation, we have:

$24 = kn^3$ ... (i)

$48 = kn^4$ ... (ii)

Dividing: $n=2$

Substituting: $k = \dfrac{24}{2^3} = 3$

$k+n=5$

MULTIPLE CHOICE QUESTIONS

76

The following graph contains a safety rating vs. maximum speed of car analysis to model every car driven in the United States. A higher safety rating means the car is extremely safe, while a lower safety rating means the car is not very safe.

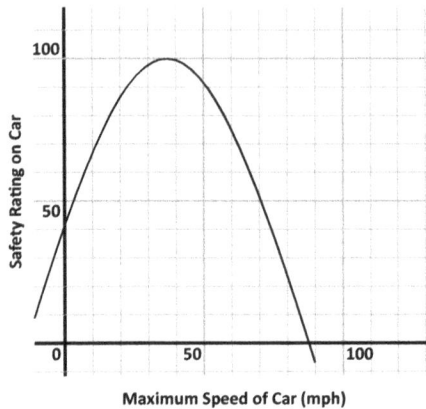

Which of the following statements is false?

A) The maximum safety rating on a car is 100 and it occurs at a speed of 45 mph.

B) The maximum speed occurs at about 85 mph and it represents a safety rating of 0.

C) There is a place on the graph where both the maximum safety rating and the maximum speed of the car are at the same point.

D) When the maximum speed of a car is 0 mph, the safety rating is about 40.

A B C D
○ ○ ○ ○

77

John is driving a car at a constant speed. After 4 hours he has travelled 256 miles. How many kilometers will John travel in 6 hours, if 1 mile is equal to 1.6 kilometers?

A) 384

B) 240

C) 409.6

D) 614.4

A B C D
○ ○ ○ ○

78

A clay ball has a diameter of 12 centimeters. The clay has a density of 1.7 grams per cubic centimeter.

What is the mass of the clay ball in grams?

A) 1537.34

B) 16782.46

C) 12298.8

D) 200560.6

A B C D
○ ○ ○ ○

79

John participated in a game where each participant was asked to pick up six cards from a box without looking at the cards. The participant with the highest total would be declared the winner. Each card had a numerical value from one to a hundred written on it. John's average in the first four cards came out to be 83. What is the lowest he can get in the sixth draw so that he still has a chance of taking his overall average to at least 88?

A) 100

B) 98

C) 96

D) 92

A B C D
○ ○ ○ ○

80

John decided to treat his friends with some chocolates. On visiting a Hershey's outlet, he found that chocolates were sold in boxes. The boxes had different number of chocolates and the prices of the boxes were also different. The prices are shown in the table below.

Number of chocolates per box	Price per box
5	$2
10	$3.6
15	$5

How much less does John spend if he buys 90 chocolates in boxes of 15 chocolates than if he buys the same in boxes of 10 chocolates?

A) $1.40

B) $2.40

C) $3.60

D) $6.00

A B C D
○ ○ ○ ○

81

$P=\{1,2,3,4,5...25\}$. How many sets of integers can you pick from the set P so that they start with 1, end with 25 and consecutive numbers in the set have a constant gap between them?

For example, one way of selecting such a set of numbers is $\{1, 7, 13, 19, 25\}$ (since the set starts with 1, ends in 25 and consecutive numbers are at a constant gap of 6).

A) 4

B) 5

C) 8

D) 10

A B C D
○ ○ ○ ○

82

The Washington Post has a daily quota of 60 advertisements. The percentage of advertisements on each page and the corresponding cost of putting an advertisement is as given:

Position of advertisement	Percentage of number of advertisements	Price of each advertisement
Page one	25%	$1000
Page three	60%	$200
Back page	15%	$400

Approximately, what percentage of total revenue from advertisements is generated from the advertisements on the back page?

A) 14%

B) 15%

C) 20%

D) 30%

A B C D
○ ○ ○ ○

83

The graph below gives the production and consumption of crude oil in certain countries of the world.

Figures below the names of the countries indicate crude reserves in million tonnes. Shortfall / (excess) between production and consumption is met by imports / (exports)

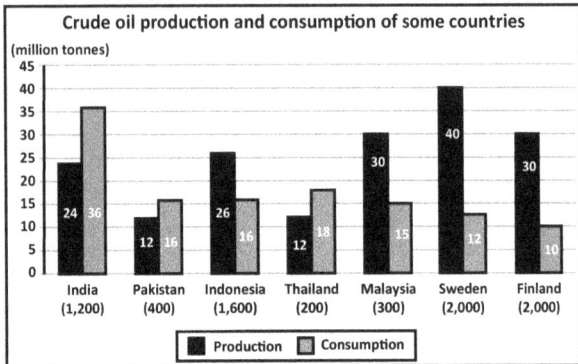

Crude oil production and consumption of some countries

If India's entire import of crude oil is from Finland, what percentages of Finland's exports are not to India?

A) 40%

B) 50%

C) 60%

D) 75%

A B C D
○ ○ ○ ○

84

Napster offers discounts on purchase of three garment pieces at a time. On purchase of every garment at the listed price, there is a 10% discount on offer on the remaining two garments. All garments are priced the same. If the garments are listed at 25% above the cost price of $120, what is the profit made by the store if a customer purchases three pieces of garments?

A) $30

B) $45

C) $60

D) $90

A B C D
○ ○ ○ ○

GRID-IN

85

Please use the provided data to answer the question below.

Data Set	1	2	2	2	4	7	2	5	1	9	8	7	4	40	5	6	8	1	3

How much does the mean change if the outlier (*data point that differs significantly from other values in the data set*) is replaced by the mode?

86

There is a hole in a water tank. Water is leaking at a constant speed 10 milliliters per minute.

What is a water leaking speed in liter per hour?

87

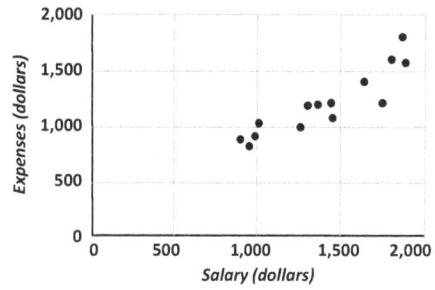

The scatterplot above shows the monthly salary and expenses of 14 people.

What percent of the people have expenses less than $1000?

88

Martin visited a juice shop and found that there were three varieties of mango juices available Rich, Sweet and Tangy. The details for these varieties is as in the table:

Name	Price (per 60ml)	Concentration of mango syrup
Rich	$45	80%
Sweet	$20	70%
Tangy	$15	60%

Martin wanted to mix exactly two of these varieties to make a juice having 70% concentration. What would be the price (in dollars per 60 ml) of such a mixture?

89

n and p are two positive integers. If it is known that $3n$ is a perfect square and $12n^2 p$ is a perfect cube, what is the smallest possible value of np?

76. Topic: Key Features of a Graph

The correct answer is C.

The answer is C. The maximum safety rating is at approximately (45,100), while the maximum speed is at approximately (85,0). These maximums do not occur at the same point.

77. Topic: Interpreting linear functions

The correct answer is D

John travels $\dfrac{256}{4} = 64$ miles per hour.

Hence, after 6 hours John will travel 64 (6)=384 miles.

Since 1 mile = 1.6 kilometers, we get 384(1.6) = 614.4 kilometers.

Hence, the correct answer is D.

78. Topic: Units

The correct answer is A

First, we find the volume of the clay ball:

$\dfrac{4}{3} 6^3\, 3.14 = 904.32$.

(The radius of the ball is $\dfrac{12}{2} = 6$)

Hence the mass is 904.32 × 1.7=1537.34 grams.

Hence, the correct answer is A.

79. Topic: Data inferences

The correct answer is C

In order that John gets the lowest possible number in his sixth draw, he needs to maximize his total in the fifth test. The maximum he can get in the fifth draw is 100.

Since John needs to get at least 88 as the overall average, in his first four draws, John is (88–83)×4=20 behind.

If he gets 100 in the fifth draw, he makes up (100–88)=12.

So, he is still 20–12=8 behind.

Thus, John needs to draw a number which is at least 8 more than 88 or 88+8=96 in the sixth draw so that he can be sure to get an average of 88 overall.

Hence, the answer is C.

80. Topic: Table data

The correct answer is B

If John wants to buy the boxes containing 15 chocolates, he will require $\dfrac{90}{15} = 6$ boxes.

Cost of each such box = $5.

Hence, his total cost = $5×6=$30.

However, if John wants to buy the boxes containing 10 chocolates, he will require $\dfrac{90}{10} = 9$ boxes.

Cost of each such box = $3.6.

Hence, his total cost = $3.6 × 9 = $32.40.

Hence, John saves $32.40 – $30 = $2.40.

Hence, the answer is B.

81. Topic: Data Inferences

The correct answer is C

The minimum number on the set P is 1 and the maximum number is 25.

Thus, the gap between them = 25 –1=24.

In order to pick integers from P so that they start with 1, end with 25 and consecutive numbers in the set have a constant gap between them, we need to pick numbers whose gap is a factor of 24.

Thus, possible gaps are 1, 2, 3, 4, 6, 8, 12 and 24.

The set of integers are:

Gap is 1: the numbers are all the integers in the set P i.e. 1, 2, 3, 4 … 23, 24, and 25.

Gap is 2: the numbers are the following integers: 1, 3, 5, 7, 9, 11, 13, 15, 17, 19, 21, 23, and 25.

Gap is 3: the numbers are the following integers: 1, 4, 7, 10, 13, 16, 19, 22, and 25.

Gap is 4: the numbers are the following integers: 1, 5, 9, 13, 17, 21, and 25.

Gap is 6: the numbers are the following integers: 1, 7, 13, 19, and 25.

Gap is 8: the numbers are the following integers: 1, 9, 17, and 25.

Gap is 12: the numbers are the following integers: 1, 13, and 25.

Gap is 24: the numbers are the following integers: 1 and 25.

Thus, there are 8 possible sets of integers that can be selected from P satisfying all the conditions.

Hence, the correct answer is C.

82. Topic: Table data

The correct answer is A

Let us assume that the total number of advertisements be 100 (since this is a percentage question, the choice of the initial value does not have any effect on the final answer).

So, the breakup of the advertisements can be formed as shown below:

Position	Number of advertisements	Price of each advertisement	Revenue
Page one	25	$1000	$1000x25= $25000
Page three	60	$200	$200x60= $12000
Back page	15	$400	$400x15= $6000
Total Revenue			$43000

Thus, percentage of total revenue generated from advertisements on the back page

$$= \frac{6000}{43000} \times 100 = 13.95\% \sim 14\%$$

Hence, the answer is A.

83. Topic: Data collection and conclusions

The correct answer is A

Amount of oil imported by India = (36 – 24) million = 12 million tonnes

Total exports by Finland = (30 – 10) million = 20 million tonnes

Since India's entire import of crude oil is from Finland, we have:

Export of oil other than India = 8 million tones

Thus, the required percent

$$= \frac{8}{20} \times 100$$

$$= 40\%$$

84. Topic: Percents

The correct answer is C

The cost of each garment = $120.

Hence, the list price of each garment = $(120+25% of 120)=$150.

Profit made by the store when it sells a garment at $150 is $(150–120)=$30.

Thus, discount offered on a garment = 10% of 150=$15.

Thus, price after discount = $(150–15)=$135.

Profit made by the store when it sells a garment at $135 is $(135–120)=$15.

Thus, when a customer purchases three pieces of garments he pays $150 for the first and $135 for each of the remaining two pieces.

Hence, the profit made by the store = $(30+2×15)=$60.

Hence, the answer is C.

85. Topic: Center, Spread, and Shape of Distributions

The correct answer is 1.9

The mode is 2. The mean of the original data set is obtained by adding all of the values and dividing by the total number of values:

$$\text{Mean}=\frac{117}{20}=5.85$$

If you replace the outlier 40 with the

mode 2, you obtain the following:

$$\text{Mean}=\frac{79}{20}=3.95$$

To find how much the mean changes, subtract the new mean from the old mean to get 5.85–3.95=1.9. Therefore, the answer is 1.9.

86. Topic: Units

The correct answer is $0.6\dfrac{liter}{hour}$

The speed is $\dfrac{10ml}{1minute}$.

$$1\,liter=1000\,ml => 1\,ml=\frac{1}{1000}\,liter$$

$$1\,hour=60\,minutes => 1\,minutes=\frac{1}{60}\,hour$$

$$\frac{10\,ml}{1\,minute}=\frac{10\,\dfrac{1}{1000}\,liter}{\dfrac{1}{60}\,hour}=>$$

$$\frac{6}{10}\,\frac{liter}{hour}=0.6\,\frac{liter}{hour}$$

87. Topic: Scatterplots

The correct answer is 28.57%

From the scatterplot we see that there are 4 people with expenses less than $1000.

Since there are 14 people in total, we get

$$\frac{4}{14}=28.57\%$$

.

88. Topic: Table data

The correct answer is 30

Since Martin wants to mix two varieties of juices to create a juice with 70% concentration, he cannot use the Sweet variety since it itself has 70% and mixing it with any other variety would change its concentration from 70%.

Thus, Martin needs to mix the Rich and the Tangy varieties.

We can observe that the Rich variety has 80% concentration and the Tangy variety has 60% concentration. The required concentration i.e. 70% is the simple average of 60% and 80% since

$$\frac{60+80}{2} = 70\%$$

Thus, it is definite that he must mix the Rich and Tangy varieties in equal proportion.

Hence, the price of the resulting mixture would

have a price = $\$\dfrac{45+15}{2} = \$30 \; per \; 60ml$

Hence, the answer is 30.

89. Topic: Relationships between variables

The correct answer is 6

Since $3n$ is a perfect square and 3 is not a perfect square in itself, we can conclude that n must be 3 times a perfect square.

Thus, n can be numbers like 3,3×4=12,3×9=27 etc.

Again, since $12n^2 p$ is a perfect cube

($12 = 2^2 \times 3$, is not a perfect cube), we can conclude that $n^2 p$ must be $(2 \times 3^2 = 18)$ or 18 times some other perfect cube.

Thus, $n^2 p$ can be numbers like 18,18×8=144, 18×27=486 etc.

Now, we need to find the minimum possible value of np.

We see that we can take $n=3$ and in that case, if $n^2 p = 18$, we have $p=2$.

These are the minimum possible values of n and p.

Thus, minimum possible value of np=3×2=6.

Hence, the answer is 6.

Chapter 5
Additional Topics in Math

MULTIPLE CHOICE QUESTIONS

1

What are the coordinates of the center of the circle represented by the following equation?

$(x-2)^2 + (y+3)^2 = 16$

A) (3,2)

B) (2,–3)

C) (–2,3)

D) (16,2)

A B C D
○ ○ ○ ○

2

Which of the following expressions is equal to (2+i)(3–i)?

A) $6 - i^2$

B) 5

C) $6 + i + i^2$

D) $7 + i$

A B C D
○ ○ ○ ○

3

What is the area of the circle with the following triangle inscribed?

Please note, $XY=6, YZ=8, XZ=10$, and XZ crosses through the center O.

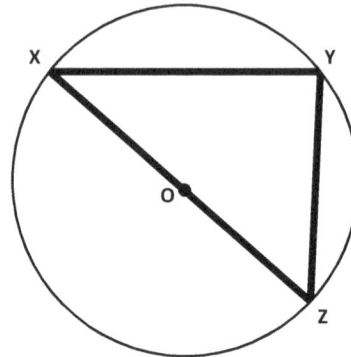

A) 5π

B) 25π

C) 10π

D) 6π

A B C D
○ ○ ○ ○

4

The imaginary number i is defined such that $i^2 = -1$. Which of the following options is equivalent to $\left(\dfrac{1}{i} + \dfrac{1}{i^2} + \dfrac{1}{i^3} + \dfrac{1}{i^4}\right)$?

A) –1

B) 0

C) 1

D) –i

A B C D
○ ○ ○ ○

GRID-IN

5

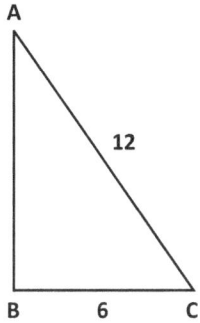

In the figure shown above, *ABC* is a triangle right angled at *B*. What is the value of angle *A*, in degrees?

6

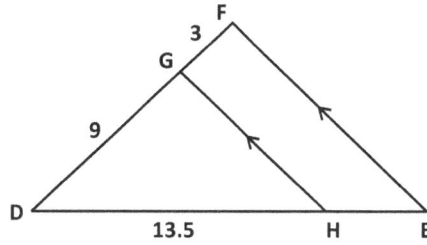

In the figure *GH*||*EF*. What is the length of *HE*?

1. **Topic:** Circle Equations

   The correct answer is B

   The equation of a circle is
   $(x - a)^2 + (y - b)^2 = r^2$, where (a, b) is the center and r is the radius. So, the center point of the circle is located at $(2, -3)$.

2. **Topic:** Complex Numbers

   The correct answer is D

   FOIL to simplify first. You obtain $6+3i-2i-i^2$. Combine like terms to get $6+i-i^2$.

   Because $i = \sqrt{-1}, i^2 = -1$. Plugging into our previous expression, we get $6+i-(-1)$.

   This becomes $7+i$ and the solution is Choice D.

3. **Topic:** Circle Equation

   The correct answer is B

   Side XZ represents the diameter, which is 10. So the radius is 5. The area is then found by using the formula $A = \pi r^2$. Plug in 5 for r and obtain $A=25\pi$, which is Choice B.

4. **Topic:** Complex numbers

   The correct answer is B

   We have:

   $$\frac{1}{i} + \frac{1}{i^2} + \frac{1}{i^3} + \frac{1}{i^4} =$$

   $$i^{-1} + i^{-2} + i^{-3} + i^{-4} =$$

   $$i - 4 \times (i^3 + i^2 + i + 1) =$$

   $$\frac{(i^3 + i^2 + i + 1)}{i^4}$$

   $$i = \sqrt{-1}$$

   $$i^2 = \sqrt{-1} \times \sqrt{-1} = -1$$

   $$i^3 = i \times i^2 = i \times (-1) = -i$$

   $$i^4 = i \times i^3 = i \times (-i) = -(-1) = 1$$

   Thus,

   $$\frac{1}{i} + \frac{1}{i^2} + \frac{1}{i^3} + \frac{1}{i^4} =>$$

   $$\frac{(i^3 + i^2 + i + 1)}{i^4} =>$$

   $$\frac{(-i) + (-1) + i + 1}{1} = 0$$

   Hence, the correct answer is B.

5. **Topic:** Angles, arc lengths, and trig functions

The correct answer is 30

In the triangle, corresponding to angle A, we know the values of the opposite side and the hypotenuse. Hence, we work with $Sin\ A$.

$$\sin A = \frac{BC}{AC} = \frac{6}{12} = \frac{1}{2}$$

We know that $\sin 30° = \frac{1}{2}$

Thus, $A = 30°$.

Hence, the correct option is 30.

6. **Topic:** Congruence and similarity

The correct answer is 4.5

Triangles DGH and DFE are similar since $\angle DGH = \angle DFE$ and $\angle DHG = \angle DEF$ (corresponding angles)

Thus, we have:

$$\frac{DG}{DF} = \frac{DH}{DE} =>$$

$$\frac{9}{12} = \frac{13.5}{DE} =>$$

$$DE = 18$$
$$HE = 18 - 13.5 = 4.5$$

MULTIPLE CHOICE QUESTIONS

7

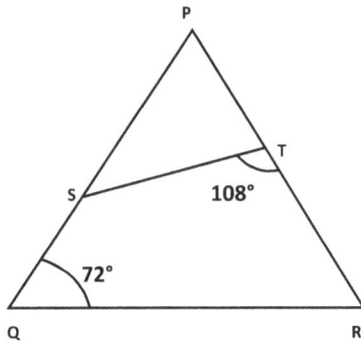

If $\dfrac{PS}{PR} = \dfrac{1}{2}$, $PT = 6$ and $QS = 4$, what is the length of PS?

A) 12

B) 10

C) 9

D) 8

A B C D
○ ○ ○ ○

8

The imaginary number i is such that $i^2 = -1$. Which of the following options is equivalent to $\left(\dfrac{1-2i}{2+3i}\right)$?

A) $-\dfrac{4}{7} - i$

B) $\dfrac{4}{7} + i$

C) $8 - 7i$

D) $\dfrac{8}{7} + i$

A B C D
○ ○ ○ ○

9

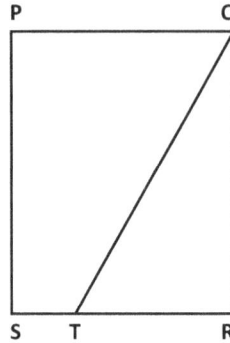

$PQRS$ is a rectangle. T is a point on RS such that $ST = 2$. If the area of the triangle QRT is 24 and $QR : RS = 2 : 1$, what is the measure of QR?

A) 12

B) 14

C) 15

D) 16

A B C D
○ ○ ○ ○

10

A well, $2m$ radius and $40m$ deep, is being dug. The excavated soil is transported using a truck of size $5m \times 2m \times \pi m$. How many trips will the truck have to clear the excavated soil if it can be filled to 80% of its height?

A) 10

B) 12

C) 20

D) 24

A B C D
○ ○ ○ ○

11

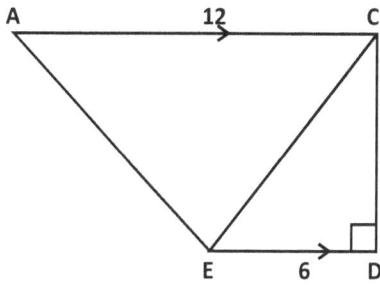

In the figure shown, area of triangle *ACE* is 48. If *AC* is parallel to *DE*, what is the length *CE*?

A) 6

B) 8

C) 10

D) 11

A B C D
○ ○ ○ ○

7. **Topic:** Congruence and similarity

   The correct answer is D

   Triangles PST and PRQ are similar since $\angle P$ is common to both and $\angle PTS = \angle PQR = 72°$.

   Thus,

   $$\frac{PS}{PR} = \frac{PT}{PQ} = \frac{1}{2} =>$$

   $$PO = 2PT = 12$$

   Thus, $PS = PQ - QS = 8$

   Hence, the correct option is D

8. **Topic:** Complex numbers

   The correct answer is A

   We have a term $(2+3i)$ in the denominator of the expression. We need to rationalize it so that the denominator does not have any i present.

   To do that, we need to multiply the denominator with its conjugate. Thus, we have:

   $$\left(\frac{1-2i}{2+3i}\right) = \left(\frac{1-2i}{2+3i}\right) \times \left(\frac{2-3i}{2-3i}\right) =>$$

   $$\frac{(1-2i)\times(2-3i)}{(2+3i)\times(2-3i)} => \frac{2-3i-4i+6i^2}{4-6i+6i-9i^2} =>$$

   $$\frac{2-7i-6}{4+9} = -\frac{4+7i}{13} = -\frac{4}{7} - i$$

   Hence, the correct option is A.

9. **Topic:** Right triangle geometry

   The correct answer is A

   We have: $QR : RS = 2 : 1 => QR = 2x$ and $RS = x$

   $RT = RS - ST = x - 2$

   Thus, area of $\triangle QRT = \frac{1}{2} \times (2x) \times (x-2) = 24$

   $x(x-2) = 6(6-2) => x = 6$

   $QR = 2x = 12$

   The correct answer is option A.

10. **Topic:** Volume word problems

    The correct answer is C

    Volume of the well $= \pi \times 2^2 \times 40 = 160\pi$ cubic meters

    Volume of the truck $= 5 \times 2 \times \pi = 10\pi$ cubic meters

    Volume of soil that can be filled in the truck = 80% of $10\pi = 8\pi$ cubic meters

    Thus, number of trips required $= \frac{160\pi}{8\pi} = 20$

11. **Topic:** Right triangle geometry

    The correct answer is C

    Area of

    $$\triangle ACE = \frac{1}{2} \times AC \times h =>$$

    $$\frac{1}{2} \times AC \times CD = 48$$

    $$CD = 8$$

    $$CE^2 = ED^2 + CD^2 = 36 + 64 = 100$$

    $$CE = 10$$

    The correct answer is option C.

GRID-IN

12

1 What is the value of $\overset{\frown}{MN}$ if $\overline{MN} = 20$ inches and the distance from $\overline{MN}$ to the center of the circle, labeled O, is $10\sqrt{3}$ inches? Approximate π as 3 to simplify your calculations.

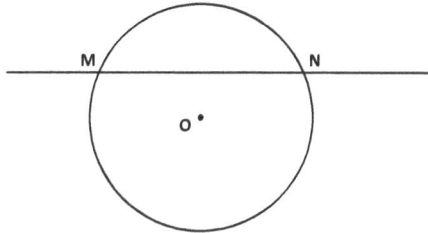

12. Topic: Circle Theorems

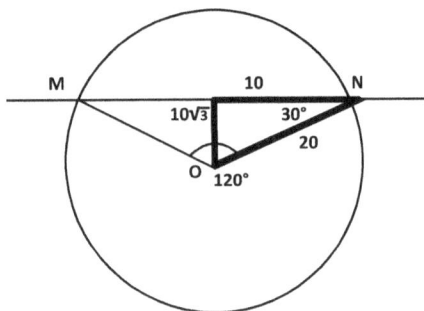

The origin can create a perpendicular bisector to $\overline{MN}$.

The length of the perpendicular bisector would be $10\sqrt{3}$ inches, while the bisected lengths would be 10 inches each. You can then create a right triangle with one part of the bisected side and the perpendicular bisector.

This is a 30, 60, 90 triangle. Now we know the side ON (from the center to the point N) is $2(10)$ or 20, by using 30–60–90 triangle properties. We also now know the angle measure of the angle closest to N. It is 30 degrees.

Doing the same thing on the other side gives us another 30° triangle. Combining the smaller triangles to make a large one incorporating the center angle gives us a 30–30–120 triangle.

Now that we know the center angle measure and the radius (given by side ON), we know the measure of the arc. Arc measures can be calculated by using the following formula:

$$Arc = 2\pi r \frac{\theta}{360},$$

where θ is the central angle. Therefore, plugging r and θ in as 20 and 120 respectively, you get

$$2(3)(20)\left(\frac{120}{360}\right) = 40.$$

The arc measure is 40. An additional diagram is provided for explanation clarity.

MULTIPLE CHOICE QUESTIONS

13

If the cone is 2/3 full of ice cream, how many cubic inches of ice cream is there in the cone?

Using the following diagram and the equation of a cone:

$$V = \frac{1}{3}\pi r^2 h$$

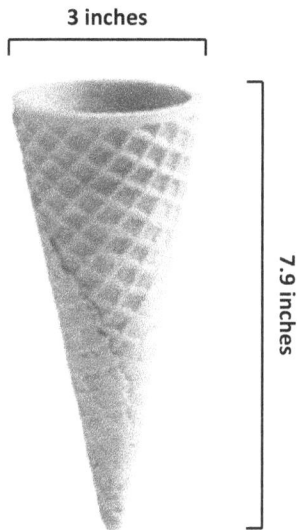

3 inches

7.9 inches

A) 12.4 cubic inches

B) 18.6 cubic inches

C) 6.2 cubic inches

D) 74.4 cubic inches

A B C D
○ ○ ○ ○

14

What is the value of X that makes the following statement true?

$\triangle ABC \sim \triangle EDF$

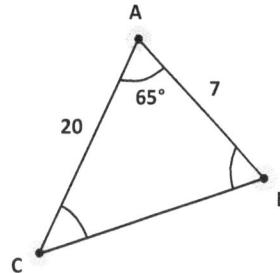

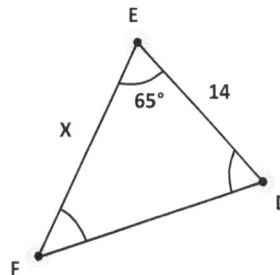

A) 10

B) 7

C) 20

D) 40

A B C D
○ ○ ○ ○

15

30 meters

60°

A hot air balloon was tied to a point on the ground using a rope 30*m* long. If the rope makes an angle of 60° with the ground, how high, in meters, is the balloon above the ground level?

A) $\dfrac{15}{\sqrt{3}}$

B) 15

C) $\dfrac{30}{\sqrt{3}}$

D) $15\sqrt{3}$

A B C D
○ ○ ○ ○

16

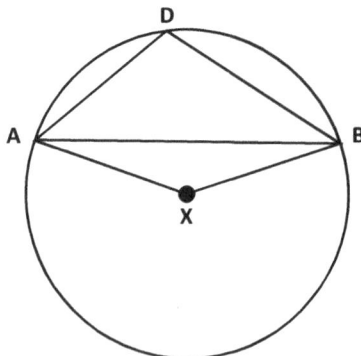

Angle *ADB* equals 110°. What is the value of angle *AXB* if *X* is the centre of the circle?

A) 220°

B) 120°

C) 140°

D) 200°

A B C D
○ ○ ○ ○

GRID-IN

17

What is the angle measure of A in the diagram below?

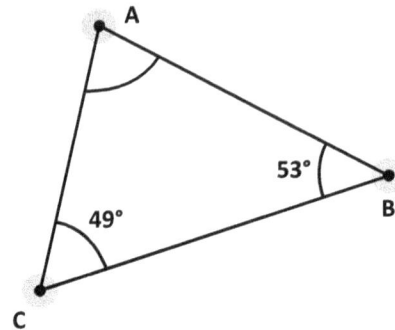

53°

49°

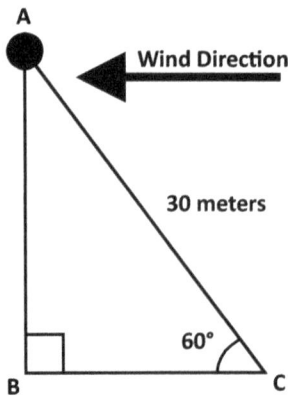

18

What is the value of side *AC* that completes the diagram below? Please round your answer to the nearest thousandth if necessary

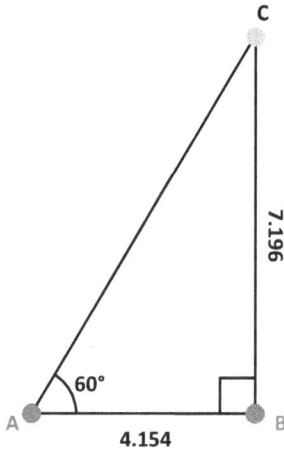

C

7.196

60°

A   4.154   B

19

F

12

B   12   Q

4   4

A   E

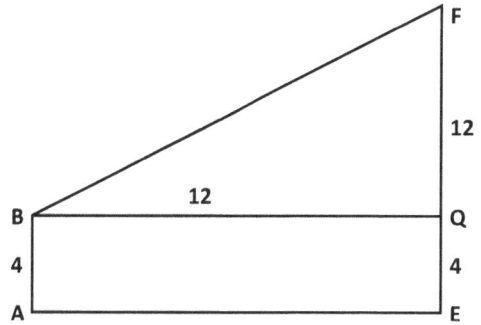

In the figure shown above, *AB* and *EF* are parallel and measure 4 and 16, respectively. If *AB* is perpendicular to *AE* and *AE* measures 12, what is the perimeter of the figure to the nearest integer?

20

In the figure $AB \| DE$, $AC = 6$, $CE = 15$ and $DB = 28$. What is the length of CD?

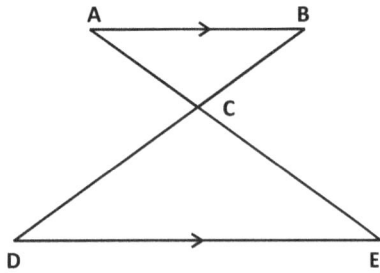

13. Topic: Volume Word Problems

The correct answer is A

In order to find the volume of the cone, plug into the equation given with $h=7.9$ and $r=1.5$, since the diameter is 3 inches.

$$V = \frac{1}{3}\pi(1.5)^2(7.9)$$

The full volume is then 18.61 cubic inches. Then multiply this by $\frac{2}{3}$ since the cone is only $\frac{2}{3}$ full. The volume of $\frac{2}{3}$ of the cone is therefore $18.61 \times \frac{2}{3}$, which is Choice A.

14. Topic: Congruence and Similarity

The correct answer is D

In order for triangles to be similar, they must have two similar sides with an equal included angle. The 65° angle for A and E are congruent. The side AB is similar to side ED by a proportion of 2. So, in order for the two triangles to be similar, side AC must be proportional to EF by a factor of two. Therefore, 2*20=40.

X must be 40 in order for these triangles to be congruent. Choice D is correct.

15. Topic: Right triangle word problems

The correct answer is D

Let the balloon be at the point A and AC is the rope with which the balloon is tied to the ground.

In triangle ABC, we have:

$$\text{Sin } 60° = \frac{AB}{AC} => \frac{\sqrt{3}}{2} = \frac{AB}{30} =>$$
$$AB = 15\sqrt{3}\ m$$

The correct option is D.

16. Topic: Circle theorems

The correct answer is A

Reflex $\angle AXB = 220°$ (Since angle at the centre = Twice the angle at circumference)

Hence, the correct answer is Option A.

17. Topic: Angles, Arc Lengths, and Trig Functions

The correct answer is 78

In order to find the measure of angle A, you must use the Triangle Angle Sum Theorem, which states that the sum of the three angles of a triangle must add up to 180. So, A+49+53=180. Subtract 49 and 53 from 180 to get 78. The measure of Angle A is 78.

18. Topic: Right Triangle Geometry

The correct answer is 8.309.

Use the Pythagorean theorem to calculate the value of the hypotenuse.

The Pythagorean theorem is $a^2+b^2=c^2$. The two legs are a and b, and you are solving for c. Plugging in the two legs creates the equation $(4.154)^2+(7.196)^2=c^2$. Squaring the two terms on the left and combining them give you 69.038132. To find the length of the hypotenuse, the side AC, you need to take the square root of this value, which is 8.30891882257. Rounding to the thousandths place gives you an answer of 8.309.

19. Topic: Right triangle geometry

The correct answer is 49

$AB=EQ=4$, $AE=BQ=12$ and $FQ=12$

From Pythagoras' theorem:

$$BF = \sqrt{BQ^2 + QF^2} =>$$

$$\sqrt{12^2 + 12^2} = 12\sqrt{2} =>$$

$$16.97 \approx 17$$

Thus, perimeter of the figure

$=4+12+16+17=49$

The correct answer is 49.

20. Topic: Congruence and similarity

The correct answer is 20

Triangles DCE and BCA are similar since $\angle CDE = \angle CBA$ and $\angle CED = \angle CAB$ (alternate angles)

Thus, we have:

$$\frac{AC}{CE} = \frac{BC}{DC} => \frac{6}{15} = \frac{BC}{DC} => \frac{BC}{DC} = \frac{2}{5}$$

Since $BD = 28$, we have:

$$CD = \frac{5}{2+5} \times 28 = 20$$

MULTIPLE CHOICE QUESTIONS

21

A solid cube is put in a sphere. What is the least percentage of the volume of the sphere not occupied by the cube?

A) 44.44%

B) 50%

C) 57.66%

D) 63.24%

A B C D
○ ○ ○ ○

22

In a right–angled triangle ABC, right angled at B, an altitude BD is dropped on AC. If $AB = 8$ and $BC = 6$, what is the length of AD?

A) 2.4

B) 3.6

C) 4.8

D) 6.4

A B C D
○ ○ ○ ○

23

If $a + ib = (5 + 3i)(6i + 1)$, what is the value of $a^2 + b^2$?

A) 1258

B) 1528

C) 2158

D) 3168

A B C D
○ ○ ○ ○

24

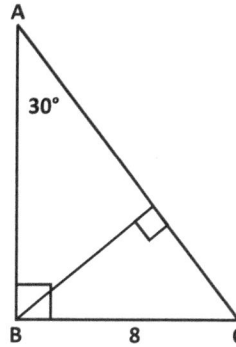

In the figure shown, ABC is a triangle, right angled at B. Through B, a line is drawn perpendicular to AC which meets AC in D. What is the length of BD?

A) $\dfrac{4}{\sqrt{3}}$

B) $\dfrac{8}{\sqrt{3}}$

C) $2\sqrt{3}$

D) $4\sqrt{3}$

A B C D
○ ○ ○ ○

25

In $\triangle ABC$, D and E are the mid-points of AB and AC. Again, F and G are the mid-points of DB and EC. If $BC = 12$, what is the length of FG?

A) 4

B) 6

C) 8

D) 9

A B C D
○ ○ ○ ○

26

What is the perimeter, to the nearest integer, of an equilateral triangle inscribed in circle whose circumference is 6π units?

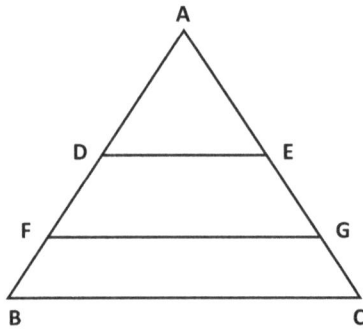

21. **Topic:** Volume word problems

    The correct answer is D

    The required percent would be the least if the largest cube is placed in the sphere.

    Let each side of the cube be s

    Thus, the body diagonal = $s\sqrt{3}$

    Also, volume of the sphere = s^3

    Thus, diameter of the sphere = The body diagonal = $s\sqrt{3}$

    Radius of the sphere = $\dfrac{s\sqrt{3}}{2}$

    Thus, volume of the sphere =

    $$\dfrac{4\pi}{3}\left(\dfrac{s\sqrt{3}}{2}\right)^3 = \dfrac{\pi\sqrt{3}}{2}s^3 = 2.72s^3$$

    Thus, volume of the sphere not occupied by the cube = $2.72s^3 - s^3 = 1.72s^3$

    Thus, required percent =

    $$\dfrac{1.72s^3}{2.72s^3}\times 100 = 63.24\%$$

    The correct answer is option D.

22. **Topic:** Congruence and similarity

    The correct answer is D

    From Pythagoras' theorem:

    $$AC^2 = AB^2 + BC^2 = 64 + 36 = 100$$

    $$AC = 10$$

    From the diagram, it is clear that triangle ABD is similar to triangle ACB

    $$\dfrac{AB}{AC} = \dfrac{AD}{AB} \Rightarrow \dfrac{8}{10} = \dfrac{AD}{8}$$

    $$AD = 6.4$$

    The correct answer is option D.

23. **Topic:** Complex numbers

    The correct answer is A

    Let us first simplify the given expression.

    $$a + ib = (5 + 3i)(6i + 1)$$

    $$a + ib = 30i + 5 + 18i^2 + 3i$$

    $$a + ib = -13 + 33i$$

    $$a = -13, b = 33$$

    $$a^2 + b^2 = 169 + 1089 = 1258$$

    Hence, the correct answer is option A.

24. **Topic:** Angles, arc lengths, and trig functions

The correct answer is D

We know that angle B is 90° and angle A is 30°.

Thus, angle C = 180°–(90°+30°)=60°.

In triangle BDC, with respect to angle C, BD is the opposite side and BC is the hypotenuse.

Thus, in order to relate these two sides, we use $\sin \theta$.

Thus, $\sin C = \sin 60° = \dfrac{BD}{BC}$ =>

$$\dfrac{\sqrt{3}}{2} = \dfrac{BD}{8} => BD = 4\sqrt{3}$$

25. **Topic:** Congruence and similarity

The correct answer is D

Triangles *ADE*, *AFG* and *ABC* are similar

Thus, we have:

$AD : AF : AB = DE : FG : BC$

Since $AD = DB$ and $DF = FB$,

we have: $AD : DF : FB = 2 : 1 : 1$

$AD : AF : AB = 2 : 3 : 4$

$DE : FG : BC = 2 : 3 : 4$

Since $BC = 12$, we have:

$DE : FG : 12 = 2 : 3 : 4 = 6 : 9 : 12$

$FG = 9$

The correct answer is option D.

26. **Topic:** Circle theorems

The correct answer is 16

$2\pi r = 6\pi => r = 3$

Let the side of equilateral triangle be s

Thus, height of the triangle = $\dfrac{\sqrt{3}s}{2}$

Thus, we have:

$$r + \dfrac{r}{2} = \dfrac{\sqrt{3}s}{2}$$

$$=> \dfrac{\sqrt{3}s}{2} = \dfrac{9}{2}$$

$$=> s = 3\sqrt{3}$$

Thus, perimeter = $3s = 9\sqrt{3} = 15.59 \approx 16$

Hence, the correct answer is 16

MULTIPLE CHOICE QUESTIONS

27

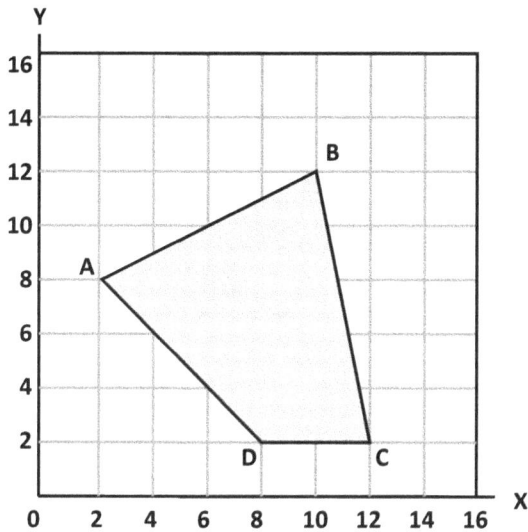

What is the area of the quadrilateral *ABCD* as shown in the figure above?

A) 74

B) 72

C) 28

D) 56

A B C D
○ ○ ○ ○

28

Two friends, Amy and Bob, are standing in line with a lamp post. The shadows of both friends meet at the same point on the ground. If the heights of the lamp post, Amy and Bob are 6 meters, 1.8 meters and 0.9 meters respectively, and Amy is standing 2 meters away from the post, then how far (in meters) is Bob standing from Amy?

A) 0.43

B) 0.90

C) 1.80

D) 2.00

A B C D
○ ○ ○ ○

27. Topic: Right triangle geometry

The correct answer is D

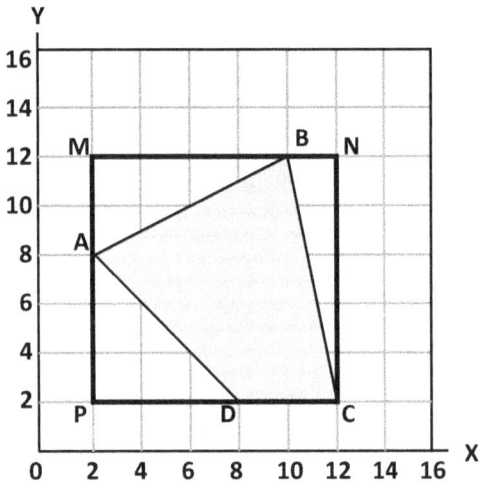

The required area $ABCD$ = Area $MNCP$ – (Area AMB + Area BNC + Area APD)

The coordinates of M, N, C and P are

(2, 12), (12, 12), (12, 2) and (2, 2) respectively.

The coordinates of A, B and D are

(2, 8), (10, 12), (12, 2) and (2, 2) respectively.

Thus, we have: $AM = 4$, $MB = 8$, $BN = 2$, $NC = 10$, $CD = 4$, $PD = 6$, $PA = 6$, $MP = 10$ and $MN = 10$.

Area $MNCP = MP \times MN = 10 \times 10 = 100$ sq units.

Area $AMB = \dfrac{1}{2} \times AM \times MB = \dfrac{1}{2} \times 4 \times 8 = 16$ sq units.

Area $BNC = \dfrac{1}{2} \times BN \times NC = \dfrac{1}{2} \times 2 \times 10 = 10$ sq units.

Area $APD = \dfrac{1}{2} \times AP \times PD = \dfrac{1}{2} \times 6 \times 6 = 18$ sq units.

Hence, area $ABCD = 100 - (16 + 10 + 18) = 56$ sq units.

Hence, the correct answer is D.

28. Topic: Right triangle word problems

The correct answer is A.

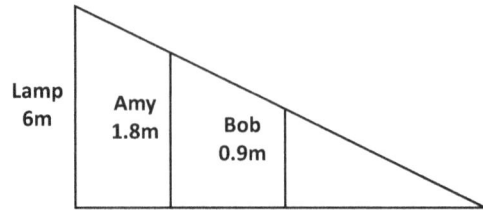

From similar triangles, we have:

$$\frac{6}{2+x+y} = \frac{1.8}{x+y} = \frac{0.9}{y}$$

$$\frac{6-1.8}{(2+x+y)-(x+y)} = \frac{1.8-0.9}{(x+y)-y}$$

$$\frac{4.2}{2} = \frac{0.9}{x} \Rightarrow x = 0.43\,\text{m}$$

Chapter 6
Math Practice Test

Math Test - No Calculator
25 MINUTES, 20 QUESTIONS

Turn to Section 3 of your answer sheet to answer the questions in this section.

DIRECTIONS

For questions 1-15, solve each problem, choose the best answer from the choices provided, and fill in the corresponding circle on your answer sheet. **For questions 16-20**, solve the problem and enter your answer in the grid on the answer sheet. Please refer to the directions before question 16 on how to enter your answers in the grid. You may use any available space in your test booklet for scratch work.

NOTES

1. The use of a calculator **is not permitted.**

2. All variables and expressions used represent real numbers unless otherwise indicated.

3. Figures provided in this test are drawn to scale unless otherwise indicated.

4. All figures lie in a plane unless otherwise indicated.

5. Unless otherwise indicated, the domain of a given function f is the set of all real numbers x for which $f(x)$ is a real number.

REFERENCE

$A = \pi r^2$
$C = 2\pi r$

$A = \ell w$

$A = \frac{1}{2}bh$

$c^2 = a^2 + b^2$

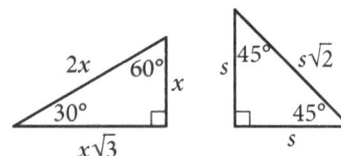

Special Right Triangles

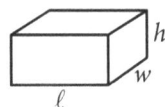

$V = \ell wh$

$V = \pi r^2 h$

$V = \frac{4}{3}\pi r^3$

$V = \frac{1}{3}\pi r^2 h$

$V = \frac{1}{3}\ell wh$

The number of degrees of arc in a circle is 360.

The number of radians of arc in a circle is 2π.

The sum of the measures in degrees of the angles of a triangle is 180.

MULTIPLE CHOICE QUESTIONS

1

Adam bought 23 pencils, 15 erasers and 20 sharpeners from a stationery shop and spent a total of $111. Bob bought 19 erasers, 12 pencils and 40 sharpeners from the same stationery shop and spent $10 more than Adam. Which of the two equations satisfy the above two conditions, if the price of a pencil is $a, price of an eraser is $b and price of a sharpener is $c?

A) $23a+15b+20c=111, 19a+12b+40c=101$

B) $23a+15b+20c=111, 19a+12b+40c=121$

C) $23a+15b+20c=111, 12a+19b+40c=101$

D) $23a+15b+20c=111, 12a+19b+40c=121$

A B C D
○ ○ ○ ○

2

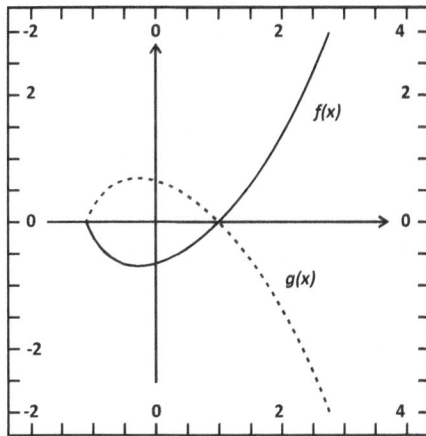

The graphs of $f(x)$ and $g(x)$ are shown above. Which option is true?

A) $f(x) = g(-x)$

B) $f(x) = g(x)-x$

C) $f(x) = -g(x)$

D) $f(x) = -g(-x)$

A B C D
○ ○ ○ ○

3

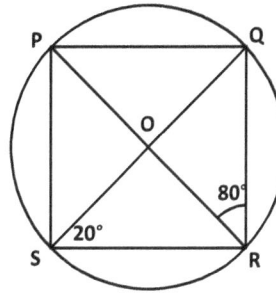

PQRS is a cyclic quadrilateral, its diagonals intersect at O. If $\angle PRQ = 80°$, and $\angle QSR = 20°$, what is the measure, in degrees, of $\angle PSR$?

A) 45°

B) 50°

C) 80°

D) 100°

A B C D
○ ○ ○ ○

4

For all numbers x, let $f(x) = x^2 - 6x + 8$, and $g(x) = x + 2$. For how many integer values of x is $g(x) \geq f(x)$?

A) 1

B) 2

C) 3

D) 4

A B C D
○ ○ ○ ○

5

If $a^3b^4c^7d^2$ is negative, where a,b,c,d are integers, all of the following statements are incorrect EXCEPT

A) ab^2cd^2 is positive

B) b^2d is positive

C) bc^2d is positive

D) a^3b^2c is negative

A B C D
○ ○ ○ ○

6

The relation between the numbers of pieces p Amy has learnt to sing at the end ofn weeks of singing lessons is given as: $p = 2n+3$

After how many weeks would Amy be able to sing 17 pieces?

A) 5

B) 6

C) 7

D) 8

A B C D
○ ○ ○ ○

7

The height of the tree (*in centimeters*) is represented by the formula $H=160+8t$, where t is a number of months, since the three's height was measured for the first time. How many months does the tree need to be at least 312 centimeters high?

A) 10

B) 19

C) 20

D) 17

A B C D
○ ○ ○ ○

8

How many integer values of x satisfy $2|2x-3|<14$?

A) 8

B) 6

C) 4

D) 3

A B C D
○ ○ ○ ○

9

It was observed in an experiment that the number of bacteria doubles every hour. It was found that the number of bacteria twelve hours from the start of observation was 40960. After how many hours from the start of the experiment would the number of bacteria has been one–fourth of the final number of bacteria?

A) 11

B) 10

C) 8

D) 6

A B C D
○ ○ ○ ○

10

The cost, in dollars, of producing tires by a manufacturing firm is determined by the following equation: $C=120+90\times W+78\times N$, where '$C$' represents the cost incurred, 'W' represents the number of workers, 'N' represents the number of units produced. If 10 units have to be produced, what is the maximum number of workers that can be employed so that the total cost doesn't exceed $2700?

A) 18

B) 19

C) 20

D) 21

A B C D
○ ○ ○ ○

11

$f(x) = x^2 - 6x + 8$ and $g(x) = x - 2$. At how many points do the graphs of the two functions intersect?

A) 0

B) 1

C) 2

D) 3

A B C D
○ ○ ○ ○

12

$$N = 4^{61} + 4^{61} + 4^{61} + 4^{62} + 4^{62} + 4^{62}$$

Choose the correct statement(s):

I. N is divisible by 3.

II. N is divisible by 5.

III. N is a perfect square.

A) Only I

B) Only II

C) Only III

D) Only I and II

A B C D
○ ○ ○ ○

13

Abe reads a book every day, some pages in the morning and some in the evening. He reads 23 pages every morning and 31 pages every evening.

The number of pages completed by Abe after some number of days can be written as a function of the number of pages read in the morning and number of pages read in the evening.

If the number of days is represented by 'N', the number of pages read in the mornings be 'M' and the number of pages read in the evenings be 'E', which of the following represents the number of days for which Abe read the book?

It is known that if Abe read in the morning, he did not read in the evening and vice versa.

A) $N = 23M + 31E$

B) $N = 31M + 23E$

C) $N = \dfrac{M}{23} + \dfrac{E}{31}$

D) $N = \dfrac{M}{31} + \dfrac{E}{23}$

A B C D
○ ○ ○ ○

14

If the linear equation $5x-27=6(15-x)+bx$ has no solution, which of the following could be the value of b?

A) 5

B) –10

C) 117

D) 11

A B C D
○ ○ ○ ○

15

Which of the following statements are true regarding the expression $f(x) = x^2 - 6x + 11$?

I. The expression has a least value of 11

II. The value of the expression is always positive for any value of x

III. The roots of $f(x)=0$ are real

A) Only I

B) Only II

C) Both I and II

D) Both II and III

A B C D
○ ○ ○ ○

DIRECTIONS

For questions 16–20, solve the problem and enter your answer in the grid, as described below, on the answer sheet.

1. Although not required, it is suggested that you write your answer in the boxes at the top of the columns to help you fill in the circles accurately. You will receive credit only if the circles are filled in correctly.
2. Mark no more than one circle in any column.
3. No question has a negative answer.
4. Some problems may have more than one correct answer. In such cases, grid only one answer.
5. **Mixed numbers** such as $3\frac{1}{2}$ must be gridded as 3.5 or 7/2. (If 3 1 / 2 is entered into the grid, it will be interpreted as $\frac{31}{2}$, not $3\frac{1}{2}$.)
6. **Decimal answers:** If you obtain a decimal answer with more digits than the grid can accommodate, it may be either rounded or truncated, but it must fill the entire grid.

Answer: $\frac{7}{12}$ Answer: 2.5

Write answer in boxes. ← Fraction line

Grid in result.

← Decimal point

Acceptable ways to grid $\frac{2}{3}$ are:

Answer: 201 – either position is correct

NOTE: You may start your answers in any column, space permitting. Columns you don't need to use should be left blank.

GRID-IN

16

If the correct form of $2i^4 + 4i^3 - i^2 + 3i$ is $a + ib$, where the imaginary number i is such that $i^2 = -1$, what is the value of $(a+b)$?

17

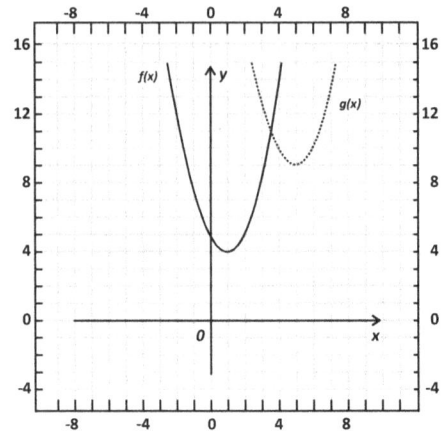

The graphs of $f(x)$ and $g(x)$ are shown below.

If $g(x) = f(x+k) - m$, what is the value of $|k+m|$?

18

Peter, Rene and Andrew were playing a game of marbles. In the game, at a point of time, Peter gave one–fourth of his marbles to Rene, who in turn gave half of what she received to Andrew. If the difference between the marbles left with Peter and the marbles received by Andrew is 30, then how many marbles did Rene receive from Peter?

19

Some friends decided to buy a Nikon camera priced at $300 by contributing equal amount of money. At the time of purchase, one more friend decided to contribute along with the others, thus reducing the contribution of each friend by $10. How many friends were there originally?

20

Matt has a garden in the shape of a right–angled triangle with one of the acute angles as 30°. If the longest side of the triangle is 4 m long, what is the perimeter, in meters, of the garden?

1. **Level of Difficulty:** Easy

   Category: Heart of Algebra

   Topic: Linear function (word problems)

   The correct answer is D

   As the cost of a pencil is 'a', the cost an eraser is 'b', the cost of a sharpener is 'c', then Adam should have spent $23a+15b+20c$, which must be equal to $70

   $23a+15b+20c=111$ … (i)

   Also, Bob must have spent $19b+12a+40c$ and as he spent $10 more than Adam, this spending must be equal to $(70 + 2) = 121.

   $19b+12a+40c=121$ … (ii)

   The answer is option D.

2. **Level of Difficulty:** Easy

   Category: Advanced Math

   Topic: Nonlinear equation graphs

   The correct answer is C

   It appears that the graph of $g(x)$ has been reflected about the X–$axis$ to get the graph of $f(x)$.

   Thus, $f(x)=-g(x)$.

   Say,

   $$x = \frac{1}{2}, g\left(\frac{1}{2}\right) = \frac{1}{2} \text{ and } f\left(\frac{1}{2}\right) = -\frac{1}{2} =>$$

   $$f\left(\frac{1}{2}\right) = -g\left(\frac{1}{2}\right)$$

   Similarly, we can check for all other points.

   Thus, $f(x)=-g(x)$.

   Hence, the correct answer is C.

3. **Level of Difficulty:** Easy

   Category: Additional Math

   Topic: Circle theorems

   The correct answer is D

   $\angle QPR = \angle QSR = 20°$ [angle made by the chord QR]

   $\therefore \angle PQR = 180° - (80° + 20°) = 80°$

   $\therefore \angle PSR = 180° - 80° = 100°$

   Hence, the correct answer is Option D.

4. **Level of Difficulty:** Easy

   Category: Advanced Math

   Topic: Linear and quadratic systems

   The correct answer is D

   Solving $g(x) \geq f(x)$:

   $x - 2 \geq x^2 - 6x + 8$

   $x^2 - 7x + 10 \leq 0$

   $(x - 2)(x - 5) \leq 0$

   $2 \leq x \leq 5$

   Thus, the integer values of x are: 2, 3, 4 and 5.

   Thus, there are 4 possible values of x.

   The correct answer is option D.

5. **Level of Difficulty:** Easy

   Category: Advanced Math

   Topic: Radicals and rational exponents

   The correct answer is D

   We know that an even exponent of any number is always positive irrespective of whether the original number is positive or negative.

   We have: $a^3 b^4 c^7 d^2 = a^2 b^4 c^6 d^2 \times ac$

   We can say that $a^2 b^4 c^6 d^2$ has all even exponents. Hence, it is positive.

   However, since the given expression is negative, we can conclude that ac must be negative.

   Working with options:

   A): $ab^2 cd^2 = b^2 d^2 \times ac$

   $b^2 d^2$ is positive (*even exponents*) and ac is negative. Hence, the product is negative.

   Thus, this option is incorrect.

   B): In $b^2 d$, we can say that b^2 is positive. But we do not know whether d is positive or negative.

   Hence, $b^2 d$ can be either positive or negative depending on d.

   Thus, this option is incorrect.

   C): In $bc^2 d$, we can say that c^2 is positive. However, we do not know the nature of b and d. Hence, $bc^2 d$, can be either positive or negative depending on b and d.

   Thus, this option is incorrect.

   Hence, D must be our answer.

   Let us verify D:

   D): $a^3 b^2 c = a^2 b^2 \times ac$ We can say that $a^2 b^2$ is positive. Also, we know that ac is negative. Hence, $a^3 b^2 c$ must be negative.

   Thus, this option is correct.

   Hence, the answer is D.

6. **Level of Difficulty:** Easy

   Category: Heart of Algebra

   Topic: Interpreting linear functions

   The correct answer is C

   $p=2n+3$

   Thus, for $p=17$: $17=2n+3 => n=7$

7. **Level of Difficulty:** Easy

   Category: Heart of Algebra

   Topic: Linear inequality and equation (word problems)

   The correct answer is B

   Since tree should be at least 312 centimeters high we get the inequality $160+8t \geq 312$.

   Then we get $8t \geq 152 => t \geq 19$.

   Hence, the correct answer is B.

8. **Level of Difficulty:** Easy

   Category: Heart of Algebra

   Topic: Solving linear equations and inequalities

   The correct answer is B

   $2\,|\,2x-3\,|< 14 => |\,2x-3\,|< 7$

   $-7 < 2x-3 < 7 => -7+3 < 2x < 7+3 =>$

   $-4 < 2x < 1 => -2 < x < 5$

   Thus, the possible integer values of x are: $\{-1,0,1,2,3,4\}$

   Hence, there are 6 possible integer values of x satisfying the inequality.

   Hence, the correct answer is B.

9. **Level of Difficulty:** Easy

   Category: Passport to Advanced Math

   Topic: Quadratic and exponential (word problems)

   The correct answer is B.

   Let the number of bacteria initially be N. The number of bacteria doubles in every hour.

   Using the above information, we can calculate the number of bacteria in 12 hours and equate with the value mentioned. Then, we can calculate when the number of bacteria would have been one–fourth of the final value.

   However, such calculations are unnecessary as we can solve the problem using a simple logic as mentioned below:

   We know that the number of bacteria doubles every hour.

   Thus, we can say that the time taken for the bacteria to double in value from

   $\dfrac{1}{2} \times 40960$ to 40960 would have taken only one hour.

   Similarly, we can say that the time taken for the bacteria to double in value from

   $\dfrac{1}{4} \times 40960$ to $\dfrac{1}{2} \times 40960$ would also have taken only one hour.

   Since the number of bacteria was 40960 after 12 hours from start of the experiment, the number of bacteria was one–fourth of that number two hours before i.e. 10 hours from the start of the experiment.

   Hence, the correct answer is B.

10. **Level of Difficulty:** Medium

    Category: Heart of Algebra

    Topic: Interpreting linear functions

    The correct answer is A

    $C=120+90\times W+78\times N$

    For 10 units, total cost = $120+90W+780=900+90W$

    Thus: $900+90W \leq 2700$

    $W \leq 20$

    The correct answer is option C.

11. **Level of Difficulty:** Medium

    Category: Advanced Math

    Topic: Functions

    The correct answer is C

    At the points where $f(x)$ and $g(x)$ intersect, the values of the functions will be equal.

    Thus:
    $$f(x) = g(x) =>$$
    $$x^2 - 6x + 8 = x - 2 =>$$
    $$x^2 - 7x + 10 = 0 =>$$
    $$(x - 2)(x - 5) = 0 =>$$
    $$x = 2 \text{ or } 5$$

    Thus, the two graphs intersect at two points, $x=2$ and $x=5$.

    Hence, the correct answer is C.

12. **Level of Difficulty:** Medium

Category: Advanced Math

Topic: Radicals and rational exponents

The correct answer is D

We have:

$$N = 4^{61} + 4^{61} + 4^{61} + 4^{62} + 4^{62} + 4^{62} =>$$

$$4^{61}(1+1+1+4+4+4) = 4^{61} \times 15$$

Hence, we can see that N is divisible by both 3 and 5.

Hence, both the first and second statements are correct.

Now, we can also write

$$N = 4^{61} \times 15 = 4^{61} \times 3 \times 5 = 2^{122} \times 3 \times 5$$

Since all the exponents of the prime factors are not even numbers, N is not a perfect square.

Hence, the third statement is not correct.

Hence, the answer is D.

13. **Level of Difficulty:** Medium

Category: Heart of Algebra

Topic: Linear function (word problems)

The correct answer is C

As Abe reads 23 pages every morning, number of mornings he read $= \dfrac{M}{23}$

Also, as Abe reads 31 pages every evening, number of evenings he read $= \dfrac{E}{31}$

Since Abe did not read in morning and evening of the same day, the number of days he read

$$N = \dfrac{M}{23} + \dfrac{E}{31}$$

The correct answer is option C.

14. **Level of Difficulty:** Difficult

Category: Heart of Algebra

Topic: Solving linear equations and inequalities

The correct answer is D

$$5x - 27 = 6(15 - x) + bx =>$$

$$5x - 27 = 90 - 6x + bx =>$$

$$(11 - b)x = 117$$

If $b=11$, the equation is equivalent to the false statement 0=117. Therefore, the equation has no solution when $b=11$.

Hence, the correct answer is D.

15. **Level of Difficulty:** Difficult

Category: Passport to Advanced Math

Topic: Rational expressions and polynomials

The correct answer is B

We have

$$f(x) = x^2 - 6x + 11$$

$$(x - 3)^2 + 2$$

Since $(x - 3)^2$ is a perfect square, it is non-negative.

Hence, the lease value of $f(x)$ occurs if the perfect square term becomes zero (which happens if $x=3$).

In that case, the value of $f(x)$ becomes 2.

Thus, the least value of $f(x)$ is 2.

Hence, statement I is false.

Again, since $f(x) = (x - 3)^2 + 2$ and $(x - 3)^2$ is non-negative, we can conclude that the value of $f(x)$ for any value of x will always be positive.

Hence, statement II is true.

In a quadratic equation $ax^2 + bx + c = 0$, the roots are imaginary if $b^2 - 4ac < 0$.

Here, $a=1$, $b=-6$, $c=11$. Thus,

$$b^2 - 4ac = 36 - 44 = -8 < 0$$

Thus, the roots of the equation $f(x)=0$ are imaginary.

Hence, statement III is false.

Hence, the correct answer is B.

16. Level of Difficulty: Easy

Category: Additional Math

Topic: Complex numbers

The correct answer is 2

We know that the imaginary number i is such that $i^2 = -1$.

Therefore, $i^4 = (i^2)^2 = (-1)^2 = 1$.

Similarly, $i^3 = i \times i^2 = i \times (-1) = -i$.

Therefore, we can write the given expression as $2i^4 + 4i^3 - i^2 + 3i$

$= 2 \times 1 + 4(-i) - (-1) + 3i$

$= 2 - 4i + 1 + 3i$

$= 3 - i$

$\Rightarrow a = 3, b = -1 \Rightarrow a + b = 2$

Hence, the correct answer is 2.

17. Level of Difficulty: Medium

Category: Advanced Math

Topic: Nonlinear equation graphs

The correct answer is 9

We can see from the graph that the graph of $f(x)$ has shifted right and up.

In order to find the amount of the shift, let us pick a reference point on the graphs.

The easiest point to check is the lowest point on the graphs.

The lowest point on $f(x)$ is at $(1, 4)$ and the corresponding point on $g(x)$ is $(5, 9)$.

Thus, $f(x)$ has shifted 4 units right and 5 units up.

We know that if the function $f(x)$ is modified to $f(x+a)$, then the graph shifts a units left and if the function is modified to $f(x-a)$, then the graph shifts a units right where a is positive.

Again, if the function $f(x)$ is modified to $f(x)+b$, then the graph shifts b units up and if the function is modified to $f(x)-b$, then the graph shifts b units down where b is positive.

Since $f(x)$ has shifted 4 units right and 5 units up, the modified function $(x)=f(x-4)+5$.

Comparing with the given form: $g(x)=f(x+k)-m$, we get $k=-4$, $m=-5$.

Thus, $|k+m|=|-4-5|=9$.

Thus, the correct answer is 9.

18. Level of Difficulty: Medium

Category: Heart of Algebra

Topic: Linear inequality and equation (word problems)

The correct answer is 12

Let the number of marbles with Peter be $8p$ (we assumed the number of marbles with Peter as $8p$ since Peter would give one-fourth of his marbles to Rene who would give away half of that to Andrew.

It would be Easy to work if we assume the number of marbles with him as a multiple of $4 \times 2 = 8$).

When Peter gives one-fourth of his marbles to Rene, he gives away $\frac{1}{4} \times 8p = 2p$ marbles to Rene.

Thus, number of marbles left with Peter = $8p-2p=6p$.

Rene gives away half of what she received to Andrew, i.e. $\frac{1}{2} \times 2p = p$.

Thus, the number of marbles received by Andrew = p.

Thus, we have: $6p-p=30 \Rightarrow 5p=30 \Rightarrow p=6$.

Thus, the number of marbles Rene received from Peter = $2p=2 \times 6=12$.

Hence, the answer is 12.

19. Level of Difficulty: Difficult

Category: Advanced Math

Topic: Quadratic and exponential (word problems)

The correct answer is 5

Let the number of friends be x.

Price of the camera = $300.

Thus, contribution from each friend = $\$\dfrac{300}{x}$.

Contribution from each friend after one more friend joined = $\$\dfrac{300}{x+1}$.

we have:

$$\left(\frac{300}{x} - \frac{300}{x+1}\right) = 10 \Rightarrow$$

$$\frac{30}{x} - \frac{30}{x+1} = 1 \Rightarrow$$

$$\frac{30}{x^2 + x} = 1 \Rightarrow$$

$$x^2 + x - 30 = 0$$

$$(x+6)(x-5) = 0 \Rightarrow$$

$$x = -6 \text{ or } 5$$

Thus, the numbers of friends originally were 5.

Hence, the correct answer is 5.

20. Level of Difficulty: Difficult

Category: Additional Topics in Math

Topic: Angles, arc lengths, and trig functions

The correct answer is 9.46

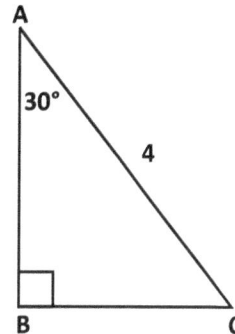

Let the garden be the triangle ABC as shown, right angled at B.

The longest side i.e. the hypotenuse is 4 m long.

We need to use $\operatorname{Sin}\theta$ and $\operatorname{Cos}\theta$ to find the other two sides of the triangle since only these two ratios relate the sides to the hypotenuse.

$$\operatorname{Sin}30° = \frac{BC}{AC} \Rightarrow \frac{1}{2} = \frac{BC}{4} \Rightarrow BC = 2m$$

$$\operatorname{Cos}30° = \frac{AB}{AC} \Rightarrow \frac{\sqrt{3}}{2} = \frac{AB}{4} \Rightarrow AB = 2\sqrt{3}\ m$$

Thus, perimeter of the triangle = $AB + BC + AC \Rightarrow$

$$2\sqrt{3} + 2 + 4 = (6 + 2\sqrt{3})m \Rightarrow$$

$$6 + 2 \times 1.73 = 9.46m$$

Hence, the correct answer is 9.46

Math Test – Calculator

55 MINUTES, 38 QUESTIONS

Turn to Section 4 of your answer sheet to answer the questions in this section.

For questions 1-30, solve each problem, choose the best answer from the choices provided, and fill in the corresponding circle on your answer sheet. **For questions 31-38**, solve the problem and enter your answer in the grid on the answer sheet. Please refer to the directions before question 16 on how to enter your answers in the grid. You may use any available space in your test booklet for scratch work.

NOTES

1. The use of a calculator **is permitted.**

2. All variables and expressions used represent real numbers unless otherwise indicated.

3. Figures provided in this test are drawn to scale unless otherwise indicated.

4. All figures lie in a plane unless otherwise indicated.

5. Unless otherwise indicated, the domain of a given function f is the set of all real numbers x for which $f(x)$ is a real number.

REFERENCE

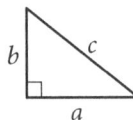 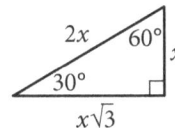 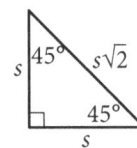

$A = \pi r^2$ $A = \ell w$ $A = \frac{1}{2}bh$ $c^2 = a^2 + b^2$ Special Right Triangles
$C = 2\pi r$

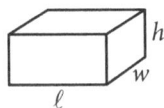 

$V = \ell wh$ $V = \pi r^2 h$ $V = \frac{4}{3}\pi r^3$ $V = \frac{1}{3}\pi r^2 h$ $V = \frac{1}{3}\ell wh$

The number of degrees of arc in a circle is 360.

The number of radians of arc in a circle is 2π.

The sum of the measures in degrees of the angles of a triangle is 180.

MULTIPLE CHOICE QUESTIONS

1

Among 40 employees in an office, 60% are men. Out of them, 33.33% play rugby. If 30% of the total employees play rugby, how many of the total employees are women who do not play rugby?

A) 4

B) 12

C) 16

D) 20

A B C D
○ ○ ○ ○

2

Acer.com recently purchased 30 printers, each at $120. The store then sold the printers, to a dealer, all at the same price. Had the store sold each printer for $10 more than what it actually did, the total profit made would have been $1800. What was the selling price of each printer?

A) $50

B) $120

C) $150

D) $170

A B C D
○ ○ ○ ○

3

The profit, in dollars, of a company is determined by the following equation: $P=50.5\times N-210.5$, where 'P' represents the profit of the company and 'N' represents number of units manufactured by the company. When can the company expect a profit of $92.50?

A) When the number of units manufactured is 2

B) When the number of units manufactured is 3

C) When the number of units manufactured is 4

D) When the number of units manufactured is 6

A B C D
○ ○ ○ ○

4

The following graph shows the breakup of the type of employees of company from 1997-2000: Managerial, Staff, Unskilled and Temporary.

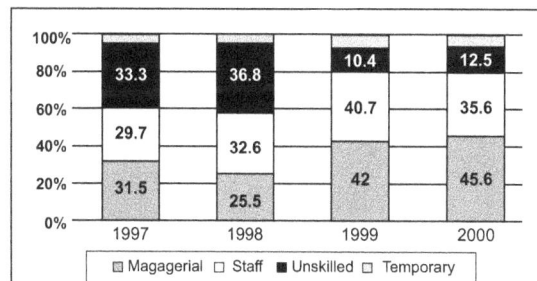

If the total number of employees remained the same throughout, what is the approximate percent increase in the number of staff employees between 1997 and 1998?

A) 16.4%

B) 9.8%

C) 8.9%

D) 2.9%

A B C D
○ ○ ○ ○

5

A man earns $40 for a period of 5 hours that he works per day. Thereafter, for every additional hour, he earns $5 per hour. If the man earns $P in a day by working for t hours, where t>5 and is an integer, and P≤60, which of the following sets of values of P and t satisfy the above conditions?

A) $P=60, t=10$

B) $P=55, t=10$

C) $P=50, t=9$

D) $P=50, t=7$

A B C D
○ ○ ○ ○

6

Amy, Joe and Ron contributed a total of $255 for a trip to an amusement park. Had each friend managed $5 more, the ratio of their contributions would have been 2 : 3 : 4 respectively. What was the actual ratio in which they had contributed $255?

A) $11 : 17 : 23$

B) $13 : 19 : 25$

C) $5 : 6 : 9$

D) $3 : 5 : 7$

A B C D
○ ○ ○ ○

7

Which of the graphs below most closely represents the function $y=2^x$?

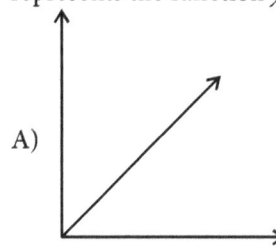

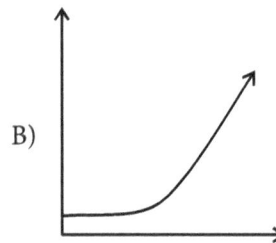

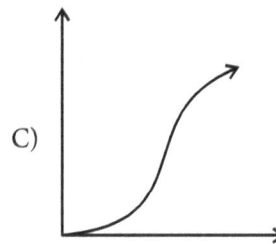

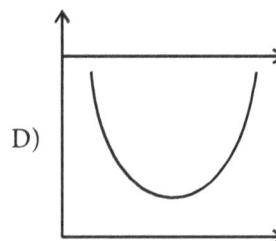

A)

B)

C)

D)

A B C D
○ ○ ○ ○

8

Rick is an independent contractor. His fee, in dollars, for working t hours is given by $F=22t+40$. What does the 22 mean in this formula?

A) The constant fee that Rick charges per project is $22.

B) The constant fee for the first hour is $22.

C) The constant fee that Rick charges per hour is $22.

D) The extra fee that Rick charges after 8 hours of work is $22.

A B C D
○ ○ ○ ○

9

In the equation $\dfrac{3y}{2x-y}-2=5x,$ what is the correct expression of y in terms of x?

A) $\dfrac{2x(5x+2)}{5(x+1)}$

B) $\dfrac{x(5x+2)}{(x+5)}$

C) $\dfrac{5x(5x+1)}{2(x+1)}$

D) $\dfrac{5x(x+5)}{2(5x+2)}$

A B C D
○ ○ ○ ○

10

A man buys a apples and g oranges, each costing 80 cents and 60 cents respectively. If the man buys less than 18 fruits and spends less than $12, which of the following values of a and g satisfy the above conditions?

A) $a=12, g=5$

B) $a=9, g=8$

C) $a=11, g=6$

D) $a=8, g=9$

A B C D
○ ○ ○ ○

11

The average of five positive distinct integers is 60. If the largest integer is 70, what is the minimum possible value of the smallest integer?

A) 0

B) 1

C) 20

D) 26

A B C D
○ ○ ○ ○

12

The population of a town increases by 20% in each year starting 2010. If the total population of the town in 2013 is 77940, what was the population of the town in 2010?

A) 60000

B) 45000

C) 40000

D) 35000

A B C D
○ ○ ○ ○

13

The triangle *ABC* bounded by the graphs of $f(x)=x-1$ and $g(x)=4x-8$ and the *X*–axis as shown in the graph below.

What is the area of *ABC*, if *B* and *C* have coordinates (1,0) and (2,0), respectively.

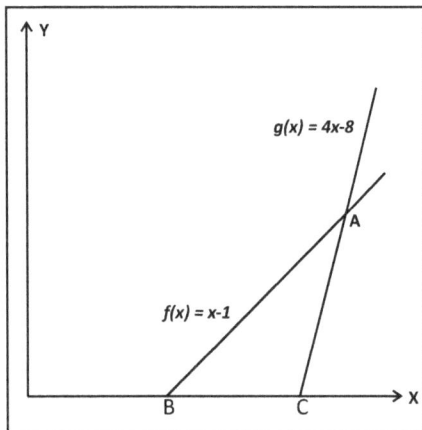

A) 2/3

B) 1

C) 4/3

D) 2

A B C D
○ ○ ○ ○

14

If the total strength of all employees in 1997 was 5000, and there was a 20% increase in total strength for every year from 1997, what is the number of employees in 1999?

A) 6000

B) 7200

C) 6800

D) 7000

A B C D
○ ○ ○ ○

15

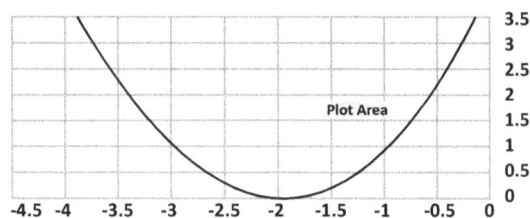

According to the graph above, what was the approximate average temperature of these three cities on July 5th, 2005?

A) 96

B) 105

C) 80

D) 90

A B C D
○ ○ ○ ○

16

Jessica decides to drive across the country on a road trip. If the trip is 2,669 miles and she wants to drive at most 250 miles a day, how many weeks will it take her to complete the trip if she drives the maximum distance every day? Round your answer to the nearest tenth.

A) 1.5

B) 10.7

C) 2.1

D) 0.7

A B C D
○ ○ ○ ○

17

Student Population at Greendale School	
Grade	Number of Students
2nd	74
3rd	73
4th	81
5th	90
6th	75
7th	82

Based on the data in the table above, what grade would the median student be in at Greendale School?

A) 3

B) 4

C) 5

D) 6

A B C D
◯ ◯ ◯ ◯

18

Joe throws a ball upwards from a certain height above the ground level. The height of the ball above the ground after time t seconds from when the ball was thrown is given by the expression $h(t) = -(t-4)^2 + b$.

The ball reaches a maximum height of 25 feet after 4 seconds. After how much time (in seconds) will the ball reach the ground level?

A) 6

B) 7

C) 8

D) 9

A B C D
◯ ◯ ◯ ◯

19

In a sequence of terms, the first term is (– 1). Each term thereafter is obtained by multiplying the previous number with (– 2). How many of the first 40 terms of the series are less than 10?

A) 3

B) 28

C) 22

D) 30

A B C D
◯ ◯ ◯ ◯

20

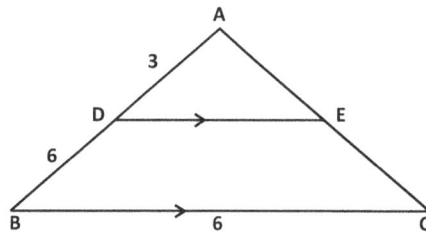

In the

$$\triangle ABC, DE \parallel BC, AD = 3,$$
$$BD = 6, \text{ and } BC = 6$$

What is the ratio of the areas of triangle ADE and trapezium $BDEC$?

A) 1 : 3

B) 1 : 4

C) 1 : 8

D) 1 : 9

A B C D
◯ ◯ ◯ ◯

21

In a field trip organized by a school for the 6th grade students, it was decided that there should be at least one teacher for every 8 students.

A total of 48 teachers and students combined participated in the trip.

How many students were there in the trip?

A) 40

B) 41

C) 42

D) 43

A B C D
○ ○ ○ ○

22

There was a sale on sofas at a furniture store for 60% off the original price of any sofa, with an additional 40% off your entire purchase if you purchase a matching armchair for a fixed price of $450. Which expression represents the final total of your purchase if you buy a sofa that is originally $s and an armchair for $a?

A) $0.4(0.6s + a)$

B) $0.6(0.4s + 450)$

C) $0.4s + 0.6a$

D) $0.24(s + 450)$

A B C D
○ ○ ○ ○

23

During the NBA playoffs, Chicago Bulls, last year's basketball champion, scored 88 points in their fifth game of the season. As a result, their initial average points from that season increased by an integer value.

Which of the following could have been their initial average points i.e. average of the points scored in the initial four games in the season?

A) 67

B) 78

C) 91

D) 93

A B C D
○ ○ ○ ○

24

Mike is painting the wall. After t hours of work, Mike still needs to paint $A = 315 - \dfrac{t}{46}$ square feet of the wall.

What does 46 mean in the equation?

A) Mike needs 46 hours to paint one square feet of the wall.

B) 46 square feet of the wall were initially painted.

C) Mike needs 46 hours to finish painting.

D) Mike is painting 46 square feet of the wall per hour.

A B C D
○ ○ ○ ○

25

The Farm–Fresh fruit store in California stocks *Apples*, *Peaches* and *Lychees*. While ordering fruits for its store, the owner wanted the fruits in particular ratios as depicted in the table below:

Fruits	Required Ratio
Apples : Peaches	4 : 3
Apples : Lychees	3 : 5

What fraction of the total fruits are *Apples*?

A) $\dfrac{16}{42}$

B) $\dfrac{12}{41}$

C) $\dfrac{41}{25}$

D) $\dfrac{24}{15}$

A B C D
◯ ◯ ◯ ◯

26

Joe was asked to fill up the missing digits A and B in the number $25A7B$ subject to the condition that the resulting number has to be divisible by 45. What is the value of $(A+B)$ if A and B are positive digits?

A) 4

B) 8

C) 9

D) 13

A B C D
◯ ◯ ◯ ◯

27

If $2w = \dfrac{3}{2}x = y = \dfrac{5}{3}z$ for four positive integers w, x, y and z, which of the following expressions can represent an integer?

A) $\dfrac{wx}{yz}$

B) $\dfrac{x}{w}$

C) $\dfrac{4x}{y}$

D) $\dfrac{x^2}{y}$

A B C D
◯ ◯ ◯ ◯

28

If $x^2 > x^3 > x$, which of the following statements must be correct?

I) $x^6 > x^7$

II) x can take any value between 0 and 1

III) $-1 < x < 0$

A) Only I

B) Only III

C) Only II

D) Both I and III

A B C D
◯ ◯ ◯ ◯

29

After multiplying by 5, each of the following numbers will have the same number of factors that are made by squaring a whole number,

i.e. perfect square factors, *EXCEPT*

A) 350

B) 290

C) 250

D) 12

A B C D
○ ○ ○ ○

30

If $x > x^3$, then all the options may be correct *EXCEPT*

A) $x^3 > x^5$

B) $x^2 > x$

C) $x^2 > x^3$

D) $\dfrac{1}{x} > \dfrac{1}{x^2}$

A B C D
○ ○ ○ ○

DIRECTIONS

For questions 31–38, solve the problem and enter your answer in the grid, as described below, on the answer sheet.

1. Although not required, it is suggested that you write your answer in the boxes at the top of the columns to help you fill in the circles accurately. You will receive credit only if the circles are filled in correctly.

2. Mark no more than one circle in any column.

3. No question has a negative answer.

4. Some problems may have more than one correct answer. In such cases, grid only one answer.

5. **Mixed numbers** such as $3\frac{1}{2}$ must be gridded as 3.5 or 7/2. (If the grid $3\,1\,/\,2$ is entered into the grid, it will be interpreted as $\frac{31}{2}$, not $3\frac{1}{2}$.)

6. **Decimal answers:** If you obtain a decimal answer with more digits than the grid can accommodate, it may be either rounded or truncated, but it must fill the entire grid.

Answer: $\frac{7}{12}$

Write answer in boxes. → Grid in result.

← Fraction line

Answer: 2.5

← Decimal point

Acceptable ways to grid $\frac{2}{3}$ are:

Answer: 201 – either position is correct

NOTE: You may start your answers in any column, space permitting. Columns you don't need to use should be left blank.

GRID-IN

Two marbles are picked simultaneously from a box containing three red and five blue marbles. What is the probability that the marbles are of the same color?

32

What is the value of $\left\{ \dfrac{(a+b)^2 - (a^2+b)^2}{(a+b)^2 - (a-b)^2} \right\}$?

33

Jane is riding a bicycle from the office to her house at constant speed.

The remaining distance is given by the formula $D = -4t + 3{,}600$, where D is measured in meters and t is measured in seconds.

How many meters does Jane need to ride after 10 minutes?

34

If $\dfrac{1}{x} + \dfrac{1}{y} = 2$ and $\dfrac{3}{x} + \dfrac{4}{y} = 7$, what is the value of $(x + y)$?

35

Given that the equation $(3x+2)k+5=12x+7m$ has infinite solutions, what is the value of $(k+m)$?

36

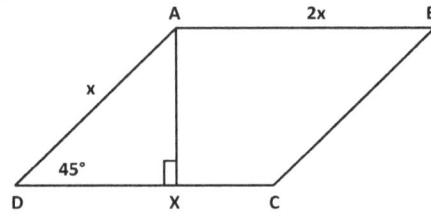

In a parallelogram, the ratio of the two adjacent sides is 1 : 2. If the area of the parallelogram is 20 square units and the angle between the two sides is 45°, what is the area, to the nearest integer, of the rectangle having the sides equal to that of the parallelogram?

37

A, B, C and D are four distinct positive integers lying between 1 and 5, both inclusive; such that $C+D=A$ and $D-C=B$. What is the maximum possible value of $(B + C)$ if none of the numbers is 4?

/		○	○	
.	○	○	○	○
0	○	○	○	○
1	○	○	○	○
2	○	○	○	○
3	○	○	○	○
4	○	○	○	○
5	○	○	○	○
6	○	○	○	○
7	○	○	○	○
8	○	○	○	○
9	○	○	○	○

38

If the equation of the circle having the coordinates of the ends of its diameter as (3,5) and (5,11) is $(x-a)^2+(y-b)^2=r^2$, what is the value of $(a+b+r)$ to the nearest tenth?

/		○	○	
.	○	○	○	○
0	○	○	○	○
1	○	○	○	○
2	○	○	○	○
3	○	○	○	○
4	○	○	○	○
5	○	○	○	○
6	○	○	○	○
7	○	○	○	○
8	○	○	○	○
9	○	○	○	○

1. **Level of Difficulty:** Easy

   Category: Problem Solving and Data Analysis

   Topic: Data inferences

   The correct answer is B

   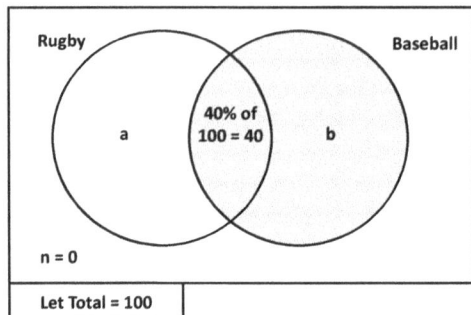

   Number of men = 60% of 40 = 24.

   Number of women = 40 – 24 = 16.

   Number of men who play rugby = 33.33% of 24 = 8.

   Number of employees who play rugby = 30% of 40 = 12.

   Thus, number of women who play rugby = 12 – 8 = 4.

   Thus, the number of women who do not play rugby = 16 – 4 = 12.

   Hence, the correct answer is B.

2. **Level of Difficulty:** Easy

   Category: Problem Solving and Data Analysis

   Topic: Percents

   The correct answer is D

   If the price of each printer was increased by $10, additional profit generated = $10×30=$300.

   Thus, initially, the total profit generated on selling 30 printers = $(1800-300)=$1500.

   Thus, profit made on each printer =

   $$= \$\frac{1500}{30} = \$50$$

   Cost of each printer = $120.

   Hence, the selling price of each printer = $(120+50)=$170.

   Hence, the answer is D.

3. **Level of Difficulty:** Easy

   Category: Heart of Algebra

   Topic: Interpreting linear functions

   The correct answer is D

   If we put P= 92.50, we get

   $$92.5 = 50.5 \times N = 210.5$$

   $$50.5N = 303 => N = \frac{303}{50.5} = 6$$

   $$N = 6$$

   The correct answer is option D.

4. **Level of Difficulty:** Easy

    Category: Problem Solving and Data Analysis

    Topic: Data collection and conclusions

    The correct answer is B

    Since the number of employees remains the same throughout, the above percent values are equivalent to the actual number of people under each category.

    Thus, the required percent change =

    $$= \frac{32.6 - 29.7}{29.7} \times 100 = 9.76\% \approx 9.8\%$$

5. **Level of Difficulty:** Easy

    Category: Heart of Algebra

    Topic: Systems of linear inequalities (word problems)

    The correct answer is D

    Earnings for the first 5 hours = $40

    Earnings for the remaining (t-5) hours = ${5(t-5)}=$(5t-25)$

    Since he earns P: $P=40+(5t-25)$

    $P=5t+15$

    Since $P{\leq}60 => 5t+15{\leq}60 => t{\leq}9$

    Thus, only options C and D are possible.

    If $t=9$, $P=5t+15=60$

    Thus, option C is not correct.

    The correct answer is option D.

6. **Level of Difficulty:** Easy

    Category: Problem Solving and Data Analysis

    Topic: Ratios, rates, and proportions

    The correct answer is A

    If each friend had contributed $5 more than what they did, they would have managed to have $5 × 3 = $15 more than $255 i.e. $270.

    The ratio in which they would have contributed $270 is 2 : 3 : 4.

    Hence, contribution of Amy =

    $$\$\left(\frac{2}{2+3+4} \times 270\right) = \$60$$
    .

    Contribution of Joe =

    $$\$\left(\frac{3}{2+3+4} \times 270\right) = \$90$$
    .

    Contribution of Ron =

    $$\$\left(\frac{4}{2+3+4} \times 270\right) = \$120$$

    Thus, before contributing $5 extra, their respective contributions were

    $$= (60 - 5) : (90 - 5) : (120 - 5) =>$$

    $$55 : 85 : 115 =>$$

    $$11 : 17 : 23$$

    Hence, the answer is A.

7. **Level of Difficulty:** Easy

    Category: Passport to Advanced Math

    Topic: Nonlinear equation graphs

    The correct answer is B

    The equation $y = 2^x$ is an exponential function, and the graph in Choice B is the only graph that features exponential growth.

    Choice A is incorrect because it features a linear equation, Choice C and D are incorrect because they do not feature exponential growth.

8. **Level of Difficulty:** Easy

   Category: Heart of Algebra

   Topic: Interpreting linear functions.

   The correct answer is C

   We see that t is increasing by 1 every hour. Hence, 22 is Rick's hourly rate, $22.

   The correct answer is option C.

9. **Level of Difficulty:** Medium

   Category: Advanced Math

   Topic: Isolating quantities

   The correct answer is A

   $$\frac{3y}{2x-y} - 2 = 5x$$

   $$\frac{3y}{2x-y} = 5x+2$$

   $$\frac{2x-y}{3y} = \frac{1}{5x+2}$$

   $$\frac{2x}{3y} - \frac{1}{3} = \frac{1}{5x+2}$$

   $$\frac{2x}{3y} = \frac{1}{5x+2} = \frac{1}{3} = \frac{5x+5}{3(5x+2)}$$

   $$\frac{3y}{2x} = \frac{3(5x+2)}{5(x+1)}$$

   $$y = \frac{2x(5x+2)}{5(x+1)}$$

   Alternative: Plug in $x=1$ in the given expression:

   The value of $y=1.4$

   Plugging in $x=1$ in each option, only option A gives $y=1.4$

   The correct answer is option A.

10. **Level of Difficulty:** Medium

    Category: Heart of Algebra

    Topic: Systems of linear inequalities (word problems)

    The correct answer is D

    Since total number of fruits is less than 15, we have: $a+g<18$

    Since total amount spent is less than $12, we have: $80a+60r<1200 => 4a+3r<60$

    Each of the options satisfies the first condition.

    We need to verify the second condition regarding the amount spent.

    Only Option D satisfies that condition since $4a+3g=32+27=59<60$.

    The correct answer is option D.

11. **Level of Difficulty:** Medium

    Category: Problem Solving and Data Analysis

    Topic: Center, spread and shape of distributions

    The correct answer is D

    The total of the five integers $= 60 \times 5=300$.

    The largest integer is 70.

    Since we need to minimize the smallest integer, we need to assign the largest possible values of the remaining three integers (leaving out the largest and the smallest from the set of five integers).

    Thus, the other three integers are 69, 68 and 67 which add up to 204.

    Thus, the minimum possible value of the smallest integer =

    $300 - (70+ 204) = 300 - 274 = 26$.

    Hence, the correct answer is D.

12. **Level of Difficulty:** Medium

    Category: Problem Solving and Data Analysis

    Topic: Linear and exponential growth

    The correct answer is B

    If the population of the town increases by 20%, the new population becomes $\dfrac{120}{100}$ times the original population.

    Therefore, population in every year becomes $\left(\dfrac{120}{100}\right) = \dfrac{6}{5}$ times the population of previous year.

    Let us consider the population of 2010 as x.

    Therefore, with 20% increase, the population in 2011 will become $\left(\dfrac{6}{5}\right)x$.

    The population in 2012 will be again $\left(\dfrac{6}{5}\right)$ times the population of 2011 and so on. Hence, we get

    $$\left(\dfrac{6}{5}\right)^3 \times x = 77940$$

    $$\dfrac{216}{125} \times x = 77940$$

    $$x = 77940 \times \dfrac{125}{216}$$

    $$x = 45000$$

    The correct answer is option B.

13. **Level of Difficulty:** Medium

    Category: Heart of Algebra

    Topic: Graphing linear equations

    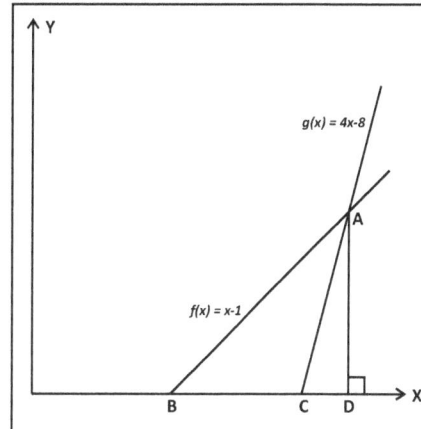

    The correct answer is A

    We need to find the coordinates of A, B and C. Solving $f(x) = g(x)$:

    $$x - 1 = 4x - 8 \Rightarrow x = \dfrac{7}{3} \Rightarrow f\left(\dfrac{7}{3}\right) = \dfrac{7}{3} - 1 = \dfrac{4}{3}$$

    Thus, $f\left(\dfrac{7}{3}\right) = g\left(\dfrac{7}{3}\right) = \dfrac{4}{3}$.

    Thus, coordinates of A are $\left(\dfrac{7}{3}, \dfrac{4}{3}\right)$

    Thus, length of $BC = 2 - 1 = 1$ unit.

    Height of triangle ABC i.e. $AD = \dfrac{4}{3}$ units.

    Hence, area of triangle

    $$ABC = \dfrac{1}{2} \times bas \times height = \dfrac{1}{2} \times BC \times AD \Rightarrow$$

    $$\dfrac{1}{2} \times 1 \times \dfrac{4}{3} = \dfrac{2}{3} \text{ square units}$$

    Hence, the correct answer is A.

14. **Level of Difficulty:** Medium

    Category: Problem Solving and Data Analysis

    Topic: Data collection and conclusions

    The correct answer is B

    The total number of employees in 1997 = 5000.

    Thus, the number of employees in 1999, at a 20% growth rate

    $$= 5000 \times \left(1 + \frac{20}{100}\right)^2 = 7200$$

15. **Level of Difficulty:** Medium

    Category: Problem Solving and Data Analysis

    Topic: Center, Spread, and Shape of Distributions

    The correct answer is A

    To find the average temperature, first identify the approximate temperatures of the three

    cities: *New York* = 98 *DC* 102, *Chicago* 87.

    Find the average 98+102+87 = 287÷ 3 = 95.67.

    Therefore,

    Choice C is the closest approximate value. Choices B, C, and D are incorrect because they do not represent the average of the temperatures listed in the graph.

16. **Level of Difficulty:** Medium

    Category: Problem Solving and Data Analysis

    Topic: Data Inferences

    The correct answer is A

    If Jessica drives 250 miles every day and the total trip is 2,669 miles, then one must divide 2669 ÷ 250 =10.676.

    This value represents the number of days it will take her to complete the trip but to find the number of weeks, divide your answer by 7, so that 10.676 ÷ 7=1.525.

    Rounded to the nearest tenth is then 1.5. Choices B is incorrect because it is the number of days the trip would take, not weeks.

    Choices C and D are incorrect and are mostly likely the result of arithmetic errors.

17. **Level of Difficulty:** Medium

    Category: Problem Solving and Data Analysis

    Topic: Center, Spread, and Shape of Distributions

    The correct answer is C

    To find the median value of the data set, start by finding the total number of students in the school, 74+73+81+90+75+82=475.

    The median, or halfway point, would then be half of 475 or 237.5.

    The 237th student falls in the 5th grade row (students 228 through 318), so the median student is in the 5th grade.

    Choices A, B and D are incorrect and most likely result from errors in calculating the total number of students to find the median value.

18. **Level of Difficulty:** Medium

    Category: Passport to Advanced Math

    Topic: Quadratic and exponential (word problems)

    The correct answer is D

    The maximum height reached is 25 feet after 4 seconds.

    Hence, $h(4) = -(4-4)^2 + b = 25$

    Thus, $b=25$.

    Thus, we need to find when

    $h(t) = 0 =>$

    $-(t-4)^2 + 25 = 0 =>$

    $(t-4)^2 = 25$

    $t - 4 = \pm 5 => t = 4 \pm 5 =>$

    $t = 9$ or -1

    Since time cannot be negative, we get $t=9$.

    Thus, the ball reaches the ground level after 9 seconds.

    Hence, the correct answer is D.

19. **Level of Difficulty:** Medium

    Category: Passport to Advanced Math

    Topic: Quadratic and exponential (word problems)

    The correct answer is C

    Let us write the first few terms of the sequence:

    $t_1 = -1$

    $t_2 = (-1) \times (-2) = 2$

    $t_3 = (2) \times (-2) = -4$

    $t_4 = (-4) \times (-2) = 8$

    $t_5 = (8) \times (-2) = -16$

    and so on.

    Thus, we can see that every odd positioned term, $t_1, t_3, t_5 \ldots t_{49}$ is negative and hence is less than 10.

    There are $\dfrac{40}{2} = 20$ such terms.

Again, the even positioned terms are positive. The first few terms are less than 10, however, as the magnitude increases, they would exceed 10.

We need to find the number of such terms less than 10.

We observe that successive such terms get multiplied with 4.

Thus, we get:

$t_2 = 2$

$t_4 = 2 \times 4 = 8$

$t_6 = 8 \times 4 = 32$

Thus, we see that only 2 such terms are less than 10.

Thus, we have a total of 20 + 2 = 22 terms which are less than 10.

Hence, the correct answer is C.

20. **Level of Difficulty:** Medium

    Category: Additional Topics in Math

    Topic: Congruence and similarity

    The correct answer is C

    $\triangle ADE$ and $\triangle ABC$ are similar since

    $\angle ADE \cong \angle ABC$ and $\angle AED \cong \angle ACB$

    (corresponding angles)

    $\dfrac{AD}{AB} = \dfrac{AE}{EC} = \dfrac{3}{9} = \dfrac{1}{3}$

    Also, we have:

    $\dfrac{Area\ of\ \triangle ADE}{Area\ of\ \triangle ABC} = \left(\dfrac{AD}{AB}\right)^2 = \dfrac{1}{9}$

    $\dfrac{Area\ of\ \triangle ADE}{Area\ of\ trapezium\ BDEC} = \dfrac{1}{9-1} = \dfrac{1}{8}$

    The correct answer is option C.

21. Level of Difficulty: Difficult

Category: Problem Solving and Data Analysis

Topic: Ratios, rates, and proportions

The correct answer is C

We know that the ratio of teachers to students should be 1:8 or more (i.e. there can be more than one teacher per 8 students).

Let the number of teachers be x, so the number of students = $8x$.

Thus, total participants in the field trip = $x+8x=9x$.

Thus, we have: $9x = 48 => x = \dfrac{48}{9} = 5.33$

However, the number of teachers cannot be a fractional number. So, the value of x will be either 5 or 6.

But, with 5 teachers and 48-5=43 students, the required ratio of one teacher per 8 students won't be satisfied.

Thus, the number of teachers should be more than 5.33 i.e. 6.

Thus, number of students = 48-6=42 (observe that teacher to student ratio = 6:42=1:7 is more than the required ratio of 1:8).

Hence, the answer is C.

22. Level of Difficulty: Difficult

Category: Problem Solving and Data Analysis

Topic: Percents

The correct answer is B

In order to correctly represent the situation, one must match the correct variable with the correct percentage.

The sofa is 60% off, so the total price is in fact 40% of the original price or $0.4s$.

The armchair price is fixed price of $450, and the sum of $0.44s$ and $450 is the discounted again by 40% or 60% of the original price, which can be rewritten as $0.6(0.4s +450)$ Choices A,C and D are incorrect because they represent errors in writing discounts as percentages and errors in matching variables and prices with the correct discount.

23. Level of Difficulty: Difficult

Category: Heart of Algebra

Topic: Linear inequality and equation (word problems)

The correct answer is B

Let the average in the first four games be x points.

Thus, total points across the four games = $4x$.

Since the team scored 88 points in their fifth game, the total points across the five games = $(4x+88)$.

Thus, average across five games = $\dfrac{4x+88}{5}$.

Thus, increase in average =

$$\dfrac{4x+88}{5} - x = \dfrac{88-x}{5}$$

This increase is given to be an integer.

Now, when 88 is divided by 5, the remainder is 3.

Thus, x should be a number such that when it is divided by 5, the remainder is 3 as well so that the remainders cancel each other out in (88-x).

From the options, we can see that options B and D leave a remainder 3 when divided by 5.

However, according to the question, the initial average must have been less than 88 as only then the average would increase.

Hence, the answer is B.

24. Level of Difficulty: Hard

Category: Heart of Algebra

Topic: Interpreting linear functions.

The correct answer is D

Since A is measured in square feet, $\dfrac{t}{46}$ is also measured in square feet.

Then

$$\dfrac{hours}{46} = square\ feet =>$$

$$45 = \dfrac{hours}{sqaure\ feet}$$

We see that 46 is how many square feet Mike is painting per hour.

The correct answer is option D.

25. Level of Difficulty: Difficult

Category: Problem Solving and Data Analysis

Topic: Ratios, rates, and proportions

The correct answer is B

We have the following information:

Apples : Peaches = 4 : 3,

Apples : Lychees = 3 : 5.

We can see that *Apples* have numbers 4 and 3 respectively.

So, we assume the number of *apples* as the *LCM* of 4 and 3 i.e. 12.

Thus, to maintain the ratio of *Apples* and *Peaches*, the number of *Peaches* = 3×3=9.

Again, to maintain the ratio of *Apples* to *Lychees*, the number of *Lychees* =4×5=20.

Thus, the final ratio of *Apples : Peaches : Lychees* =12 : 9 : 20.

Thus, *Apples* as a fraction of total fruits

$$= \dfrac{12}{12 + 9 + 20} = \dfrac{12}{41}$$

Hence, the answer is B.

26. Level of Difficulty: Difficult

Category: Passport to Advanced Math

Topic: Isolating Quantities

The correct answer is D

To check the divisibility by 45, we need to check the divisibility by 5 and 9.

For 5, the last digits of the number i.e. B should be 0 or 5.

We know that B is positive, hence B = 5.

For 9, sum of all digits of the number i.e. $2+5+A+7+B=(14+A+5)=19+A$ should be divisible by 9.

In order that $(19+A)$ is divisible by 9, we must have $A=8$ (since $19+8=27$ is divisible by 9).

Thus, $A+B=8+5=13$.

Hence, the answer is D.

27. Level of Difficulty: Difficult

Category: Problem Solving and Data Analysis

Topic: Ratios, rates, and proportions

The correct answer is D

Here, the relation between four *integers,w,x,y,z* is given.

Since $2w = \dfrac{3}{2}x = y = \dfrac{5}{3}z,$ let us assume that all of these are equal to k.

Thus, $w = \dfrac{k}{2}, x = \dfrac{2k}{3}, y = k, z = \dfrac{3k}{5}$

So, the ratio

$$w : x : y : z = \frac{k}{2} : \frac{2k}{3} : k : \frac{3k}{5} = \frac{1}{2} : \frac{2}{3} : 1 : \frac{3}{5}$$

To make the ratio as integers, we multiply it with the *LCM* of the denominators i.e. 2,3,5=30.

Thus, the ratio

$$w : x : y : z = \frac{30}{2} : \frac{60}{3} : 30 : \frac{90}{5} = 15 : 20 : 30 : 18$$

Then, from the ratio, we have: $w=15m$, $x=20m$, $y=30m$, $z=18m$ where m is some constant.

Now, we need to substitute the values of w,x,y,z in the options to check which option can result in an integer.

Option A: $\dfrac{wx}{vz} = \dfrac{(15m)(20m)}{(30m)(18m)} = \dfrac{5}{9}$

This is not an integer.

Option B: $\dfrac{x}{w} = \dfrac{20m}{15m} = \dfrac{4}{3}$

This is not an integer.

Option C: $\dfrac{4x}{v} = \dfrac{4(20m)}{30m} = \dfrac{8}{3}$

This is not an integer.

Hence, option D must be the one which can be an integer. In fact, $\dfrac{x^2}{v} = \dfrac{(20m)^2}{30m} = \dfrac{40m}{3}$

This can become an integer if we choose m as a multiple of 3.

Hence, the answer is (D).

28. Level of Difficulty: Difficult

Category: Passport to Advanced Math

Topic: Interpreting nonlinear expressions

The correct answer is D

Let us check statement I.

Since $x^2 > x^3$, we can multiply both sides of the inequality by x^4 : $x^2 \times x^4 > x^3 \times x^4 => x^6 > x^7$ (since x^4 is always non-negative, multiplying an inequality by x^4 will not reverse the inequality).

Hence, the first statement is correct.

To verify the second statement:

Let us pick a number between 0 and 1, say 0.5 and see if it satisfies the condition. Thus, we have: $x^2 = 0.5^2 = 0.25, x^3 = 0.5^3 = 0.125$.

We see that $x > x^2 > x^3$.

Hence, the second statement is not correct.

To verify the third statement: Let us pick one number between 0 and -1, say -0.5.

Let us see if $x=-0.5$ satisfies the condition.

Thus, we have: $x^2 = 0.25, x^3 = -0.125$

We find $x^2 > x^3 > x$

Hence, the condition is satisfied.

Hence, the third statement is correct.

Hence, the answer is D.

29. Level of Difficulty: Difficult

Category: Passport to Advanced Math

Topic: Radicals and rational exponents

The correct answer is C

We need to find the number of factors of each of the numbers which are perfect squares after the numbers are multiplied by 5.

Thus, we need to break the numbers in their prime form. Working with options, we have:

(A): $350 \times 5 = 2 \times 5^3 \times 7$

Hence, the factors which are perfect squares are 1 and 5^2. Thus, there are two such factors.

(B): $290 \times 5 = 29 \times 2 \times 5^2$

Hence, the factors which are perfect squares are 1 and 5^2. Thus, there are two such factors.

Since both options (A) and (B) have the same number of perfect square factors, any option that does not have two perfect square factors must be the answer.

(C): $250 \times 5 = 2 \times 5^4$

Hence, the factors which are perfect squares are $1, 5^2$ and 5^4. Thus, there are three such factors.

Hence, we know that (C) must be the answer.

It can be verified that options (D) does not have perfect square factor:

(D): $12 \times 5 = 2^2 \times 3 \times 5 => 1$ and 2^2

Hence, the answer is C.

30. Level of Difficulty: Difficult

Category: Passport to Advanced Math

Topic: Interpreting nonlinear expressions

The correct answer is D

While solving these types of questions, it is best to divide the number line in the four parts as shown below:

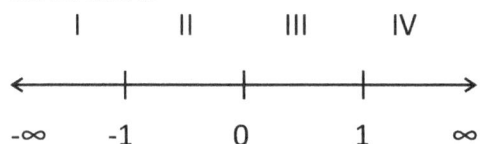

We now need to pick a number from the regions (I, II, III and IV) and check which region(s) satisfy.

Region I: Say $x=-2$. Thus, $x^3=-8$. Hence, $x > x^3$. Thus, region I satisfies the condition.

Region II: Say $x=-0.5$. Thus, $x^3=-0.125$. Hence, $x^3 > x$. Thus, region II doesn't satisfy the condition.

Region III: Say $x=0.5$. Thus, $x^3=0.125$. Hence, $x > x^3$. Thus, region III satisfies the condition.

Region IV: Say $x=2$. Thus, $x^3=8$.

Hence, $x^3 > x$. Thus, region IV doesn't satisfy the condition.

Thus, the regions satisfying the given condition are I and III.

Going by options:

A): $x^3 > x^5$: This is satisfied by the point $x=-2$ in Region I since $(-2)^3 = -8 > (-2)^5 = -32$

B): $x^2 > x$: This is satisfied by the point $x=-2$ in Region I since $(-2)^2 = 4 > -2$

C): $x^2 > x^3$: This is satisfied by the point $x=0.5$ in Region III since $(0.5)^2 = 0.25 > (0.5)^3 = 0.125$

This is also satisfied by the point $x=-2$ in Region I since $(-2)^2 = 4 > (-2)^3 = -8$

D): $\dfrac{1}{x} > \dfrac{1}{x^2}$: Let us multiply x^2 to both sides (since x^2 is positive, it will not reverse the inequality).

As a result, we get: $\dfrac{x^2}{x} > \dfrac{x^2}{x^2} => x > 1$.

However, we know that $x > 1$ (i.e. Region IV) is not a correct solution to the given condition. Thus, this option is not correct.

Hence, the answer is D.

31. Level of Difficulty: Easy

Category: Problem Solving and Data Analysis

Topic: Data inferences

The correct answer is 0.46

The marbles would be of the same color if either both are red, or both are blue.

The number of ways of getting both red or both blue $= {}_3C_2 + {}_5C_2 = \dfrac{3!}{2!1!} + \dfrac{5!}{3!2!} = 13$.

Thus, there are 13 favorable cases.

Total ways of drawing 2 marbles from 3+5=8 marbles is $= {}_8C_2 = \dfrac{8!}{2!6!} = 28$.

Thus, required probability $= \dfrac{13}{28} = 0.46$

Hence, the correct answer is 0.46.

32. Level of Difficulty: Easy

Category: Advanced Math

Topic: Structure in expressions

The correct answer is 0.5

$$\dfrac{(a+b)^2 - (a^2+b^2)}{(a+b)^2 - (a-b)^2}$$

$$= \dfrac{a^2 + 2ab + b^2 - (a^2+b^2)}{(a^2+2ab+b^2) - (a^2-2ab+b^2)}$$

$$= \dfrac{2ab}{4ab} = 0.5$$

The correct answer is option 0.5.

33. **Level of Difficulty:** Easy

    Category: Heart of Algebra

    Topic: Interpreting linear functions.

    The correct answer is 1,200

    10 minutes is equal to 10(60) = 600 seconds.

    Then substituting t=600 seconds to the equation of D, we get D= -4(600)+3,600=1,200 meters.

34. **Level of Difficulty:** Medium

    Category: Problem Solving and Data Analysis

    Topic: Solving systems of linear equations

    The correct answer is 2

    Let $\dfrac{1}{x} = a$ and $\dfrac{1}{y} = b$

    $a+b=2$ … (i)

    $3a+4b=7$ … (ii)

    From (ii) – (i) x^3: $b=1$=>$a=1$

    $x+y=2$

    The correct answer is 2.

35. **Level of Difficulty:** Medium

    Category: Heart of Algebra

    Topic: Solving systems of linear equations

    The correct answer is 5.86

    $Ax+B=Cx+D$

    The above has infinite solutions if: $A=C$ and $B=D$

    $(3x + 2)k + 5 = 12x + 7m$

    $3kx + (2k + 5) = 12x + 7m$

    $3k = 12$ and $2k + 5 = 7m$

    $k = 4$ and $m = \dfrac{13}{7} = 1.86$

    $k + m = 5.86$

36. **Level of Difficulty:** Medium

    Category: Additional Topics in Math

    Topic: Right triangle geometry

    The correct answer is 28

    Let the parallelogram be $ABCD$, with

    $AB : BC = 1 : 2$

    $AB = CD = 2x$ and $AD = BC = x$

    AX is drawn perpendicular to CD.

    In triangle ADX: $AX = DX$

    $AD = \sqrt{AX^2 - DX^2} = AX\sqrt{2}$ =>

    $AX = \dfrac{AD}{\sqrt{2}} = \dfrac{x}{\sqrt{2}}$

    Area of the parallelogram = $(AX)(CD)$

    $20 = \dfrac{x}{\sqrt{2}} \times 2x$ =>

    $\sqrt{2}x^2 = 20$

    Thus, area of the required rectangle

    $= (AD)(CD) = (x)(2x)$ =>

    $2x^2 = 20\sqrt{2} = 28$

37. Level of Difficulty: Difficult

Category: Heart of Algebra

Topic: Solving linear equations and inequalities

The correct answer is 8

We have:

$C + D = A$ ... (i)

$D - C = B$ ... (ii)

Adding the above two equations: $2D = A + B$ ... (iii)

Since $2D$ is even, $A + B$ must be even. Thus, A and B can be the following couples of numbers: 1 and 3, 1 and 5, or 3 and 5.

Since we need to maximize the sum $B + C$, we should choose the maximum possible value of B.

Let us check each combination.

$A = 1, B = 3 => 2D = 1 + 3 => D = 2$.

Hence, $C = 5$ and $B + C = 3 + 5 = 8$.

$A = 1, B = 5 => 2D = 1 + 5 => D = 3$.

Hence, $C = 2$ and $B + C = 5 + 2 = 7$.

$A = 3, B = 5 => 2D = 3 + 5 => D = 4$.

However, we cannot have any number as 4.

Thus, the maximum $B + C = 8$.

Hence, the answer is 8

38. Level of Difficulty: Difficult

Category: Additional Topics in Math

Topic: Circle equations

The correct answer is 15.2.

Coordinates of the centre = Midpoint of the line joining the ends of the diameter

$$= \left(\frac{3+5}{2}, \frac{5+11}{2} \right) = (4,8)$$

Radius = Distance between the centre and one end of the diameter

$$= \sqrt{(4-3)^2 + (8-5)^2} = \sqrt{10}$$

Thus, the required equation:

$$(x-4)^2 + (y-8)^2 = \left(\sqrt{10} \right)^2$$

$$a + b + r = 4 + 8 + \sqrt{10} = 15.16 \approx = 15.2$$

Hence, the correct answer is 15.2Sa in teristi, nem aus. Quit facciendam tudam ta, nos spervit parius. Huis egilis host? Issulum convoltus es Cast? Omnonve roximan trions es in virmandium in reore henatiam, tem fir ublius is hocchum ponsum must omne in vero unt, adem, cre tam iac mac ma, sil utus es, popopublisse culto no. Sereortus.

www.ingramcontent.com/pod-product-compliance
Lightning Source LLC
Chambersburg PA
CBHW080357030426
42334CB00024B/2907